AROUND THE WORLD, 1932-1934

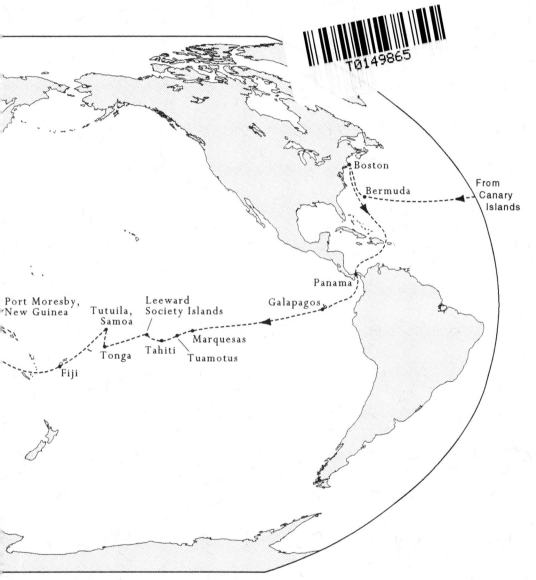

Boston

Bermuda

From Canary Islands

Panama

Galapagos

Port Moresby, New Guinea

Tutuila, Samoa

Leeward Society Islands

Marquesas

Tonga

Tahiti

Tuamotus

Fiji

The Schooner
Pilgrim's
Progress

The Schooner *Pilgrim*   ©Mystic Seaport Museum, Inc., Rosenfeld Collection, Mystic, Connecticut

THE SCHOONER
PILGRIM'S
PROGRESS

A Voyage Around the World
1932–1934

DONALD C. STARR

With supplemental material by
Harold Peters and Horace W. Fuller

INTRODUCTION BY JOHN ROUSMANIERE

PEABODY ESSEX MUSEUM
SALEM, MASSACHUSETTS

MYSTIC SEAPORT MUSEUM
MYSTIC, CONNECTICUT

Special Supplement to *The American Neptune*
Volume 56, 1996

Acknowledgments

This book would not have been published without the attention and support of Donald's wife, Polly Thayer Starr.

Richard M. Dey edited Donald Starr's manuscript, interwove excerpts from the ship's log and Horace W. Fuller's journal, and produced most of the appendix material.

Preparation for publication was carried out by Dori Phillips, Assistant Publisher of *The American Neptune*. Charles Anezis served as copy editor. The Peabody Essex Museum, repository of the Starr yachting papers and maritime artifacts, oversaw publication, and assisted photographically and in other areas.

John Rousmaniere has provided cogent support and assistance.

For permission to quote from Horace W. Fuller's journal, the editors thank Benjamin A. G. Fuller.

We thank Kym Pappathanasi of Salem State College for drawing the *Track of the Schooner* Pilgrim *Around the World* as the end papers of this book.

Peabody Essex Museum photograph of the jacket watercolor by Jeffrey Dykes.

Printed in the United States of America
BookCrafters, Chelsea, Michigan
©1996 by The Peabody Essex Museum
Salem, Massachusetts

Contents

Introduction, by John Rousmaniere

❂

❂

Introduction

by John Rousmaniere

YOU WHO ARE ABOUT TO READ this lively, first-hand story of a pioneering sailing voyage around the world will soon learn (if you do not know already) how well a good cruise can be brought to life by a talented sailor and writer. Here is Donald Starr's story, which he describes, with characteristic understatement and grace, as "some 28,500 miles of days and nights of life afloat with good companions, threading the channels and ports of strange but friendly waters and lands with no disasters to mar the recollection."

I first heard about the circumnavigation of the John Alden-designed, 85-foot schooner *Pilgrim* from the author, who told me yarns in the cockpits and cabins of various boats as we knocked around various bodies of water. I met Donald in 1964, thirty years after the *Pilgrim* made her way to Boston. I was a nineteen-year-old college dropout looking for some sailing, he was a sixty-four-year-old retired attorney. We were helping his old shipmate Hod Fuller deliver a big ketch from San Diego to Greece, where Fuller (whom you will soon come to know in these pages as the fun-loving Chief) put her into charter service. Over the next twenty years, I sailed happily under Donald's command in several of the small cruising boats he owned — happily, but not enough. Writing now, three years after his death at the age of ninety-one,

I am sure that I spent far too few days under sail with Donald Starr.

Donald was what used to be called a "cruising man." He hardly ever raced, he deeply loved all handsome and sturdy cruising boats, and when he was under sail, in reality or in his thoughts, his soul danced to the same rhythm of tide and wind that guides a boat's lifetime. He was a wonderful shipmate — handy as a seaman, a craftsman, and a cook, and playfully full of songs and harmonica tunes and jokes. As I stood watch with Donald on our first night out on the Pacific in 1964, he traced the constellations above our heads as though greeting old friends, ending with the great warrior whom Donald, in a brogue, saluted as "the only Irishman in the sky, O'Ryan."

His cheerful, pragmatic traditionalism marked his friendship with boats. He owned ten of them over half a century. While *Pilgrim* was by far the largest and had the longest legs, most of his vessels were, like her, commissioned by him to meet specific goals. A couple of them had especially shallow draft so they could fit the thin waters of the Bahamas; another was a roomy motor sailer perfect for cruising the canals of France; and his last was a 26-foot traditional gaff-rigged, Maine-built Friendship sloop whose aesthetics and old-fashioned gear met Donald's desire in his later years to have something handsome and intricate to fuss with afloat and in his woodworking shop ashore. These yachts he rewarded with names redolent of a long ocean voyage or of nature: *Morning Watch, Circe, Milky Way, Northern Crown, Cornflower, Morning Glory.* As for *Pilgrim*, the title of this book suggests how she was inspired by the wide-ranging seeker after truth and salvation who is the narrator of John Bunyan's classic, *The Pilgrim's Progress.*

Donald certainly was a traditionalist at heart, and sometimes an emphatic one, yet he was not inflexible. When he launched the canal boat at her Dutch yard, he named her *Tansy*, a French name for a life-giving medicinal herb. Bringing her to America after several summers of delightful cruises in French waterways, he blithely dared the shibboleth against changing a ship's name, and she suddenly became a blooming *Morning Glory*. Of course, wood was his favorite construction material, but the experimental side of his complex nature turned him once to steel and another time to fiberglass. His last boat, the wooden Friendship sloop *Morning Watch*, was traditional in every way, yet he was constantly tinkering with her. He did some things that purists would love — replacing her metal turnbuckles with deadeyes and tarred line, for example — and others that they would hate. To douse her jib without his having to venture out on her long, slippery bowsprit, he installed a roller-furling device, and tiring of her backbreaking weather helm, he chopped six feet off her long boom, stepped a small mizzenmast, and turned her into a less unadulterated — but more seaworthy — yawl.

He was still improving *Morning Watch* when his back went out, and he had to leave the water. When I took a boat I was sailing at the time out to Martha's Vineyard, where he and his wife, Polly, had a summer home overlooking Vineyard Sound, he sadly confided that his back was so delicate that he could not risk coming aboard for a drink for fear of slipping should she roll. Yet he was not unhappy ashore. In and around his homes on the Vineyard and in Boston and nearby Hingham, his life was full of family, friends, books, and hobbies. He carved models of his boats, painted in both oils and water colors, and played his musical instruments. Setting a model of vigorous old age for us all when he gave up sailing in his eighties, he took up the cello.

All the time he continued to speak of the *Pilgrim*. Only after he died did I see his manuscript about her voyage, upon which he had worked on and off for many years. Polly asked that it be prepared for publication, and I recruited Richard M. Dey, a sailor and writer, to edit the text.

Whenever and wherever Donald told the story of *Pilgrim's* great cruise — whether in his manuscript or over rum and bitters in the cabin of *Morning Watch* — he quickly made his audience aware that this was the voyage of a young man's dreams. He makes that clear on the first page, when he informs us that *Pilgrim* cast off from Boston in 1932: "At the beginning of the ebb on the first day of summer." This is a story of hope, optimism, and bright light. Donald then was thirty-one years old, a veteran of several invigorating years as an Assistant Attorney General of the Commonwealth of Massachusetts. Born inland, he had picked up sailing from friends and bought a little yawl in which he did some extended cruising. As the seafaring dream arose in him, he went to the most famous yacht designer of the day, John Alden, and requested a new, husky schooner that could carry him anywhere. While the vessel was under construction, he asked around for capable, companionable men who would join him on the adventure. It being the middle of the Great Depression, he found them (or, rather, they found him). Hod Fuller once told me that his out-of-pocket expenses for the two-year voyage amounted to all of $400, which, he said, was a great deal less than he would have spent looking for a job back in Boston.

The adventurous pilgrims were undertaking a great and rare enterprise. To cruise across an ocean or two is the adventure of any sailor's lifetime, but today it is not the rare adventure that it was that summer solstice over sixty years ago. The oceans were then almost empty of amateur sailors. The *Pilgrim* stumbled upon a handful of them (in Panama, Starr met the courageous Harry Pidgeon in his little *Islander*), yet her story is not about the Americans she encountered, but about the extraordinary places, interesting people, and curious stories that Donald and his friends came across in their travels. In the Galapagos Islands, there lies a mystery hinting of jealousy and violence. In Tahiti — the old, unspoiled, pre-tourist, pre-jet airline Tahiti — there is an intriguing mix of pragmatic, hospitable Polynesians and eccentric Westerners. Then come the little islands of the South Pacific, which Donald loved more than any other destination on his meandering route, and from there across the Indian Ocean into the vicious Red Sea gales to the Suez Canal, and through the Mediterranean into the cold North Atlantic and back to Boston. Of his habitual curiosity, which surfaces here on every page, Donald says simply: "To someone with most of his life ahead of him and no financial or other reasons for hastening home, much of this area invites investigation."

These investigations include reflection on the source of the pleasures of life under way in a blue-water cruising boat. He describes the schooner's offshore gear, including a squaresail that made a lark of running before the wind, and in Chapter 19 he presents one of the most succinct descriptions of the workings of Trade winds that I have ever read. He writes of the joys of good food, lively conversation, a dry bunk, and a shipboard cat — the *Pilgrim*'s many felines play prominent roles in her crew's contentment. A dream voyage this may have been, but Donald is never dreamily romantic about it. "Every winged flight across the water," he accurately tells us, "is a race from one base of supplies to the next." This acknowledges the probability of problems, and *Pilgrim* had a few. Almost fatal to the voyage was a confounding and dangerous leak in the schooner's bottom. The voyage stalled in Panama until, after backbreaking work, they discovered the cause, which was due to careless construction by the shipyard. The leak was plugged and *Pilgrim* headed on into the Pacific. Otherwise, as long-distance cruises go, this one was relatively free of unhappy events. Many modern day sailors will be amazed a crew this small had so little trouble with such a big vessel and her bulky sails, heavy spars, and 300-pound anchors. The first damage to the rig occurred some 12,000 miles out when, off New Guinea, a lazy jack parted without consequence.

While Donald touches on technology when it is important, his chief interest lies in the people and customs he encounters along the way. He is always respectful and thoughtful, even as his eye is peeled for irony. He tells us with glee that the impresario of a cockfighting championship in Bali is the widow of a bishop, that the little household fire is, for New Guineans, both a source of warmth and a status symbol, and that the simple nutmeg tree in the Dutch Banda islands is at the center of a whirlwind of complex international finance. He chuckles, "As the nutmeg ripens at all times of the year, this unhurried harvesting never ends, bringing in a steady flow of guilders from the consumers of apple pies and eggnog."

To these discoveries, Donald is led sometimes by locals, sometimes by his nose, and sometimes by his friends — for example, the able Swedish professional sailor Joe Ekelund, of whom Donald writes, "Joe's capacity for finding the strange, wonderful, or enjoyable in any port was almost infinite." (A wonderful seaman, Joe went on to care for General George Patton's Alden schooner _When and If._)

Joe is one of the few characters here called by his own name. The many nicknames may leave the reader confused as to who is who, and so Richard Dey has compiled a scorecard in Appendix A. You should now mark the three leading players — "The Commander," "The Chief," and "The Skipper." The first is Starr, and "The Chief" is Fuller, so named because he was chief engineer. (Richard Dey has also placed apt and lively excerpts from Fuller's light-hearted, observant journal in the text, along with the many relevant log entries.) More explanation is required for "The Skipper." While the captain or skipper of a boat usually is the owner, Donald, who was rigorously objective about the limits of his own sailing experience, assigned himself the job of first mate and handed command to an older man who had wrung more gallons of salt water out of his socks. "The Skipper," then, is his friend Harold Peters. Peters also wrote the two chapters covering the rough trip to the Mediterranean from Singapore, where Donald, according to the log, "took temporary leave of the schooner and embarked on a Dutch steamer for Genoa." Donald was not giving up on the cruise but, rather, giving in to his heart. He went to marry Polly Thayer, a painter from Boston whom he had known for many years. He rejoined the vessel in Genoa, and Polly greeted him a few weeks later when *Pilgrim* came home to Boston.

"Ahead lay a life of another sort," Donald writes at the end. His was a rich life lasting another six decades. He went back to practicing law, played a key role in the creation of the park along the embankment of Boston's Charles River Basin, and surrounded himself with books, art, music, woodworking tools, boats, and companions of all ages. In 1964, he went to sea again with Fuller and (fortunately for me) me. Eight years later, when he was in his early seventies, he helped deliver a yawl through a series of gales to Bermuda.

The last of the young men of *Pilgrim*'s dream cruise, Donald died in March 1992. He was survived by Polly, their two daughters, and many friends who had been privileged to know him in many ways and places. If they were especially lucky, they knew him in and around boats.

John Rousmaniere
Author, "*Fastnet, Force 10*"; *The Annapolis Book of Seamanship; The Golden Pastime,* and other books.

November, 1995

chapter 1

Boston to Panama

AT THE BEGINNING OF THE EBB TIDE on the first day of summer, the schooner *Pilgrim* headed down Boston Harbor, bound for Panama and seas west. It was 11:40 on a bright morning, and the year was 1932. A throng of relatives, friends, and acquaintances of the ship's company, recent temporary employees of the ship, and strangers not just then occupied in watching steam shovels waved good-bye and shouted their farewells across the water widening from Commercial Wharf, Boston. The Western world was well into the Great Depression, and the spectacle of eight men in a yacht sailing away from it had elicited congratulations from the well-wishers and not a little envy. The economic situation was so much on everyone's mind, in fact, that others characterized the venture as a case of escapism — that is, of repulsion, a misconception that placed a low estimate on the attraction of the things we expected to do and see over the next 30,000 miles. In any case, the voyage around the world meant employment to John Vranken, cook, and to Joe Ekelund, boat-swain. To the other six of us, it seemed at the time like a good idea.

"Let go forward!" the Skipper called.

I watched Joe lift the bow line off the piling and swing into the rigging. "All gone for'ard, Skipper," Joe called back in his thick Scandinavian accent. Joe is not an emotional man, but he called those words with a note of exultation that made them a kind of song.

The *Pilgrim* was a brand-new schooner, but as she threaded her way down the main ship channel, dodging the East Boston ferry and bucking the turbulent swirls of the Metropolitan sewer outlet off Deer Island, she did not look it. A black automobile tire that had served as a fender hung over her white hull, on the starboard quarter. Her once gleaming topsides were soiled with the marks of three weeks of close contact with the old pilings and rich, iridescent fluids of Boston Harbor. After a shakedown cruise from the builder's yard in Boothbay Harbor, Maine, we had made our final preparations. I had hoped that little would remain to be done but to take aboard provisions, tell the paper boy not to call until further notice, and head for the Pacific. But as the hurricane season grew closer, those things which ought to have been done, and those things which had been done as they ought not to have been done, reared their mocking heads.

Due to several serious defects in the installation of the engine, the after part of the vessel had been a workshop for a corps of mechanics who left their occupational spoor on the crisp white pine decks and fresh paint work. Ten tons of tarred sash weights used for ballast had been lifted up from the bilge so that ceilings could be fitted along the frames inside the ship to protect the outer planking from their heavy load. The weights had been placed on every horizontal surface on deck and below and then replaced, one by one, together with an additional ten tons of fifty-pound each lead pigs. These were installed by the Skipper, Harold Peters of Boston. He had the same pride in his judgment for the disposition of ballast that many have for building wood fires. Although muffled complaints about the tendency of the pigs to smash his fingertips rose up from under the cabin sole where he was wedged, he would not let anyone relieve him.

While work on the engine and ceiling was underway, the provisions were coming aboard. Food for eight men for six months, stacked in cases on deck, looked so much bulkier than the available stowage space that, if only to dispel an initial hopeless despair, we broke open the cases and proceeded piecemeal. For three days, tins of beef, tomatoes, pears, grapefruit, butter, condensed milk, corn, and more beef were tossed singly down through the main hatch. The game of trying to pitch faster than the others could catch and stow raised this operation to a high level of intensity and added to the general disorder and noise. Friends and the friends of friends were always found about the deck, below, and even up in the rigging, while a constant flow of perfect strangers who wanted to go along with us came aboard from the waterfront. During the three weeks of repair work and outfitting, the spreaders and cockbilled yard were the roosting place of the Atlantic Avenue Local of the Boston Pigeon's Union, and their droppings aloft showed it. Over the whole of the schooner fell, day and night, the constant rain of a big city's atmospheric waste. The time finally came, however, when the mechanics proclaimed the diesel "better than when she was new" and the last jar of jam was crammed beneath the bunks.

As the schooner left Boston Light astern and gradually came into cleaner waters, the decks were sluiced down with buckets of brine and the less tenacious marks of the pigeons and mankind were dislodged and effaced with a deck swab. Between lingering glances at the receding mainland and outlying islands, we moved about the decks and secured all movable objects — dories, anchors, water kegs, kerosene tins — against the increasing motion of the sea. By nightfall, we were sailing in a dense dripping fog, penetrated only by the green and red glows of the *Pilgrim's* running lights and the periodic caterwauling squawks of our hand-operated foghorn. In these dismal conditions, we found our way around Nantucket Shoals by dead reckoning, listening for other horns and taking soundings with the lead line.

After two nights and days, we came out into a large open space bounded on the bottom by the bland waters of the Gulf Stream and on the top by the star-and-planet-studded firmament. With the rising of the sun, the sides of the space around the Stream receded. I saw water of rich ultramarine decorated with whitecaps and, now and again, bright ochre patches of the air-bladder seaweed characteristic of that mighty river of the ocean. We all saw our first flying fish of the voyage breaking the surface in shoals, in terrified flights for life from the jaws of ravening bonitos. They zoomed amazing distances over wave crests and swooped down into the wave troughs before vanishing far off, spent and small. Damp woolen articles were brought up from below or peeled from our backs and spread to dry in the sun. The canvas sails and manila cordage dried and stretched so much that the halyards had to be swayed taut again. With this emergence from the fog and casting off of wool, we seemed truly to have left New England behind. Furthermore, in a surprisingly brief amount of time, it seemed as though all of life before we came to be confined within the limits of the ship had faded to a remote and shadowy past even as we found ourselves, at present and for the immediate future, unconfined upon all the earth's seas.

Shortly after midnight of the fourth day, what later proved to be a momentous event occurred. The wind had increased from Force 5 to Force 7, backing from west-by-south to northwest. We took in the flying jib and then rounded-to in order to take down the mainsail. In heading up into the wind, the schooner made several plunges into the sea. We continued working until we were sailing handily under foresail and a reefed squaresail. By morning, the wind had moderated and we were running before it under the squaresail, making five to six knots, accompanied by more flying fish.

It was then the Skipper started to worry. Harold Peters always had what Joseph Conrad in *The Mirror of the Sea* called "the sense of insecurity which is so invaluable in a seaman," and he had it especially strong when things seemed to be going well. At forty-four, the Skipper was the oldest and by far the most experienced sailor aboard. He had served (after graduating from Harvard College in 1910) in various commercial sailing vessels hauling cargo downeast or to the River Plate, and catching fish on Brown's Bank, and as executive officer of a torpedo boat, navigator of a transport ship, and captain of a mine sweeper in the Great War, World War I. He sailed the 60' schooner *Lloyd W. Berry,* of which he was part-owner and master, from Boston to Europe and back in 1920 — not without enduring a hurricane in the Bay of Biscay — then in yachts on several races, including the schooner *Ladona* in the Bermuda Race of 1923 and the cutter *Highland Light* in the Transatlantic and Fastnet races of 1931, upon which he served as navigator. Joe Ekelund had sailed with him in the *Highland Light.* Having been fortunate enough to persuade Peters to come along in the *Pilgrim,* I had enough sense to yield to him the position of Captain, and his experience obviously made him the primary navigator. This is how he became "the Skipper."

Now I watched as he ambled over to the leeward deck pump and gave its handle a few tentative heaves. The result? Fresh sea water spilled onto the deck and down the scuppers. Apparently, the *Pilgrim* had started a leak. Twelve gallons taken in a few hours, while no great amount, was more than normal "weeping." We soon saw that the leak varied with changing strains on the hull and was considerably greater on the port tack. That, I thought, would place the trouble somewhere in the port half of the schooner's bottom. Discovery of the leak, however, could have gone no further at the time had the Doc (a medical student) not been in the ship's company.

Having undergone an emergency operation for appendicitis

	Bilges		Lookouts	
No.	A. M.	P. M.	Hours	Names
THE	SKIPPER	WITH	HIS FAVORITE	HAT.

The Skipper with his favorite hat. (Sketch in the log.)

while on a brief visit to Paris late in the preceding year, I was of no mind to go beyond the reach of a similar service should it be necessary again, nor to rely on the traditional ship's medicine locker, bottle of rum, and carving knife, even with extensive handbook directions. Dick Durant (a Yale graduate and oarsman) was through two of the three years of medical school at Harvard and was willing to take a year off. I had asked him to draw up a list of cutlery, pills, and whatever else the compleat ship's doctor would not like to be caught without in mid-ocean. The resulting stores, which filled a large dresser and part of an empty cabin, ranged from tongue depressors to an artificial leg, and, for particular use on this occasion, a stethoscope. Durant's first job as ship's doctor was to find the trickle. He found it eventually outside the ceiling in the way of the port fore-rigging. The stethoscope, as it turned out, was never needed again for any purpose, but as perhaps the most characteristic piece of medical equipment, it was very reassuring to have one along.

From the ship's log: June 27, 1932. 12-4 A.M. Much less wind this A.M. Standing to south'ard on starboard tack. Leak increasing from 25 to between 40 & 50 pumps per hour.... A bit over 100 miles west of Bermuda today.

What there was of wind over the next nine days continued to come from a general southwesterly direction, naturally the direction in which we were heading. Since the wind became progressively lighter as we approached the horse latitudes, the Chief went below one day to consult with the engine. Hod Fuller of Milton, Massachusetts, and Harvard College, '30, was the Chief Engineer, but he was the Chief in everything else as well. He had done a fair amount of yacht cruising, some automobile racing and airplane flying, and had been most recently selling what the Skipper called "gold bricks" for an investment banking institution. This last occupation did not suit his nature at all.

For a few hours, the Winton diesel allowed us to steer closer to our course, but, every now and again, the engine's vibration would stop and leave the schooner wallowing in a swell sent up by some distant commotion to the southeast.

From Hod Fuller's journal: Had a hell of a time with the engine all day today. It is either building up too much hydraulic pressure or not enough. I was in the engine room all day long goosing it along. I finally had to give up about 8 o'clock, it was running so rotten.

The Chief had experience with gasoline engines in automobiles (both cruising and racing types) and in airplanes, and had also attended the rebuilding of the diesel he was now looking after. If the diesel could have been made to work properly with the facilities at hand, the Chief would have done it. The trouble, however, was too fundamental.

The additional ten tons of ballast had brought the exhaust pipe in the transom down so far toward the waterline that a lop of sea found its way back through the pipe and into the engine head from time to time. The exhaust pipe had been fitted directly from the engine to the transom without a U-bend rising high above the waterline to prevent the problem. As the stops for repairs became more frequent and longer, the Chief's expressions graduated from patient technical comments exchanged with his consultant, the Trader, to expletives and vituperation. And then, just as we entered the horse latitudes, the *Pilgrim* became a pure sailing vessel.

> **Spent all day & yesterday pulling the engine to pieces.... We haven't struck the NE Trades yet, although we're 225 miles into the tradewind belt. The sea is very calm with a big swell & an occasional rain squall. Before breakfast this morning a big rain squall hit us & I went on deck & got a good bath.... The ship is now about due East of the tip of Florida & 900 miles at sea.**

People say the horse latitudes got their name because, in the old sailing days, a ship's water supply was soon exhausted in areas of no wind and the horses died of thirst and had to be thrown overboard. We had plenty of water and no horses in the *Pilgrim,* but for four days we were in the same windless situation as any unfortunate sailing vessel of two hundred years ago. During much of this time, the log line hung straight down from the taffrail. Enduring these latitudes is an experience that is undoubtedly good for building character. The masts, operating as inverted pendulums, rock the hull by exaggerating every slight motion of the ceaselessly heaving sea. If they are draped with canvas in an attempt to dampen their motion, the booms strain at relieving tackles, then crash off to what would be leeward were there any wind. The booms fetch up with vicious jars which in turn cause the block-shackles to grind in their bales and travelers, and the gaffs overhead to worry the sails as does a terrier with a rag. Sturdy gear designed to take steady strains is put to the test of repeated, sudden shocks. There is no life in a ship subject to an unforgiving roll, no sense of the ship as a living thing as there is when she's heeled to a steady breeze.

The whole business gets very tiresome. Samuel Taylor Coleridge in *The Rime of the Ancient Mariner* refers to such an experience:

> The Sun, right up above the mast,
> Had fixed her to the ocean:
> But in a minute she 'gan to stir,
> With a short uneasy motion
> Backwards and forwards half her length
> With a short uneasy motion.
>
> Then like a pawing horse let go,
> She made a sudden bound:
> It flung the blood into my head,
> And I fell down in a swound.

Our active diversions were pumping, more pumping, cleaning fire-arms, and firing at tin cans. For a change, we'd take in the mainsail to stop the slatting or set it again to stop the roll, or we'd study the small aquatic critters that came up with netted patches of seaweed. One day Joe stuck a knife in the foremast and whistled. This is a ceremony not to be performed lightly or too frequently, lest it lose its effectiveness, and Joe had waited many days before resorting to it. But still the wind did not come. Scarlet-beaked white bosun birds with long whisks of tails appeared and mocked our immobility by swooping past the lifeless fly at the main masthead and making sounds like block sheaves in need of grease.

However, as I have suggested, the schooner probably would not have run out of water. We had started with eleven hundred gallons, and in extremity the Cook might have been persuaded to rinse, if not wash, the dishes in salt water. I gradually realized there was nothing we could do in such a situation to change it. We had no radio transmitter to use, even if our case should become desperate; we might as well forget it part of the time and enjoy it for the rest. Some months later, as Harry Pidgeon was sailing down the channel from Balboa in very light air, bound for Los Angeles, I called out to him and said I hoped he'd have better winds on his voyage. His reply came back across the water slowly. "You know," he said, "sailing without an engine kind of tends to make you patient."

The slim previous acquaintance among some of the ship's company was fattened by scraps of personal history and observations on the state of the world. Langley Hawthorn had been on convoy duty with the Skipper during the First World War, but was only slightly known to the rest of us (he had done a good bit of racing on Long Island Sound). He smoked a corn-cob pipe and had been of late engaged in the chinaware business. Persistent interrogation revealed that the China included chamber-pots. Although we had no doubt that, as he insisted, chamber-pots were only a very minor item in his business, we came to refer to the business, for convenience, as having to do solely with chamber-pots. Further conversation brought out the fact that Hawthorn was the only man on board who would have been willing to accept the office of President of the United States. None of the rest of us would take it even for imagined salaries and perquisites far beyond any that Congress could possibly be expected to appropriate for the most inspired leadership.

Joe McCammon was an impressive character with a head like a genial Roman emperor surmounting his heavy-set frame. His most recent activity had been selling airplanes, a business which he said had fallen off sharply since the stock market crash of 1929. His upbringing in cosmopolitan Washington DC, along with an easy Southern manner, made him at home in the most varied company. He had stepped aboard the *Pilgrim* for the first time in Boston, attired in white flannels. His willingness to do anything, from shifting ballast with the Skipper to passing tools to the Chief, soon removed the dazzle from the flannels, and he started to grow a beard. In no time at all, one leg of the flannel pants rotted off and the beard was full. He became so disreputable in appearance, in fact, that the Skipper named him "the Trader," for a composite rum-soaked store-keeper on a remote South Sea Island.

A small black cat we called Calvin filled out the crew. For poor Calvin, who persisted in stalking, tail high, along the varnished rail cap, the slatting around in the doldrums proved fatal. Late one night, just after a particularly violent roll, a frantic feline cry pierced the blackness astern. Calvin was never heard or seen again.

The sea is very blue & the day has been perfect. All we wear for clothes is a pair of shorts & sneakers.... Last night after supper the Doc got the folding organ on deck & played & we all sang songs until it got dark. The sea was just like a mill pond then.

For a rough apportionment of capabilities and experience among the three watches, Joe and the Doc stood one watch together, Hawthorn and the Trader another, and the Chief and I the remaining one. The Cook had enough to do preparing three meals a day and the Skipper, being both captain and navigator, was also thought to have enough to do. He was never far from the wheel. We used the standard system of four-hour watches beginning at noon, but we split the hours between four and eight of the afternoon into two "dog watches" of two hours each so that no pair would be on duty at the same time two days running. This constituted a routine, but it took some getting used to.

In four days in the horse latitudes, our position altered by barely over 100 miles. Our banner day was the last, when the noon position showed 19 miles of progress in twenty-four hours, fifteen of which were logged in the final four hours. Just before that final spurt, the Skipper climbed on deck after a nap in the sunken deckhouse and lit his pipe. He ruminatively puffed the pipe and watched the smoke rise perpendicularly and undisturbed. After some minutes, he removed the pipe from his mouth and after more consideration of the flat sea, said, "Jesus, it's moderate." A strong expression, but not uttered lightly.

> **When I turned out this morning there was a dead calm & a terrific swell…. I took a swim before breakfast & dove in off the ratlines. The water here is damned warm & doesn't cool you off much. We got the balloon jib & fisherman staysail on her & the real Trades finally hit us about 8:30 or 9:00.**

The new wind held, and not many hours after living in a seemingly endless world of calm, we began to worry about the possibility of a hurricane. We were in both the region and the season proper to a hurricane, and could not get any weather signals on the radio, a small headphone receiving set installed by a hobo who had come aboard from the waterfront shortly before our departure. It was rather a specialist's apparatus and the Chief, who had but a beginner's facility with the International Morse Code, had not yet gotten the hang of it. A blinker request for a weather report from a steamer that passed in the night raised no reply. Although there were no signs of an approaching blow, I could not dismiss lightly from my mind a grim reminder of hurricane winds that I'd read in *The West Indies Pilot Supplement*. The *Pilot* itself read: "New Plymouth, on Green Turtle Cay, has a population of about 1,700." The *Supplement*, issued after a hurricane, read simply: "for 1,700 read 400."

July 9, 8-12 P.M. Beautiful going; all sails pulling fine. Reefed

main with topsail over it, fore, fisherman staysail, & ballooner.
Fine trade over quarter, backing to about East. Best days run yet
— 169 miles.

As we stood along for Mona Passage, between the western
end of Puerto Rico and the eastern tip of Hispaniola, the proximity of land was indicated progressively by floating coconuts,
green grass, freshly torn branches, a potato, and a biscuit. Interest
in the schooner's first landfall brought out all four sextants — and
all six navigators in competition for the bottle of whiskey that was
to reward the closest prognostication of the time of landfall.
Within five minutes of the winning prophecy, a loom of land on
the port bow was seen from the foremast spreaders. This was
disproportionately gratifying to the winner, who discounted
nothing for luck and conceitedly forgot, as is customary with
amateur navigators, all he owed to Euclid, John Napier, Nathaniel
Bowditch, Marcq St. Hilaire and Lieutenant Ageton.

It may not be out of place to remark here that the bottle of
whiskey was purely prospective for two reasons: the first was
that, by common agreement, no one was to drink alcohol at any
time unless the vessel was anchored or otherwise securely
attached to land. The second was that, with a prohibition market
at home, there was no point in buying ahead liquid stores that
would be cheaper and of more reliable quality in Panama. Due to
the combined effect of both of these factors, together with the
consequent passage of time, the writer believes he never did get
paid.

The West Indies Pilot warns of squalls of tornado violence in the
Mona Passage so, as we approached the area in gathering
darkness 9 July, we shortened sail down to the four lowers.
Although black clouds moved rapidly and menacingly overhead,
the wind did not carry out its threats. The wind died, leaving us
with bare steerageway.

The afternoon haze smothered the glow of the setting sun and wiped out the silhouette of Desecheo Island, which lay about a mile off the starboard bow and bore no light. It was dark when the menacing overhead clouds began to discharge their electricity in a lightning storm of terrifying brilliance and intensity. We were apparently in the center of the region of attraction, and it seemed a marvel that the *Pilgrim* was not struck. If it is a poor idea to stand near the trunk of a lone pine tree during a lightning storm ashore, it is perhaps equally so if the tree has been cleared of its branches, smoothed off, and set upright in a sailing vessel; its top is still the highest point for some distance around. The danger is not only direct to the stander, but indirect to the whole ship since, if any of many stories is to be believed, a large hole may be blown through the bottom. Where there are two masts, it may be that by favoring the shorter one you can postpone your personal fate, although you may prefer a fatal concussion to drowning. If rain comes before the lightning, it is said to provide an adequate ground between the rigging and sea. On that night in Mona Passage, the spectacular performance was dry. Perhaps I should first have promised to lead a better life, but I thought only of having conductors fitted to the topmast shrouds at the first opportunity, which was done in Panama. They were never needed again but we had them, just as we had the stethoscope.

The *Pilgrim* drifted slowly along in the lee of Puerto Rico's Point Jiguera. With the gradual passing of the disturbance, we set the light canvas to catch more of the evening zephyrs fanning off the shore. Our first land in eighteen days came in an odor of moist cane fields and wood fires. I saw the headlights of automobiles creep along the shore and, now and again, heard the "beep" of a horn mingle with the soft swish of the Caribbean air. By morning, we had drawn clear of the passage. After holding a southerly course to avoid a thick cloud bank forming over Mona Island to the west, as if nourishing one of the advertised tornadoes in its bosom, the schooner was at last squared away for Panama and the

Canal.

July 11, 8-12 A.M. Set squaresail at 11:00… raffee at 12:00. Great sailing all morning: fresh trades on the quarter & some following sea. 4-6 P.M. Fresh trades. Vessel rolling considerable, but making good time. 6-8 Ditto. 8-2 P.M. To Hell with Materialists! What a night!

It was with some relief that we passed out of the hurricane belt. We stayed purposefully some miles south of the steamer lanes across the Caribbean. As the wind was blowing from the northeast and our course was southwesterly, conditions were perfect for the use of the squaresails, which extended from the yard on the foremast. They eased the steering considerably by holding the *Pilgrim's* bow well off against the powerful broaching effect of the mainsail and foresail. The strain on the hull caused by the raffee's pulling ran the leak up to twenty-three gallons in a single hour, but I thought a little extra pumping not a small price to pay for magnificent sailing. It was not to last long. At the end of one of the great lunges with which the schooner rode the successive seas, now moderately heavy, the starboard sheet for the raffee gave way. Although parceled with leather at the nip, the wire sheet had parted cleanly inside the leather.

Perhaps nothing but chain would have stood the constant working and strain (as Conor O'Brien had already discovered with the *Saiorse*), but we had none. In any case, with the schooner rolling, it was not worth the risk for a man to go aloft and reeve a new wire. Even under the reduced rig, however, the *Pilgrim* continued to make better than seven knots, and the rate of leaking immediately dropped by half. The sensation of speed in a sailing vessel is almost entirely a matter of the degree to which she approaches her own hull speed, whether that is four or fourteen knots.

The pleasure of traveling at ten knots in the *Pilgrim* when we carried the raffee was truly exhilarating, however slow that might seem to a jet pilot or an America's Cup defender.

> **The record run of 200 miles was made from noon yesterday to noon today. We are sure making time & only 480 miles to Colon. The key came out of the pulley of the generator again & I'll have to fix it tomorrow.... We have nearly finished scraping & oiling the deck, & it gives the whole vessel a different appearance. It's a messy job getting rid of the Commercial Wharf grime & grease.**

That evening, the Southern Cross came up out of the sea. The form of the constellation is not as clearly that of a cross as I had expected, nor is the brilliance of its component stars a match for many others, which on that particular night blazed with every color of the rainbow, but the sight of it for the first time was worth my coming on deck to see. Furthermore, since the axis of the cross points approximately at the South Pole in the manner that Dubhe and Merak of the Great Dipper point to the North Pole, to see the Southern Cross as it swings around its pole seems to complete one's view of the heavenly machinery as a great revolving hollow sphere.

The following morning, the wind increased until the log showed we were making nearly nine knots. The Trader, even with his two hundred thirty-odd pounds of heft, was having difficulty holding the vessel on her course. In fact, and perhaps partly because he was engaged in a spirited conversation with Hawthorn, the schooner broached-to. A towering green sea thundered aboard, sweeping both men off their feet. We immediately took in the main topsail and mainsail and finished the four hours up to noon under squaresail alone. The day's run, even with the canvas shortened, was 208 miles, a mark that stood for many months. The breeze moderated somewhat that afternoon, but tremendous following seas continued to sweep under the counter. These seas boosted the schooner along at a fine rate of speed, in pleasant contrast to a freighter bound north-eastward, which passed pitching violently and frequently burying her entire bow under the great combers.

After supper, the Skipper and I were sitting in the chart house when a flying fish about 8 inches long came over the rail & in through the companionway door & landed on the bunks. The skipper was going to have him for breakfast but he spoiled over night. We finished scraping the deck today & it looks great.

Shortly after noon on 15 July, our twenty-fourth day out of Boston, the mountain behind the old fortified town of Porto Bello (famous in the pirate history of the Spanish Main) on the isthmus of Panama took shape through the haze. Soon after, the white pyramidal lighthouse on a high rock called Farallon Sucio appeared. However, we were not there yet. It was reported that the currents over the course to the Canal breakwater were extremely variable, especially in the wet season, May through December. The *U.S.S. Hannibal* in 1914, "at 7 knots speed made the run from Farallon Sucio to the breakwater entrance several times, and found that under different conditions the course made good varied over an arc of 23°." With that inconclusive information as a guide, the Skipper referred to a special faculty of his own and allowed a half point in our course steered for the current's set. Shortly after dusk, the flashing light on Point Toro, Colón, in the Republic of Panama, appeared nearly dead ahead. The *Pilgrim,* under half her squaresail and in the dark, slid silently in between the breakwaters, past the area expressly designated in *The West Indies Pilot* as the anchorage, to a sheltered and more convenient spot off the concrete freight wharves. There was a clatter of hoops along the yard, the rattle of anchor chain through the hawse-hole, a slow diminishing swing into the wind, now but a harbor zephyr... and the *Pilgrim* came to rest.

However uneventful and undemanding a passage may be, there is always an underlying tension at sea. This is a tension partly of the muscles from the constant necessity of accommodating one's position to the motion of the vessel, and partly of the nerves from the need of constant vigilance in surroundings which never have been man's proper element. A ship's company observed during the evening watch sprawled about the after deck, smoking tobacco and taking in the last colors of the setting sun below brightening Venus, and with this perhaps the sound of a fine tenor voice accompanied by a harmonium, might seem to be the picture of anything but tension. But the tension is there, and once the anchor is down and the gear stowed, there is a suddenly pervasive relaxation. It is a brief satisfaction, soon giving way to speculation on the nature of the new place to which we have come. Even when the place is presented to the eye in as unengaging an aspect as the stark freight sheds of Cristóbal, the sister city of Colón, it is invested with the most smashing novelty, come upon, as it is, suddenly from the sea. The sense of relaxation is commonly heightened by a drink, but on this single occasion, nature went unassisted.

Mingled reflections were interrupted by the arrival of a launch from the shore. A customs officer and the port physician climbed over the rail by the glow of the gangway lantern. After satisfying themselves that we and the vessel were wholesome, they gave us permission to go ashore. We turned in, instead, on deck. Soon we were driven below by a heavy rain squall, trying to drag five rapidly moistening mattresses through the main hatch at once. This was found to be impossible. We set the awnings next day, and it was many weeks before we took them down.

chapter 2

Panama and the Canal Zone

TOURIST STEAMERS stop for only a few hours at the American-Panamanian bi-dominium of Cristóbal-Colón, long enough for both the education and the entertainment of their passengers. It would have been long enough for us aboard the *Pilgrim* if an unpleasant surprise had not been in the making, which broke just here.

It had been planned to have the schooner's bottom sheathed in copper against the expensive and dangerous attacks of the teredo. The teredo is an infamous marine creature of tropic waters that enters an unprotected wooden ship's bottom by piercing a hole no larger than a pin-prick. Feeding on the wood through which it drills with its horny proboscis, it can grow into a worm as large as ¾" in diameter and 5' in length. Incredible as that may sound, Mr. I. Walker, operator of a shipyard in Papeete, claimed some months later to have found once a 4' teredo half consumed from the rear by another which had followed it into its tunnel. Copper paint, when first applied, provides sufficient protection against this insidious borer, but it wears thin so rapidly that it must be renewed every six months. Certain rare hard woods like the West Australian jarrah have a worm-resistant quality, but none were readily available in Maine where the *Pilgrim* was built beginning late in 1931. If it came alone, this creature would be dangerous enough, but it is apparently gregarious until the moment when it immolates itself for life in a ship's plank so that, if a ship is visited with one, she is probably infested with many. Up and down inside the plank, the teredo eats its chosen way, blind, friendless, and alone — a limited way of life but with a fairly high rating for security in ordinary circumstances.

To have coppered the *Pilgrim* in Maine would have been to affix unnecessarily soon a relatively inflexible material to a base — the planking — which inevitably "works" somewhat before settling into its final form, and to have foregone the advantages of having the work done by shipwrights familiar with the art from experience with tropical vessels. It was determined accordingly that we would carry the copper with us and have it put on in the Canal Zone. There were some six hundred sheets of sixteen-ounce copper, 14" by 48", and the magnitude of the job of putting them in place can be appreciated by the fact we also carried 450 pounds of 1" copper sheathing nails, as well as 400 sheets of tarred felt to place between the sheets and the planks. An arrangement had been made to have the work done at the Mt. Hope Drydock, near the Caribbean end of the canal. The arrival of the schooner represented a job to be done and checked off the shop list, it was soon clear. We were awaited with professional impatience and received with a personal cordiality. Before the expensive — and presumably permanent — business of coppering the hull could proceed, however, there was the matter of the leak.

❂ ❂ ❂

We had sprung a leak in the Gulf Stream. There was no question in the mind of any of us that it could be fixed at once. The copper sheathing could be slapped on, and off we would go, with the lively enthusiasm of youth, into the Pacific. So near in the future did the resumption of our voyage appear to be that in cabling to the makers of the engine in the States for new fuel pump lungers, without which, at least, the engine would not run, I requested that the parts (which were about 4" long and only slightly larger in diameter than a pencil) be sent by air. An expensive memento of our early optimism, the brown paper wrapping in which the consignment arrived, bears canceled United States postage stamps of a face value of one hundred twenty-five dollars, a sum which ensured the arrival of the package at Cristóbal some five months before we finally moved along on our voyage. An ox cart would have arrived with time to spare.

There also arrived from the north, and likewise by air so as not to delay the expedition, Charles B. G. Murphy of Detroit, and with him a long wooden box containing tweezers, bottles, scalpels, cotton, and all the paraphernalia of bird stuffing, and bearing in white letters the inscription "Tangayika Expedition." The presence on board of these scientific instruments and materials, with whatever serious purpose they implied, lent to our enterprise all that it ever had of that flavor, which was little enough. The box remained under the deckhouse during the entire voyage and was seen only when it was necessary to move it to get at the batteries. Murph was moved by a number of interests, which he followed with intense thoroughness, but curiosity about the identities, habitats, and other aspects of birds was not at that period in his life, at least, one of them.

The history of the ensuing months which circumstances forced us to spend in the Canal Zone, interesting as it might be to one versed in the construction of wooden ships, would afford little entertainment. The leak was found, or so I thought, in a split plank by the forward port chain plates, just as the Doc had more or less diagnosed at sea with his stethoscope. A new plank was put on. Furthermore, bronze spikes were driven into a number of spike holes into which someone in Maine had neglected to drive anything before capping them with wooden plugs, or "bungs." The caulking was inspected in all the seams, and several more threads of oakum were hammered in for good measure. It was also seen that more than one spot in the keel had rot, so graving pieces or "Dutchmen" were put in.

> *From the ship's log: July 21. Continued in drydock. Workmen caulking bottom & commencing to put on copper. The yard people think the Pilgrim very solid... We finished sandpapering gaffs & booms & got on a coat of flat white on each... The shore activities of this outfit are omitted from the log, partly thru lack of space & partly otherwise.*

With this done, the hull, to 4" above the water line, was covered with pitch and a layer of felt. The copper, plate by plate, was carefully fitted around the rudder-post and onto every square inch of keel and bottom-planking and fastened with copper nails. Water was then let into the drydock, and all hands went ashore for a Saturday night to look at the renowned and tawdry night-life of Colón, then goodbye to Western civilization. The next morning, we tried the pumps. One hundred fifty gallons of water splashed into the scuppers. Perhaps, we said, they were the remains of the fresh water that had been pumped into the bilge for cleaning? We waited until evening when, with four hundred strokes, came another 130 gallons of water: canal water.

> **From Hod Fuller's journal: All the repair work here is done by the government & in their repair shops all the machine shops are in big steel frame buildings with open sides & corrugated iron roofs. It seems funny to see a shop practically out of doors this way. Everything they need is made right on the spot.**

> **I took the big copper jacketed exhaust manifold off. It was one hell of a job & weighed about 250 lbs. The**

machinists took it up to the shops & put a drain petcock in it to catch any more water that might come in through the exhaust pipe.

July 28. Yard workmen continue breaking out cement to locate leak. Slow work. More window weights found embedded in the cement & a hell of a job to break out.

The *Pilgrim* went into drydock again. Surveyors from two internationally known maritime institutions (one of whom, redolent of the spirit of empire in a pith helmet, was known locally as "Hot Pants") paid us a visit. Afterwards, they delivered engrossed certificates, one bearing a seal and ribbon and stating that the *Pilgrim* was unfit to proceed on her voyage, while the other certified simply that she was unseaworthy. These inspectors did assure me privately, however, that they would pass the schooner if all the bungs were removed from the nearly five thousand spike holes, if all the spikes were set up hard, and if new bungs were driven in lead over the spike heads.

God, what a hell of a way to build a boat. The whole job looks pretty useless & as though the trip might be called off right here.

This work was being carried out when, with the lower third of the hull's planking done, it was interrupted. Because the Government wanted the use of a tug that was in the dry dock with the schooner, both vessels were refloated and moved out. After two days of marking time, the schooner went into dry dock for the third time, this time with a submarine for company. For five days, the dock crew sweated, pried, and hammered until all of the copper plates had been removed, all the spikes set up, all the bungs replaced, and all the copper tacked on a second time. The copper was getting crinkly with the constant handling. On 13 August, four weeks after our arrival, the *Pilgrim* was waterborne again. "Better try the pumps, just to be sure everything is all right at last!" Fourteen gallons an hour: more than she'd leaked before our first trip into dry dock!

> **We have two pets on board today. A coati, which is like a raccoon and Starr bought...& a little monkey given to him.... We have had great fun with them on board. Today the pipe fitters ran a pipe from the electric bilge pump into the pump well, which will make it much easier to pump the vessel out.**

It might be supposed that this series of events created in the ship's company nothing but discouragement. Indeed, the sad state of the schooner, now our only home, was itself sufficiently depressing. In addition, the conditions under which we had been living were far from the idyll of life aboard a yacht in the languorous tropics. During much of this period, the *Pilgrim* had reposed in the bottom of the great sunken cement basin that is a dry dock, resting on chocks and held in an upright position by timbers extending from the hull to the slimy walls. We slept and ate on board, but were compelled for every necessity of the toilet to cross to the bank of the dock over a gangplank in order not to further defile the dank basin below. What little air moved passed overhead. It never descended to purify or even agitate the unwholesome miasma below the tops of the dock walls.

The rainy season was in full stride. Several times a day, sudden heavy showers descended, always before the remains of the last had dried in the sun. Every article below decks was perpetually damp; a shoe, gun strap, or any leather article left uncared for soon became smothered in thick green fungus. A species of small fly penetrated the screens and attacked every portion of the flesh left exposed for relief from the suffocating humidity. The Cook developed a serious skin infection from scratching his bites and had to be shipped across the Isthmus to the Government hospital at Ancon. At one point, the Skipper remarked that if the organized laborers in America were compelled to live under the conditions in which amateur yachtsmen voluntarily find themselves, our land would convulse in bloody revolution. "Surely," I said, "if our present state were typical, their cause would be just."

I was tired not only of these squalid conditions but of supporting a small army of laborers. Viewed broadly, while the ship's company intermittently fought off the attacks of time and tropical weather above the waterline, the opposing team of professionals, whom I'd hired for good wages, was busily engaged below the waterline in immobilizing the vessel altogether. Under their earnest efforts, the condition of the ship seemed to be growing steadily worse. The leak continued. We were getting nowhere. Economically, the situation was absurd. On 19 August, we cast the *Pilgrim's* lines off from a wharf outside the Mt. Hope dry dock in order to pass through the Panama Canal. We were going for a new diagnosis and treatment at the separate and larger set of shops maintained by the Mechanical Division at the Pacific end, where the construction force was only too confident of being able to humiliate the Caribbean-end shops by sealing up the now notorious *Pilgrim* tight as an eggshell.

✿ ✿ ✿

The Panama Canal, as almost everyone used to know, opened in 1914 and is 42¼ miles (68 kilometers) long. It is composed chiefly of a level ditch, filled with water, about 85' above sea level at the Caribbean and Pacific ends. Its height was dictated by the difficulty and expense of digging it down to somewhere near the natural level of the two seas, through that part of the Andes known as the Cordillera del Bando, which extends along the Isthmus of Panama. Its maintenance is made possible by the Chagres River, which rises high enough in the hills in the northwest to flow down evenly into the raised portion of the Canal at Gatun. Ships are elevated to the level of this water-bridge and then let down by a series of locks at either end. Less known is the fact that the Canal runs from northwest to southeast, and that from a short distance outside the Atlantic end it is possible to see the sun set in the ocean, while at Balboa, at the Pacific end, the sun appears to rise from the ocean.

The phenomenon of lifting a vessel by raising the water level is itself unremarkable, and the entire Canal and all its works seemed equally unsurprising to me as the *Pilgrim* passed along its length. To be sure, the initial attempt of the French, led by Ferdinand de Lesseps, who built the Suez Canal, to construct a canal across Panama attests to the difficulty of the project, since it came to failure and survives only in a few hulks and excavating engines rusting away in a bypass that runs from Cristóbal, past Mt. Hope, to Gatun. The Americans who followed were better equipped, not only to perform the actual work of excavation, but to hold off the onslaughts of disease. To carry the project through required engineering and medical capabilities of the highest order, but the result, it seems to me, is unremarkable to view. Large, rectangular concrete basins, closed at both ends by heavy iron or steel gates, swinging open in halves, present nothing of the marvelous in form. Although the locks are indeed very large as locks go, that fact is, at most, only intellectually impressive in the presence of the actuality.

The series of heartbreaking disappointments at Culebra Cut, where landslides time and again destroyed the work of months, lives only in history. There is nothing to stir the imagination in the appearance of the sloping banks which remain. With the exception of Gatun Lake, studded with the blackened stumps of drowned trees, the Canal itself looks like a meandering fresh water stream. It is so narrow that, at many points, ordinary freighters barely have room to pass each other. Even this capacity is kept available only by the constant work of dredges which must almost daily continue the work begun by Colonel Goethals on removing thousands of tons of earth that, deprived of their former natural support, keep sliding into the Canal.

> **Gatun Lake is a very wonderful sight dotted with small wooded islands on very blue water. At the far end of the lake a range of purple mountains rise high into the sky & often their peaks show above the clouds. It was from one of these peaks that Balboa was supposed to have seen the Pacific. The Spanish must have been tough old bastards to cut through this jungle here. It's all swamp and everything is dripping wet & pungy & smells very sickly & unhealthy.**

It was for the larger vessels of the commercial lines and the United States Navy that the locks and their great waterworks were built, a fact which calls for special handling of smaller and more fragile craft in them. In order to raise the water level speedily (the Canal officials take great pride in the number of vessels that transit daily), dozens of large inlet valves in the bottom of a lock release violent submarine jets which agitate the water with strong, confused currents.

Having read of the trouble other yachtsmen had experienced from this cause, you may ask the pilot, as I did, that your yacht be kept from smashing against the lock's sides by running lines out to both sides of the dock, holding her in the middle and at a safe distance from the concrete walls. You may take a book from a shelf in the main cabin and show him this suggestion, earnestly made by a predecessor, but even if you do, the chances are you'll be told the pilot knows his business, as does the man in charge of the water valves. Your yacht, looking very small in the bottom of the first of the Gatun Locks, will be made fast to but one side of the lock by nearly vertical lines running up to bollards some 50' above. She will be held off the lock side by fenders, and yet nothing will hold her close to the lock side, preventing her from drifting toward the lock's center as the water level rises. The valve tender, with an eye on his watch, then opens wide all the valves at once, and the game begins.

As the water rises, all hands take in the slack in the lines to prevent the yacht from being carried away by the current and then dashed violently back against the concrete wall. The least tardiness at any point in this game allows one of the submarine fountains to spout up in the gap between the wall and the yacht, which then requires the strength of all hands straining to close it. While the crew is thus hauling in the bow line, the stern lines goes neglected for a few seconds. One of the submarine fountains suddenly shoots up on the outboard side of the yacht and her quarter is hurled against the wall. The crew piles aft to pull in the stern line's slack, only to see a new jet rise up forward again between the bow and the wall, and the process is repeated.

We aboard the *Pilgrim* survived the three locks at Gatun with many timber-shaking jolts but without visible damage. However, on a later passage through the Miraflores Locks, on the way from Balboa back to Paraiso, the lock tender won the game. The *Pilgrim's* fashion-piece, the aftermost timber below the waterline, was smashed. This mishap was reported by the pilot and led to a formal hearing before a three-striper sitting as a board of inquiry, with official stenographer and all witnesses present. The hearing lasted several hours and held that the Government should make repairs. There is no question but that the hearing cost the Government more than the repairs, and that both the hearing and expense could have been avoided altogether.

It's damned interesting going through the canal. We passed many vessels & went into the different locks with the *President Garfield* from San Francisco, a big passenger liner. The *Pilgrim* looked tiny in the tremen-

dous locks beside the big steamer. It seems almost impossible when you actually see some of the great hills they had to cut through.

After ten hours of passage through the roughly forty miles of the Canal, the *Pilgrim* passed the dry dock and concrete wharves at the base of Ancon Hill and anchored off the Balboa Yacht Club. In this anchorage was one of the most interesting gathering of yachts we encountered in any port of the world. At the head of my list was the 34' engineless yawl *Islander*, which Harry Pidgeon "came down out of the mountains" and built himself and sailed alone around the world. He paid us a call one day and sold us copies of his book about the voyage. He would make the circuit again, and again alone.

Ashore one afternoon, Captain Pidgeon indignantly denied the story of the trip to Bermuda when the labels washed off all the food cans stowed in the bilge, and that he was supposed to have remarked it made no difference, "It was all grub just the same." To back up his denial, he insisted we visit the *Islander* to inspect a bilge "as dry as a pantry shelf." Off we went. That it was so was plain, an observation I made with not a little envy. We watched the Captain slap a coat of bottom paint on the *Islander* before leaving for Los Angeles, without incurring the expense of dry-docking. He managed this in the time it took the 14' tide to fall below his keel and return by tying up at the shore end of the Yacht Club Wharf and remaining there, hard aground but upright. I watched this with not a little envy, too. He cast off shortly afterwards, and we later heard he was eighty-four days to Los Angeles.

The 60' schooner *Coquet* was among our neighbors. She had been built of teak in Hong Kong and was a pretty little clipper-bowed model, though a trifle short on sail. Room for all her lead ballast evidently had not been found in the orthodox places somewhere below the metacentric height. Several dozen of the pigs had been disposed along the deck. These were kept from sliding off to leeward by rusty ten-penny nails driven into the covering boards. The *Coquet's* expedition represented the abortive aspirations of a San Francisco man who had advertised for company on a voyage to the South Seas. He had never been to sea and apparently had got all he wanted of it on the run down to Balboa. The entreaties of his wife and the rest of the company, on the rare occasions when they were able to find him ashore, were unsuccessful in inducing him to resume the voyage or even to pay more than increasingly infrequent visits to the schooner. Finally, one of the crew, a rancher from Wyoming who was accustomed to finishing what he had started, arranged to dispense with the owner altogether, and the *Coquet* set off for her original goal.

The *Western Queen*, an old British 75' ketch flying the Blue Ensign, was said to be bound for Tahiti. The owner and captain, Mr. "A" as I'll call him here, wore a monocle with an air which suggested acquaintance with a sphere at least sartorially superior to that of the tramps, adventurers, and voyagers among which he found himself, and kept rather aloof from the rest of the fleet. He permitted himself, however, to try to persuade Hawthorn to abandon the *Pilgrim* and accompany him in the *Western Queen* on a cargo-carrying venture along the Costa Rican coast. Hawthorn regarded this as fully as problematical as our own enterprise and declined.

The ketch *Southern Pearl*, likewise of British aspect, seemed to have a fluctuating ship's company that revolved around an Englishman and a Russian, who were never seen ashore or even on deck but who were observed when one or the other stuck his head out of the portholes from time to time. They were reported to have only vaguely formed plans for going somewhere or other, and we never heard of her again.

From nearer home was the *Evalu*, a 46' schooner which had left Salem, Massachusetts, about three years before, carrying a

Spanish-American named Blanco, his wife and their seven-year old daughter, Evalu. Blanco had been a Spanish teacher in a midwestern university. With little sea experience and only a slight knowledge of navigation, he had set out first to visit Barcelona, where some of his relatives lived, then to continue the wandering life indefinitely. His wife died on the eastward voyage across the Atlantic and, after burying her at sea, he continued on with only Evalu as crew. Thus short-handed, it is doubtful if he would initially have attempted to make such an extensive ocean voyage, but as he discovered from necessity that he and his very small daughter could handle the vessel well enough, he had continued with his original project. If he were to take ill or become disabled, the little girl would be at a serious disadvantage; the thought might easily have appalled him. On the passage from Barcelona to the Barbadoes, which took ninety days, Blanco asserted that for forty days at a time he "never touched the wheel." Since much of the route carried him before the northeast Trades, the *Evalu* must have been not only one of those very rare vessels which would take care of themselves while running before the wind, but perhaps the only one in existence which would do so for such a long stretch of time.

When we first met Blanco at Balboa, he had returned only recently from his first attempt to sail into the Pacific. After sixteen days of slatting about in the windless wastes of the Gulf of Panama, he and Evalu had worked the vessel back into Balboa to replenish stores and have the engine doctored. The *Evalu* carried a tall, old-fashioned, one-cylinder diesel engine of the type which, when sufficiently encouraged, emits a series of sharp and distinctly separate explosions. These explosions split the air for a time at regular intervals and then suspend, at which point the owner hopes for another before the flywheel loses momentum and the harbor neighbors hope each report will be the last. Blanco, who was more of a scholar than a mechanic, had given up hopelessly heaving at the heavy flywheel but was loath to venture into the gulf again without power. The Chief put in the better part of a day among the innards of the *Evalu* and apparently penetrated its ancient secret. The pelicans of the district meanwhile soared overhead, looking vainly for the stunned fish that normally rose to the surface during blasting operations in the Canal Zone.

❂ ❂ ❂

Aug. 31. Today was terribly hot with no rain at all. I washed all my clothes & hung them all over the rigging to dry.... I guess the whole interior of the boat will have to be torn out to replank her & it will take over a month if they decide to do the job. As things are now the vessel can not be sailed back to Boston as she is unseaworthy & has no certificate from Lloyds. She can't be taken out in the Pacific; so here she stays unless they can cure the leak.

The *Pilgrim's* predicament had of course been reported to her builder. He was quite properly concerned that a product of his yard should have become notorious. Unable to diagnose the schooner's ailment at a distance of over 2,000 miles, he finally announced that he was coming to Panama to do what he could. We decided to postpone any further experiments until he arrived. For a change of scene, we spent the intervening time at the small island of Taboga, about ten miles to the southward of Balboa.

❂ ❂ ❂

September 1. Anchored at Taboga Is. Pretty hot.... Francis climbed up to the main mast head, following Joe, & stayed an hour or more. Felt very proud on reaching the deck.

While this island had been listed, according to Findlay, in the

1884 edition of *South Pacific Ocean Directory*, as the headquarters of the Pacific Mail Company ("who have here a steam factory and coal stores, also a gridiron, 300 feet long") and was visited by vessels from Panama for procuring water and supplies ("both of which are more readily obtained than at the city"), it had, some time since, surrendered these pretensions to utility. I saw that it contained only a small village of whitewashed dwellings clustered about the single street, a Spanish church, one public house run by a Chinese proprietor, and a large red clapboard structure called the "Hotel Aspinwall". The island was composed chiefly of a one thousand foot hill, rising from behind the village. Despite its somewhat dreary aspect, its lack of mechanical activity provided a soothing respite from the docks and cranes of the Canal.

> **Last evening, Murph & I climbed up to the top of the highest mountain on Taboga.... We made it in half an hour. You get a wonderful view of all the neighboring islands and the mainland. The *Pilgrim* looked like a little toy boat in the harbor way down below us.**

One compensation for the grief of Panama was our furry *coati mundi*, Francis, who weighed about eight pounds. The *coati* inhabits Central America in droves, coursing the forests in search of roots, insects, and small members of the animal kingdom, which he roots out and subdues with a tapered snout and long claws. To all of these delicacies, however, he seems to prefer a hen's egg. Viewed from behind, while running with his clumsy lope, he exhibits much of the beguiling charm of the bear. His inquisitiveness exceeds that of a monkey, his capacity for the semblances of affection, that of the cat, and his self-will, that of a dachshund.

Francis won and kept the attention of everyone on board by his aptitude for social activity, combined with his obvious disregard of whether anyone liked him or not. The game which he

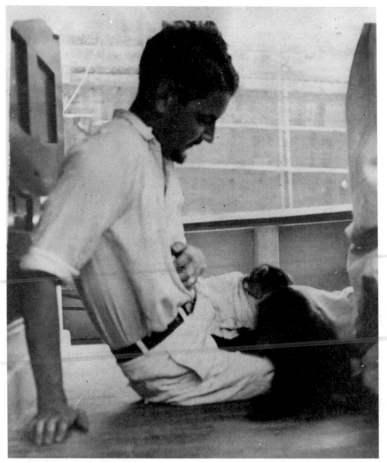

The Doc with Francis.

seemed to prefer above all others was chasing. This was simply a matter of your chasing Francis around the deck or up into the rigging or of his chasing you. Whether it was the one game or the other depended only on who started first, and both were equally absorbing to him. Boxing was another of his accomplishments. Squatting on his haunches, he would spar with a bare-handed human by the quarter-hour, chittering with excitement.

One afternoon, after a pleasant swim on the sandy isthmus

that runs out to the abandoned coal stores of the Mail Company, several of the company returned aboard to discover the Trader and the Chief attracting attention from the other side of the harbor. The Chief was running circles in the dory, shouting advice and expressions of excitement, while the Trader wrestled with a fishing rod bent nearly double and quivering with strain. The catch, when finally brought alongside, proved to be a very tired shark, 8' long. It was dispatched with gunfire and gaffed aboard, and the carcass was hung from the end of the boom in order for us to observe its effect upon its late associates.

A monster shark soon rose from below and with one chomp of its jaws severed and carried away all but the head. Immediately returning, the monster took the head with its second bite. It snapped like thread the manila line, large as a man's thumb, with which we'd hung the first shark. We were told afterwards of a local shark called "Taboga Bill," some 30' long, which had taken a small boy of the town from the shallow water, and soon afterward been caught with the evidence inside and still identifiable. Our further swimming was tentative and confined to the shallows along the beach, where there were only stingrays concealed in the sand.

Another encounter with the animal kingdom at Taboga was of a different nature. The Doc had grown a pointed, black chin-beard and mustache. The Skipper, during an exploratory walk ashore, saw on the face of a local cat black and white markings which closely approximated the pattern of the Doc's new look. He thought he'd bring the cat aboard to live with us, he later said, so that the similarity could be further studied and commented upon from all angles. The Skipper's way with animals more gently reared was not sufficiently beguiling to entrap the Taboga cat, however, and he had to ask for assistance. When the cat disappeared, the Skipper attempted to explain to an old woman in a mixture of sign language, broken English, and shattered Spanish, what he wanted. Some, at least, of this linguistic hash was understood.

A few hours later, a small boat put out from shore bearing three small boys and a large, restless, burlap sack. Once at the *Pilgrim's* rail, one of the boys upended the sack on the after deck, releasing simultaneously at least a dozen cats. Whether the bearded one was among them, the Skipper couldn't tell. Without pausing to survey their surroundings, the terrified cats rebounded from the deck as if it had been red hot and ran away in all directions so fast that it was hard to believe they had been aboard at all. Most of these directions were overboard. The boys, unpaid and disappointed, saved several as they headed back to shore. We assumed that the incident was closed until the Skipper began to complain at breakfast that something was walking across his face while he slept, or trying to. Ironically, it was only the Skipper who was subjected to these nocturnal visitations, which occurred regularly for several nights until the last cat was discovered in a remote corner of the lazarette, prodded out with an oar and repatriated.

Francis, the coati, is a great addition to the crew & a fine pet. He went ashore the other evening with the boys & got well loaded on beer.

❂ ❂ ❂

The leak continued at the rate of six to nine gallons an hour during this time, and on our return from our holiday at Taboga, 4 September, the builder, Mr. Reed, arrived. For the fourth time, the boundaries of our ship became the prison walls of a dry dock. The one improvement was that the new dry dock was 1,000' long instead of 300' as at Mt. Hope.

I got a letter from home & things sound terrible up there. I'm lucky to be out of it all.

...The latest news is that we go into drydock Tuesday, which will mean Wed. or Thursday. Simpson & Co. say they will fix us up in several days. They plan to cover the hull with tar or asbestos under the copper. This will stop the leaks while we lie at anchor but will be the same old story when we get to sea again & the vessel starts working. Hell, I'd take a chance in an unseaworthy vessel. What's the use in worrying whether you get home with your neck or not? There's nothing when you get there but worry & trouble and hard times & you might as well see what you can.

Under the builder's supervision, the copper was removed, a checked plank was replaced, a bent spike was drawn and a new one driven in. The ship's company was skeptical: it wasn't so easy as that, we had learned. And sure enough, on floating again, the pumps sang the same old tune, this time to more than eight gallons every hour. The builder said he was very sorry about the whole thing and went back to Maine.

September 25....A fine chicken dinner, prepared by the Cook in a temperature of about 300° F, was much enjoyed; but could not dispel the gloom which the persistence of the leaking has thrown over all. Even Francis seems much more quiet & not nearly so nippy...

The trip will have to be given up and the vessel junked from all appearances. I hope to hell I can get out to the East on a tramp steamer and won't have to go home from here. Such a thing as this has never happened before in yachting circles that anyone can recollect.

At about this time, the Skipper and I were called to the office of the Captain of the Port and reprimanded for going to Taboga without a pilot. No vessel of more than 65', we were told, could move in Canal waters without a pilot. I paid the bill for the pilot we had not employed and apologized. Soon after, the arrangements of the port required that the *Pilgrim* move from Pier 7 to Pier 8. This was not, of course, far distant, and lay in fact on the other side of a slip perhaps a hundred yards off. This time a pilot came aboard according to the regulations and took charge. As the schooner's engine was out of commission, we were taken under tow by a launch.

While leaving Pier 7, the pilot ran the end of the main boom into a piling, knocking the boom out of its crutch and carrying away one of the stern chocks. Cleared away for her voyage across the slip at last, the *Pilgrim* was headed by the pilot directly for a large scow. While we watched, not without admiring the last-second maneuvering with the wheel that might yet avoid collision, the pilot ran the schooner up on the scow. She took the entire strain on the bob stay, which naturally came out of the affair as slack as a hammock. Also, the outer bowsprit band, to which the bob stay is shackled, had under the strain chewed a large chunk out of the spar itself. Another official investigation followed, with sworn witnesses, stenographer, and formal procedure, resulting in free repairs and pilotage.

> *September 28. Commences tied to Pier 8. Warm & fair air. Mr. Simpson aboard & continued search for leak. Vessel having one of her peculiar good spells now: only making 2 1/3rd gal. per. hr. Sandpapered & painted big dory & peapod.*

> *September 29....Heavy showers, 9:30 A.M. Doubled up stern lines & started engine for a dock trial with the repaired valves, and to see if the vibration affects the leaking. Latter much reduced the last two days. Engine running very well. 1 P.M. Stopped engine. Leak about doubled since 9 A.M.*

I was beginning to wonder whether it was possible to repair the *Pilgrim* by any method short of replacing all of the planking. The staggering expense of such a project on top of what I had already incurred, together with the doubt that even new planking would not make her sound, kept me wondering. Still, the foreman of the Mt. Hope Yard had said in the very beginning that the schooner leaked all over in the way of her fastenings. While some of the treatment she received had been based on that theory, it might be that the treatment and not the theory was defective. If so, replanking would probably do the job. There was some good Douglas fir in the neighborhood. I sent a cable off to the builder for enough of the special bronze spikes with which she was originally fastened to replace all that would be spoiled in the pulling. He had said there were enough left over. The spikes arrived — with an invoice. They had been sent C.O.D. by the builder, who was so sorry. I shipped them back where they came from because I would not pay for them. The situation was very near to stalemate.

> *October 10. Tied to dock at Balboa. Commences calm & cloudy. Pumped bilge 10 A.M. Mr. Simpson aboard but no word yet from his office about the replanking.*

> *October 11. The vessel's owner, Mr. Starr, went to Panama Hospital this morning to have his tonsils out. Turned to scraping & varnishing blocks, cleats etc. Joe is making a new leather harness for Francis.*

> *October 13. Mr. Starr aboard from the hospital where he had his tonsils out & received a message via Mr. Simpson that Reed would replank the vessel at Boothbay Hbr or they would try to tinker up the leaky places & make the vessel tight by giving her a coat of tar!*

At this point, a yard superintendent at Balboa came forward with a scheme that, while somewhat complicated and laborious, would still be less expensive than replanking. His scheme was based on the original hypothesis that the leak was generally everywhere, contributed to by the nearly five thousand spike holes below the waterline, and was aimed directly at this condition. It had appeared first to a surveyor at Mt. Hope and later, more definitely, to a shipwright at Balboa that the diameter of the holes bored in the planking to receive the square-shanked spikes was slightly larger than the square thickness of those shanks.

Predrilling is done both to prevent the wood, in this case the 2⅜" planks of yellow pine, from splitting and to facilitate the procedure. The pilot hole, when done correctly, is of course *smaller* than the diameter of the item to follow for good. Except for the sealing effect of the spikehead, which was somewhat larger than the hole, there was a potential along each of the four sides of each spike in the *Pilgrim* for the passage of water. Each spikehead, additionally, was countersunk in a round hole in the planking, into which was driven a bung. The bungs already had been replaced with new ones, tightly driven in lead, with no perceptible sealing effect.

The superintendent's idea was to seal all of the narrow channels along all the spikes with a putty-like paste that would harden. He proposed to remove each bung and thread its hole, then insert the threaded nozzle of a specially constructed force-gun that would pump, under great pressure, a mixture of lead and litharge into the channels, after which a new threaded bung was to seal the bung hole. (Litharge is a yellow lead oxide, PbO.) The whole process, including resheathing with the copper, was estimated to cost considerably less than replanking, and take about two months. As it was out of the question to hire even a part of the 1,000' drydock for that length of time, to say nothing of living in one, it was proposed we dispense with the drydock altogether.

Again at Balboa, all the movable ballast was removed, sash-weight by sashweight and pig by pig. All but a small amount of fuel oil was pumped into dock tanks, and the sails were lugged ashore. The yard was lowered and taken ashore. The *Pilgrim* powered back into the Canal, through the Miraflores and Pedro Miguel Locks, and tied up to a scow near the dredge *Hercules* at a Black settlement named Paraiso, which is Spanish for Paradise — wildly hyperbolical in this case. Here, we lightered ashore the eighty fathoms of heavy anchor chain, two four hundred pound anchors, and the somewhat lighter kedge anchor. Joe went aloft and let go the spring, triadic, and main topmast stays between the masts.

In the meantime, Captain Mitchell of the *Hercules,* having studied a docking plan of the schooner, laid out heavy chocks on the level bank along the canal. His gang laid three strongbacks, timbers which prevent a hull's sides from being squeezed together, athwartships across the bulwarks. They passed three steel cables under the keel and up over the ends of the strong-backs, then led the three slings to a single steel hook suspended from the *Hercules'* giant crane. At the order, "Take a load!" the slings straightened, bar-taut, and I saw the *Pilgrim* take to the air. Describing a fine arc, like a flying boat in an amusement park, she floated aloft and overhead and was let down to rest on the chocks on the banks without a jar. The weight indicator in the *Hercules* registered 120 tons.

We shared the place with a collection of rusty boiler plates that was being "improved," or so it was claimed, with pneumatic hammers beginning at seven each morning. We ourselves carried on a succession of sanding and painting jobs, while the yard force labored under tarpaulins against heavy rain squalls. Paradise, indeed! From time to time, we looked wistfully at the cargo and passenger vessels that passed only yards away, flying the flags of the Netherlands, Sweden, Denmark, Norway, Great Britain, Australia, France, with now and then one from the United States or the Free City of Danzig, en route east or west to the great oceans.

The *Pilgrim* aloft in the Panama Canal Zone.

Thursday, November 24th. In spite of the general atmosphere of gloom & despair that hangs over all the members of the crew of the ill-fated *Pilgrim*, the Cook got up a wonderful Thanksgiving dinner. Last night there was general brawling & rioting on board as we all tried to forget the leaking & terrible job of driving the spikes in the planking. Hawthorne has gotten sick of hanging around and leaves Monday by steamer for Tahiti. I don't blame him at all as he only has a limited amount of time to be away from his job. Several days ago Francis slipped out of his harness and went off and has not been seen since.

With the end of our fourth month in the Zone, when the removal of a sample plank showed that the lead and litharge mixture in some instances had failed to penetrate the spike-channels, discouragement revived. The Cook went into Panama

City to attend a meeting of the local American Legion wearing a thick blue serge uniform covered with gold braid and medals and did not come back for three days. The superintendent's optimism was unaffected, at least outwardly, however. He promised he would drink all the water the schooner made when the job was done, and the work continued with that assurance.

Eventually, the last weary sheet of copper was nailed back into place, the *Pilgrim* again took to the air, and she settled back into the Canal. We ran down through the locks to Balboa, where a gang of longshoremen reloaded the ballast. Again old burlap draped the rail coaming and transom, but this time the temporary squalor of life aboard was easily endured for it meant we should soon be at sea. It would be a rare pleasure now to swing the pump handle and be rewarded for all our trouble by the suck of air from the well. The Skipper, just for practice, took a few swings. When, with a horrid gurgle and rush, the familiar dirty brown liquid poured onto the deck again, I said, "Save that, Skipper. The supervisor is going to drink it."

"Thirty-four, thirty-five.... He couldn't drink it all," the Skipper said, clenching his pipe, "but don't you think he could pump it out for us?"

"What do we do now?" Hod asked.

What indeed?

The Canal officials were incredulous. The superintendent disappeared and there was complete deadlock. The bill for the Paraiso process was presented, and since the Canal Zone Mechanical Division had not done the work on a "no cure-no pay" basis, I paid it. I was in no mood, to say nothing of financial position, now to replank the schooner. The two surveyors would not revise their previous judgment that the schooner was unseaworthy, and the Port Captain accordingly refused to grant clearance. The Cook made regular visits to the many barrooms of Panama, where he made the most of easy opportunities to tell the representatives of the Mechanical Division whom he met there what he thought of the Division, both as a whole and individually. The *Pilgrim* had become a source of embarrassment, not only to the supervisor but to all of his associates, up and down the scale.

❂ ❂ ❂

At the point when the situation looked hopelessly insoluble, the Port Captain suddenly relaxed his requirements for clearance. Why? I thought it was partly out of sympathy for our situation and partly to get rid of us.

After five months of frigging around we are off at last with the schooner still leaking after all the time & money that has been spent on her. She makes from 8-10 gals an hr, but we are going on just the same & hope for the best.

We cast off from Pier 14 at Balboa on the morning of the last day of the year 1932. As a sort of postscript, I feel compelled to relate that a pilot came aboard to make sure the schooner passed legally out through the straight, deep, unencumbered, and well-buoyed channel. In backing the schooner down past a projection from the wharf, he tore a large triangular piece of copper sheathing from just below the waterline. This served in a small way to confirm our lively satisfaction at leaving the Canal Zone, probably forever.

chapter 3

The Galapagos

THERE IS AN INVISIBLE BEATEN TRACK which extends from Balboa in a general southwesterly direction for some 900 miles to the Galapagos Islands and beyond. Not only do the steamers, taking the great circle course, pass through the islands, but virtually all the footloose mariners with the whole wide Pacific to choose from as well. They paint the names of their yachts on the shores of Tagus Cove, which lies just seconds south of the Equator on Isabela Island, then move on in a steady procession west.

A few years ago, Sunday newspaper stories fostered a new interest in the area with speculations about how two corpses came to be lying on the beach of Marchena, a relatively isolated island in the north of the group. However cold one might be to the morbid past associated with the place and its peculiar natural wonders, one will still find oneself settling irresistibly into the track of predecessors on the way to fairer scenes of the Marquesas and the Society Islands many days further down the wind. Blanco, for one, sailed his little *Evalu* clean through the group without a stop on his way to Nukuhiva.

Thanks to the Sunday supplements, one of the questions I'm most asked is whether we met the German baroness who had been associated with the two men whose bodies were discovered on the desolate lava shore beside an overturned small boat. It was widely suggested that she knew a good deal about why and how the corpses got there, but she herself has not been seen since. Another question frequently asked is, "Did you meet Dr. Ritter?"

Now, the fact that Dr. Ritter had gone to live on Floreana Island, as well as the fact that there was a Dr. Ritter at all, became known to the world through a series of articles which the doctor contributed to *The Atlantic Monthly*. He had selected that particular spot, he wrote, because it was, of all habitable places in the world, the most nearly uninhabitable and forbidding and, therefore, the least likely place to attract any other human beings who might attempt to force their company upon him. The doctor wanted above all, except for his female companion, to be let alone. However, in writing the articles for all the world to read, he could not have issued a more powerful challenge. In spite of his relative inaccessibility and his rather petulant complaints that he was not being taken at his word, an increasing number of strangers steadily found their way to his little clearing with the purpose of joining him on his adventure in solitude.

It was enough for me that Dr. Ritter said he wanted to be alone. Even though I probably should not be passing his way again and even though he was reputed to be fitted out with a full set of stainless steel teeth (a canard, it appears: it is the plate alone that is of steel), I did not attempt to penetrate the few yards of underbrush which separated his retreat from the trail up the slope from Post Office Bay. Later, it became known that the doctor had abandoned his first attitude by early 1933 and become friendly to visitors. I was not aware of that at the time, and so remain a continual disappointment to dinner partners who ask, "Did you see that German, you know, the one with the stainless steel teeth?"

❂ ❂ ❂

The *Pilgrim* had slid out from the early morning shadows of the Balboa workshops and coal cranes. She rode a fair tide down the bay past Fort Amador and green Taboguilla Island. Heading west-southwest, she raised her clipper bow to the broad Pacific swell and followed the sea-lane which leads to the islands. While our original departure from Boston had been enveloped in a stimulating aura of adventure, it dissipated gradually, first losing its freshness and then evaporating entirely as its boundaries contracted from the vast horizons of unknown oceans to the purlieus of the Zone's repair shops. Now, as we headed out for the Pacific, those boundaries expanded again to the limits of our imagination. The schooner, to be sure, was still leaking, but after the going over she had received, we felt sure that whatever the remaining leak or leaks were they could not be severe enough to challenge the pumps. Doesn't the wood of a wooden ship, once back in the water, work and swell? We were no more than three weeks out when the flow diminished to less than a gallon an hour, and it never afterward exceeded that rate.

From the ship's log: January 5, 1933. 8-12 P.M. Partly cloudy, cool & very slick. Perfect sailing. Quite a bit of moon. Latter part adds, if possible, to the perfection of sailing.

A fresh northerly was blowing on our passage out through the Gulf of Panama, and it stayed with us until we were within two degrees of the Equator, nearly 200 miles further south than is expected at that season. Fearful of losing this slant, we held a southerly course well to the east of the rhumb line and closed to within sixty miles of Galera Point, Ecuador. This lies on the bulge of the South American coast, roughly between Ecuador and Colombia, and is about 700 miles due east of the Galapagos. At that point, the friendly northern breeze disappeared in the face of colder winds from the south.

The rainy season, when the southeast trade wind gives way to a southwest monsoon was just beginning, and balmy starlit nights with porpoises making rival galaxies in the phosphorescent sea about the ship were replaced by confused seas and intermittent heavy rains. The water became colder as we passed through the northerly turning point of the Humbolt Antarctic Current, where it mixes the chill of long-melted ice floes with the warm water of the Gulf of Panama and swings to the westward, joining the Equatorial current. As we turned southwest and approached the Equator, conditions soon again became more appropriate to the latitude.

January 6. 4-8 A.M. Joe welcomed the dawn with a few snatches of Nordic melody which he refused to translate even for the Skipper. The Chief had a dream, after taking a heavy jolt of one of the Doc's remedies: "Schooner Pilgrim leaving Boston in midwinter with a load of hay on deck & pulled over the ice by a train of horses with the Skipper at the reins. All the crew were on skates & followed along beside the vessel on the ice. On the way out of the harbor the Skipper pulled up & got down off the load & went over to consult with another vessel that was just coming in drawn by horses. He was afraid the ice wasn't strong enough to hold us up. One of our crew was having a hell of a time because he had forgotten his skates. He didn't think he'd have any use for them at sea & had to ride on board with the Skipper. On rounding a sharp turn outside, the Skipper lost the whole load of hay overboard next to a fine pine grove & said, 'Hell, let's camp here. I camped here once during the war.'"

Seven days out of Panama, having used the engine for only twelve hours on the notoriously windless run, Tower Island showed up on the starboard bow. Volcanic peaks, with their monstrous lava formations, make up most of these islands and are a vivid experience when seen for the first time. For the full effect, however, I'd recommend not making Tower Island your landfall, as this alone of the fifteen islands and many islets of the archipelago is low and nondescript. It reminded the Trader of Misery Island off Manchester, Massachusetts. Darwin Bay, named for the great naturalist by William Beebe on an expedition in 1923, is a submerged crater that forms the island's only harbor. It is open to the southwest and was too deep, so far as we knew, for anchoring. So, leaving behind a straight line of breakers against a rocky shore, we turned the *Pilgrim* southward for Chatham Island where the port of entry was.

The abundant animal life, which so sharply contrasts with the starkness of the islands themselves, was first apparent in the seabirds which gathered about as the schooner approached. Among a crowd of gulls were the black Galapagos storm petrel with white rump, identified by Murph in his role as official ornithologist, and the black-browed albatross. A great frigate bird soared above the masts, while several bosun birds zoomed and side-slipped above the schooner's wake.

During the night, the loom of the peak of Santa Cruz Island rose ahead. Joe, observing its towering shape during the evening watch, reported that he smelled fire and brimstone, but this may have been his imagination. The Galapagos Current was evidently running at its greatest speed, two and a half knots, as the schooner was set well up into the channel between Marchena and Santa Cruz. The wind remained light and we spent much of the night jogging about on the Equator, which by morning we had crossed definitely though without any of the ancient and recently revived Neptune and flour paste ceremony.

Soon after I came on deck for the morning watch, the sky and sea began to separate from one another, turning from black to gray, and Venus rose above a pall of thick cloud. The gray monotony turned here to a streak of incipient yellow, there to a spot of mauve, there to pale green, each so delicate as to be scarcely discernible as color and then only by contrast with the others. The smooth and slowly heaving mounds of sea caught the

The Commander at the wheel.

light and tossed it leisurely, one to another. The scene was a
harmony of aesthetic understatement, as far removed as possible
in feeling from the ferocious life at the same moment crowding

and fighting in the waters beneath us and from the titanic forces, but resting for a moment beneath the great cones of lava among which we drifted gently along.

> *January 6. Note. We find what was sold us as an Ecuador flag is really Colombia's, the blue being dark instead of light. Several discarded pieces of cloth, including an old shirt of Commander Starr's, are believed to be the right colors...*

> *January 8. 12-4 P.M. Got our flag at the main peak & our renovated Ecuador flag at the fore top masthead.*

> *If there's one flag that I adore*
> *It is the flag of Ecuador.*
> *It's not the yellow or the red,*
> *But the baby blue suggesting bed*
> *And rattles, pap and a downy puff,*
> *And a bit of drool on papa's cuff.*
> *The Doc observes to Amy's Burt,*
> *"Who would have thought the Commander's shirt*
> *So skillfully attached by Joe*
> *Would whistle in the breezes so,*
> *Proclaiming to all on sea and shore*
> *Our great respect for Ecuador?"*

The marker for Wreck Bay on the west coast of Chatham Island is Dalrymple Rock. It has been described as resembling a ship under full sail, but as we made our approach in the late afternoon sun, it looked more like a woman's head of hair done up in curl-papers, with the added *coup de toilette* supplied by the white leavings of thousands of sea birds on its many nubbles. To the east is Kicker Rock, a boot-shaped prominence rising straight up from a thirty-fathom bottom close to the shore of the island, while further east a great natural cone rises golden from the sea, rising out of a now deep ultramarine sea. Directly ahead, burnt brown slopes resolved themselves into a shore line of tumbled black lava rocks. Above them was a band of parched scrub which blended higher up toward the summits of a line of volcano craters into the green blush of fresh vegetable life.

Between the half-submerged wreck of the Australian steamer *Canarva* on Schiavoni Reef and the estimated location of a shoal spot on the opposite side of the channel, the *Pilgrim* carried her breeze. We anchored off a little rickety pier, where a group of people stood watching our arrival with obvious expectancy. Although this was the chief port for the whole archipelago, they had no boat of any kind. It was necessary to put over one of the dories to make official contact with the government. This was represented by a small, effusive gentleman in the uniform of the Ecuadorian cavalry. Nowhere in any country did we find such courtesy and cordiality as that which immediately flowed from Major Aguilera. He shook hands all around, at the same time talking very fast. We grasped that we were extremely welcome. Had the Cook not been as well acquainted with Spanish as with English, French, Dutch, German, and possibly other languages, we might not have understood that the Major was assuring us of a supply of fresh vegetables and horses for seeing the island.

Those parts of the Galapagos which are visible in any detail from the sea are of the most barren appearance. The shore, at most points, presents a confused aggregation of enormous lava and sandstone boulders which in past ages have tumbled down the slopes of the hundreds of craters on the heights. From the shore to the woodline, where the terrain rises dramatically, the color from a distance is uniformly dusty. Closer up, you see it is a jumble of more boulders, loose shale, and lava dust, through which is spread a stubborn but seemingly lifeless growth of gray and brittle brush, some thin grass, and, here and there, stubby cactus. Above this is a contrasting belt of relative luxuriance. From these parts of Chatham came the pineapples, alligator pears, and, indirectly, the milk and eggs which Major Aguilera procured for us.

The following morning, guided by the Major, we set off on foot along the soft lava dust road rising to the town of Progreso. For some distance, the only signs of life among the whitened skeletons of bushes were little birds, some bright scarlet and others canary yellow, which hopped about the twigs a few feet from the road. After about three miles of climbing, the road leveled off into fields of sugar cane and pastures in which horses and their foals grazed. Amidst one cane field stood a structure that looked something like a house of cards. It was formed by sheets of rusty corrugated iron which shook and rattled to the vibrations of an engine somewhere within. Two voices in strident and simultaneous conversation could be heard above the noise of the machinery as we passed near it. This was a sugar mill, the Major told me, the principal enterprise of the island. A round but imperious figure in breeches and a wide-brimmed grass sombrero cantered up on a white horse. Drawing upon nearly all of my Spanish, I said, "Buenos días." The reply, simply but with some pride, came: "I am Cobos."

Señor Cobos was the son of an Ecuadorian entrepreneur who had, a generation before, obtained a concession on the labor of the mainland convicts who made up most of the island's population. The elder Cobos, only a few years before our arrival, had been killed by some of his subjects. The whole project had then been taken over by a government corporation, and the son, fresh from a Paris education, was engaged as overseer. He wore a holstered revolver in a prominent and convenient position.

Progreso presented a squalid appearance. It was composed of about one hundred huts with thatched roofs and dirt floors, four corrugated iron sheds, a white-washed adobe building resembling a stable, and a two-roomed shack serving as a barracks for the army post of fifteen soldiers. Donkeys, pigs, and barefooted children passed freely in and out of the sill-less doorways. The adobe building proved to be a store where the Administrator also had an office and where, after a round of warm beers, I invited four of the leading citizens to dine on board that evening. Both my omissions in not having included their families and the treat which was regarded as a meal on a yacht were attested by the appearance of not four, but ten, people at the landing place that evening. They had walked the five miles from Progreso and would walk back again at the end of the evening, uphill.

> **From Hod Fuller's journal: The Cook got in one of his grouches & we had to eat in two shifts because there was not enough gear to go around. After dinner we played the victrola & danced on deck & the Doc played "Oscar," the harmonium. They all seemed to have a great time. The Lt. and Major are fine fellows and very nice to us. We suspect the Lt. to have been sent out here to cool off as he is down to 3 cigarettes & a little wine a day & looks like the kind of lad who liked wine, women & song.**

In 1926, a group of Norwegians had come to Chatham, hoping to form an ideal agricultural community and settlement. The Ecuadorian minister at Oslo had described the island in such interesting terms that some fifty people were induced to make the long journey, which they did in a concrete ship. They were greatly disappointed, however, and most left within the year. Only a few of the more optimistic remained, among them a girl named Karin. Previous travelers had written admiringly, even lyrically, of Karin's beauty, describing a dashing Diana who rode over the moors dressed in white and carrying a pearl-handled revolver, and who managed a plantation with masculine efficiency but with no loss of femininity. It is no wonder that we aboard the *Pilgrim* looked forward to meeting this island queen. We soon enough received an invitation to dine at her house, but it was not at first recognized as coming from the almost legendary figure, as we did not know then she had become Madame Cobos.

On the way to the Cobos plantation, Joe rode a horse for the first time in his seafaring life. The unruly pony chewed through its rope bridle and proceeded to run away with him. Our boatswain managed to stay aboard, however, and in spite of the fact that, as he reported, "the rigging — clewlines, buntlines and braces — all carried away."

Shortly after, our guide led us to the cantina in Progreso where we were joined by a friendly young man from Mexico. During an exchange of good feelings induced by several appetizers of gin, washed down by chasers of a violet colored soda, the Mexican remarked in halting English that Murph looked like Dolores Del Rio's husband and that he was "pretty." Murph, while possessed of rugged good looks, had never been regarded as "pretty" before and seemed rather more embarrassed than flattered, and we took our cue from him to move on without further delay.

We were next shown the barracks where the fifteen enlisted men slept in one room, in bunks around the walls. In the other room, occupied by their two officers, a blueprint chart of the Galapagos Islands was tacked on a bare board wall next to a Geodetic Survey chart of the New England coast from Cape Cod to the Bay of Fundy. The enlisted men wore clothing of olive drab khaki but of no apparent uniformity of design. Only one rifle, an old German type with a bayonet attached, was visible, leaning against a wall. This sketchy and somewhat haphazard military presence was quite of a piece with the whole military establishment of the republic. The *Statesman's Year Book* for 1932 reports that the entire equipment of the Ecuadorian Air Force consisted of one Travelair monoplane.

Dinner at the Cobos hacienda began at three-thirty in the afternoon and, running to some nine generous courses, lasted into

the night. Madame Cobos had become in the last few years less
the dashing character and more the matronly figure, but I thought
her blue-black hair and fair skin must have lost little of their
beauty. She appeared to take great pleasure in the opportunity to
speak in Swedish with Joe. He sat next to her at dinner and
reported that she was homesick for Scandinavia.

After we had been confronted successively with eight dishes,
which included eggs, sausages, pork, chicken, and papaya, the
stimulus of our natural and our artificially induced appetites had
worn off entirely. There followed, however, a great pie. Beneath
its crust, sprinkled with sugar, was a kind of meat stew. It was
plainly regarded as the *pièce de résistance*, and there was nothing
to do but fall to and do it some kind of justice. After making a
gingerly showing with my portion, I asked the nature of the meat,
which was not quite like beef and was faintly fishy to the taste,
and was informed that we were eating lizard — marine iguana, to
be specific. Two of our company were sick afterwards.

Upon our departure from Wreck Bay, the Major presented us
with two buckets of avocados, some oranges, pineapples, and a
live land tortoise, or *galapago,* weighing about thirty pounds.

Barrington Island, one of the smaller of the Galapagos, has no
permanent inhabitants and is seldom described. There wasn't
even a large-scale chart of it. One of the Norwegians had shown
us a photograph, however, and gave directions for anchoring in
a cove on the northeast corner of the island, about 25 miles west.
As he had recommended the place for a peculiar interest, we
made it our next stop. By coasting along the eastern shore, a series
of nearly identical indentations, we finally picked out the
recommended cove. Our choice was confirmed by a bearded and
very dirty Baltic type with only one trouser leg. He came from the
shore in a boat with three Ecuadorian Indians to greet us and
point out the best anchorage. This was just inside the mouth of the
cove, about half way between the main shore and a low, rocky

islet which gives northerly protection, in four and a half fathoms.

The four men were living in a shack on the beach, catching and salting fish until their schooner returned. Their only water was in a rusty oil drum. If their vessel were not to reappear, they would stand a good chance of dying, since there is no natural supply of water on the island. There are, near the beach and marked by a single wooden cross, the graves of seven men who had been shipwrecked on the other side of the island in 1920. After crossing the island in search of water, they had died of thirst.

The water of the cove was perfectly clear. I saw not only the anchor and chain resting on the white sand bottom, but many rays or blanketfish, large turtles, and sea lions swimming under the sunken ship. As evening fell and a full moon rose through the cactus trees, I heard the barking of the sea lions on the shore and saw numerous little brown owls settle on the yard and in the rigging. The Trader put over a shark hook baited with pork on a chain leader, and in no time hooked a 10' shark. He hoisted it on deck with a dory tackle. It was then dispatched with a marlin spike by Joe and robbed of its tail for a bowsprit decoration.

Other sailors have recorded extensive swimming while catching sea turtles, but we saw so many determined sharks, some as long as 16', that the risk seemed too great. These sea wolves often bit large pieces out of the groupers and other fish we caught from the dory. On one occasion, I saw three of them follow a wounded sea lion into the rocky shallows to where their backs were well out of water, then drag him back into deep water for the finish. A shark which the Trader struck a mighty but glancing blow on the head with a harpoon was so little deterred by the experience that he was back again inside of five minutes. This time, the harpoon landed squarely and went clean through its body, emerging from its belly. This one was clearly not of the breed of which they will tell you in Tahiti that merely slapping the water with the hand drives them away.

Some of us climbed to a ridge above the little cove where the seven mariners had stumbled and died thirteen years before. Low rolling hills stretched away toward the interior. Even for us, well-fed and shod, the going was like a nightmare of recurring obstacles. It must have been heartbreaking for the shipwrecked men. It was almost impossible to pick a horizontal trail between the giant lava boulders and through the thorny brush. Progress was a series of climbs up and slides down the rough, baking hot sides of the rocks. We were on the lookout for wild goats, the descendants of some reputed to have been left by whalers as a stock of live provisions, and at length we saw three making off along the opposite ridge. With a lucky shot, I brought one down. It was well over an hour before we were able to reach where it lay. A suitable reward for climbing back to the shore with the warm, bloody, and fragrant carcass would have been a real gastronomic treat; the meager and rank goat meat decidedly was not. Were it not for the Skipper's robust and catholic stomach, the poor creature would have died in vain.

During this shore expedition, we saw a number of land iguanas resting beneath cactus and rock. These reptiles are about 20" long in the body, with tails more than twice as long again, and are light green. A row of vertical spines extends from the head to the rump, those just behind the neck being perhaps 3" long, gradually decreasing in length down the spine. The four feet are equipped with sharp claws. The skin, marked by reticulated creases, makes a loose pouch below the jaw. Its whole aspect when hissing through bared teeth is sinister, indeed. While it looks like a dangerous customer, however, it is in fact quite harmless.

Many sea lions are seen all along the shore stretched out in the sun & taking it easy. They are very tame & not afraid of human beings & are almost human the way they look at you. The Skipper came right up to a

big one asleep & woke him up & he roared like hell &
made lunges with his head but never bothered to move.
This evening the sea lions are making a hell of a racket
on the point about 15 yards off our stern.

From Barrington, we powered south through a calm the 38
miles to Post Office Bay on Floreana Island. A tall cylinder of
whitened oil drums with a dead lantern on top behind the beach
caused some confusion at first. Finally, we located the proper
range of a white flag staff and the middle of a weathered wooden
house and anchored in six fathoms. There were no letters for me
or anyone else in the painted cask mounted on a post ashore. This
was the most recent replacement of the famous original box used
by whalers to transfer mail to homeward bound vessels and from
which the bay took its name.

From the post box, we moved toward the only house down a
path through the sand. The path was bordered by small round
stones, but the border failed to lend an air of either formality or
care to the general forsaken appearance of the place. The door and
windows of the shack were locked. Through the glass, I saw an
overturned chair, a bare table, and a barrel freight marked with a
point of origin in Germany. Some household china had been
unpacked and left on the floor. There were no other signs of
present habitancy, but the cackling of hens from a smaller shack
behind it suggested that someone was making frequent visits.

We had been told that the baroness, who was reputedly the
granddaughter of Richard Wagner, the German composer and
poet, had settled with two guests in the hills above the bay. We
decided to make them the object of our afternoon expedition. The
going here was not nearly as hard as it had been on Barrington, as
a trail had been broken through the bush. The only difficulty was
in walking on pieces of lava about the size of footballs. There were
fresh horse or donkey droppings on the trail.

When we reached the higher and more fertile ground, where

bare sandstone and lava gave way to grass and orange trees, I saw evidence of wild cattle as well as a number of animal skulls and skeletons on the ground. After two hours of climbing, the sun was closing with the horizon. There was no further sign of settlement. Since we had no lights and were winded to boot, the Skipper and I forewent the satisfaction of meeting the granddaughter and her small following for the certainty of sleeping in our own bunks rather than among cacti or iguanas. Joe and Murph continued on. Later, they reported briefly and without enthusiasm on their short visit with the camp's inmates, after being guided back to the shore in the dark by one of the young men.

On the following morning, both of the men, Philipson and Lorenz, came down to the shore and signaled to be brought aboard. They have since become famous — Philipson through the mystery of his disappearance with the baroness, Lorenz through his association with them and his own death. Philipson, the taller of the two and the one who would naturally be named first in any reference to the pair, had recently shaved and seemed to be in fairly good physical condition.

Lorenz, on the other hand, was slight and thin. Among the sparse pale whiskers of several weeks' growth on his face were numerous sores. Although his stout walking boots were in good condition, his dirty trousers were torn off at the knees. In three months, I learned, they had become thoroughly "fed up" with the island. Neither, however, suggested that I help them get away. We put them ashore with a quantity of cigarettes (somewhat mildewed from the Canal Zone rainy season), an old pair of trousers (likewise mildewed but whole), some shotgun shells, and a length of manila rope. This last they were to substitute for the rawhide thongs which they had been using to tether their cattle and which were constantly eaten by rats.

About three miles to the east of Post Office Bay, the tip of a dead volcano protrudes from the sea, making the tiny island of

Onslow. Its precipitous sides are of solid, deeply ribbed, and indented lava in which, here and there, large bubbles have left cave-ins. As we approached the narrow beach, a dozen sea lions reared their heads to watch us land. Others, like dogs chasing an automobile, broke water alongside the boat and dove beneath it. They appear to have no fear of humans, although the older ones are suspicious. A baby sea lion approached the Chief from behind and sniffed at his calf, giving him quite a start, but when he made to capture it, the mother swept in and carried her baby off and into the water with her teeth.

> On the E shore of this island is a wonderful sea lion rookery. We landed in the midst of them & had a great time. There must have been 300 in all. Apparently there were two bulls in charge of two large herds of females & they kept herding them inshore. One of them grew very annoyed & finally came charging at me through the water to the shore & stopped about 10 yards from me roaring like hell. The Trader tried to pick up a baby about 20" long & its mother came flapping up & picked it up in her mouth & made for the water with him.

The waters around Floreana abound not only in turtles, sea lions, sharks, mantas, grouper, and many smaller fish but also in blackfish or pilot whales. During a short trip in the sailing dory along the northwest coast, we encountered a school of these whales, each one weighing perhaps eight hundred pounds. They approached us head-on in a column about fifty yards wide. They were moving very fast and jumping 6' to 8' into the air. I was greatly relieved that they parted when they came to the dory and passed on either side. The rear of their expedition was brought up by two sharks. Presumably, they were hoping for leftovers from what the blackfish were snatching in their wild career. If a story told me in Panama was true, they were not looking for a chance to attack the blackfish themselves. A Taboga man, who was to be sure well along in drink at the time, said he'd seen a school of blackfish bounce a shark from one to the other on their backs, from deep water to the shore, where they left it nearly senseless, if not dead, on the beach.

As large as all the rest of the Galapagos Islands put together, Isabela sprawls some 100 miles from just north of the Equator to the south and west. Shaped like an inverted "L," it marks the western end of the archipelago of which she is, by virtue of name and size, the queen. Huddled close to the shank of the "L" and separated from it by a two-mile strait is the much smaller island of Fernandina. With the southerly breeze continuing very light, the run over from Floreana in the *Pilgrim* was accomplished to the tune of the diesel and with the assistance of nearly one and a half knots of a following set, past the southwest end of Isabela.

Keeping about two miles off the precipitous rocky shore on which broke the southwesterly swell, we came into a kind of sound between the larger and smaller islands. The sun was just then setting. When we were about five miles off a shallow bight marked on the chart as "Webb Cove," we slowed down so we wouldn't close with either shore before daybreak. As darkness came on, the 4,000' peaks, of which there are five on the large island and one on the small, seemed to rise into the sky and lean in toward the schooner. The space between, in which we would be confined for the next eight hours, seemed very narrow. Before the loom of the mountains became entirely indistinguishable, I took bearings on all but one, which was hidden in clouds. The bearings, which normally reassure you of your position, did not cross each other at anything like the same point; careful verification of them did not help create a proper fix, either.

A year and a half earlier, although I did not know it, Temple Utley aboard the *Inyala* had made similarly unsatisfactory observations. From an anchorage on the southwest shore of

Isabela, he also took bearings of one peak on Fernandina and four on Isabela. He found his position was Webb Cove, although the plan of the harbor he was in matched Iguana Cove, which was supposed to lie nine miles south. South of Utley's cove, moreover, there was no other. What could account for this other than that the positions of the peaks on the chart were wrong? This discovery was mildly disquieting to me in the *Pilgrim,* but as the weather remained calm, we did not move enough during the night to create any risk of running ashore.

In the morning, Fernandina lay off to port. One could see it was formed almost entirely of black lava which had cooled in rolling ridges and bubbles. To starboard, behind the cliffs of Isabella's shore, the sun filtering through the mists disclosed many smaller craters and blowholes with black lava flows striating the sandstone slopes. The sea long ago had broken through the wall of a crater near to the shore and formed one of the best harbors anywhere — Tagus Cove.

> *January 16....Ran in between 2 hills into the crater forming Tagus Cove where we anchored near the head at 8:40 A.M., 8 fathom of water, 30 fathom of chain, sandy bottom. Very slick place, perfectly bare... In the evening had the usual shark hunt, getting a couple of pretty big ones. Heavy williwaws blowing around the cove suggest great possibilities of fouled anchor.*

The steeply sloping walls of rock are indeed bare of any natural growth, either sprouting from, clinging to or running along their sterile surfaces. A closer inspection of the landscape reveals a good deal of the peculiar fauna of the region — some of it, like the flightless cormorant, even peculiar to Tagus Cove. It is here that the most careless inspection could not miss the marks of man which confront you like loud shouts from the northeast corner as you enter. But for these marks, no sign would remain of the visitors over the centuries. The cove, with its border of thousands of marine iguanas, its playing manatees, its blue-footed boobies, and its pelicans, would truly be a museum of distant ages. A few years ago, however, some visiting mariner yielded to the impulse to paint the name of his vessel and the date of call in large white block letters on the rock face above the water's edge. Many who have followed have apparently approved his imagination, enterprise, and loyalty by doing likewise. The result is interesting as a directory, although not in proportion to the height of the letters, which in some cases are as much as 6'.

As it was from here that we were to make the passage of some 3,000 miles to the Marquesas Islands, the schooner came in for a careful inspection. Joe found the splices in the main throat and fore peak halyards short of his high standards and respliced them. He wormed, parceled, and canvas-coated wire lifelines, then rove them through bronze stanchions from the main rigging to the boom gallows. Out from the musty depths of the lazarette we dragged the trysail, the spare jib, and the board-like folds of the spare foresail, to open them to the sun for a few hours and restow. It was some days now since we had been near the centers of civilization where dirt is produced, and the schooner's white topsides, varnished rail, and light green house tops looked as clean as the shale which the waters of Tagus Cove had been washing for thousands of years.

The chart of the cove, based on the British survey made in 1835 by Robert FitzRoy, captain of *H.M.S. Beagle* and shipmate of Charles Darwin, indicated a source of water at a break in the cliffs a short distance to the south, but we could find no sign of it. Most of the shoreline was so precipitous that if the dory were cast ashore, I could not possibly have gained a foothold. Some of the gigantic boulders even leaned out over the water, having apparently lost momentum on some far off and violent day, just short of one more hyperborean somersault. From the rim of the crater above the harbor, which I eventually managed to climb, the absence of water at the spot marked by FitzRoy seemed to be explained by a black lava flow about a mile wide which filled the valley above it. However, Charles Hubbard, who visited the spot later in the *Zavorah*, reported finding a trickle there and with great patience filled his beakers.

The old Tanganyika spirit arose in Murph at this point, and he set off alone into the hills to look for a volcano marked on the chart as having been active in 1928. Walking along the shore was not nearly as difficult here as in some other parts of the group — or as on other parts of Isabela, where Utley and his party had nearly died of exhaustion and thirst a few months before — but making a solo expedition into the badly charted interior was still a stout-hearted project. Murph returned the next morning. He reported he'd spent the night in a bed of volcano ash without a blanket, and without having found the crater he sought.

January 17. The Commander, Murph, the Trader and the Skipper made an all day expedition across the strait 12 & ½ miles or so by sailing dory to Fernandina. Shores of this island covered with rough lava which practically prevents reaching the interior.... A great many iguanas scrambling around on the rocks close to the water, especially points, & a few sea lions, birds & a big hawk. Wildest & most recent of these volcanic islands. The iguanas are very tame & some would sit & let you scratch them with a stick. Also a couple of big wingless cormorants.

One aspect of the Galapagos which alone attracted many visitors is fishing. At each of the islands visited by the *Pilgrim*, Murph and the Trader tried their luck, trolling from the dory powered by an outboard we'd acquired in Balboa. They caught hundreds of fish in a very short time. Most were groupers, often weighing as much as thirty pounds, with an occasional wahoo, and still others we couldn't identify were brightly colored: red — what a philosopher would call carmine — fish were quite

common, and now and then bright green, and gold. On one
occasion, when I took the rod in hand near Tagus Cove, the fish
were so thick and so voracious that the spoon hardly met the
water before there was a strike. Although sharks sometimes took
a chunk out of a fish, the dory was soon loaded with more than
we could use. We donated several dory loads to the fishermen at
Barrington Island. There are also many swordfish and marlin
among the islands, but we did not have the engine power or the
right rods and reels to go after them. We were not equipped,
either, to catch the manta. We saw several of them as wide as 10',
often leaping clear of the water and turning, crashing flip-flops to
rid themselves of parasites or to stun fish for eating.

I have mentioned Temple Utley in connection with the
position of Webb Cove. It is difficult for me to think of the islands
now without recalling his sojourn there, which had ended about
a year before my arrival. Utley had come out from England by
way of Barbados in the old 54' yawl *Inyala* on his way to the
islands further to the southwest. Here he embarked on some of
the most arduous and dangerous adventures. Physically handi-
capped by having only one good lung, he repeatedly found
himself cut off from water or provisions by miles of uncharted,
almost impassable lava country. He sustained himself by eating
the occasional tortoise and sucking on cactus pads. To one of his
companions, these conditions proved fatal. The remarkable fact
about his survival was not that he survived, but that he found, in
the grueling hardship of it, a simplicity of living which led him to
refer to the Galapagos episode as one of the highest points of his
life — a life which was far from prosaic. After his ordeal, Utley
("by the light of a bit of hide floating in tortoise fat") wrote in *A
Modern Sea Beggar*:

> ...I have a beard and a mane of hair, I wear no shoes and am
> clothed in rags. I live on tortoise flesh and sweet potatoes which
> I eat with my fingers, and I sleep on straw with a coat for a

pillow. I live a precarious life and have been near disaster in the last few weeks, yet I am thoroughly contented and happy.

Surely, there are few places in the world where the conditions of living are more propitious to the attainment of the stoic ideal.

To none of the members of the *Pilgrim's* company, however, did the rock piles of the Galapagos appear as either Elysium or a challenge — except, of course, to Murph, who had his sortie in search of a live volcano. After eleven days, we were ready to leave the rock piles to the lizards and the tortoises and strike out for the islands of the South Seas. Strictly speaking, we had been in the South Seas ever since we entered the waters first seen from the "peak in Darién," but the natural abundance and hospitality to humans that so happily characterize the rest of the islands in the South Pacific are so markedly absent from the Galapagos group that it is more natural to see the region not as a corner of the South Seas, but as a world apart.

January 19.... Have spent the last couple of days getting things all set for crossing the Pacific. Joe has nailed one of the large shark tails on the end of our bowsprit & given it a coat of varnish.

The barren amphitheater of Tagus Cove echoed with the rattle and clank of many fathoms of anchor chain coming in through the hawse-hole, accompanied first by the unintelligible remarks from the Trader as he tiered the heavy links of chain in the locker below, then by the rumble and purr of the engine. Somnolent iguanas blinked their eyes indifferently, and two sea lions slid off the beach for a last gambol around the hull as we moved out of the cove for the long run to the Marquesas Islands. Leaving on the starboard quarter the wide bay named for Sir Joseph Banks, the opulent and eccentric naturalist on Captain Cook's first voyage, we ran along the north shore of Fernandina Island and took departure from its termination in Cabo Douglas.

chapter 4

The Galapagos to the Marquesas

From Hod Fuller's journal: Course all day SW by W ¾ W & nice breeze from aft. During morning set balloon jib & fisherman staysail & have been rolling along 5-6 knots all day long. Fine sunny days & great sailing. Joe has been fixing over the life rings which were falling to pieces after the spell of Panama wet season. This afternoon I found the electric hot head heater was busted on the Petter Engine. I frigged around with two busted ones & managed to make one good one of them & rigged it up & she works fine.

From the ship's log: January 21. 8-12 A.M. Excellent PEA SOUP for lunch. Nothing like pea soup.

We still have on the balloon jib, foresail, main, fisherman staysail & gaff topsail & this evening most of the breeze has died out & we are rolling around with the booms slatting like hell, still in the region of equatorial calms & variables & do not expect strong trades until 4°-5° south lat.

January 23. 12-4 P.M. 500 miles from Tagus Cove at noon today. Excellent performance for the vessel, considering the light airs.

January 26. 12-4 A.M. Commences vessel slipping along nicely, making 6 knots with a light trade well abeam.... The famous leak, having fallen to between 5 & 6 gallons per four-hour watch, holds steady and, we hope, will fall even further as Mr. Gregg (who is doubtless stowed away in the bilge) finds his thirst increasing with the westing.

January 28. 4-8 A.M. Breeze freshened between 6 & 7 & at 7:15 main staysail halyard parted again & we took the sail in. Under the ballooner & fisherman's staysail alone 6 & ¼ miles were logged between 7 & 8.

Fine fresh trade well aft. Took in ballooner, which has pulled us along for 1,000 miles & set squaresail & raffee. Took in fisherman staysail, which has a record nearly equal to that of the ballooner.

January 30. 8-12 A.M. Fine trade SExE. Moderate sea. Making 6 to 7 knots. PEA SOUP today! Joe has the record of 3 bowls in 5 minutes. The Skipper can handle 3 bowls also, but takes longer.

After supper spent awhile learning the constellations & looking up different stars. I know about 20 - 25 now. With this breeze there is a damned good swell & the schooner rolls a bit. Here is a poem I made up about the Skipper who threatened anyone who looses what little breeze there is:

Towards sunset the wind showed signs of letting go,
Which let the booms go crash, to & fro;
The Skipper, "Pea Soup Peters," barked to his aides:
"I'll keel haul the barstard who looses these trades."

February 1. 8-12 P.M. Same conditions, nearly dead before it.

Today is the birthday, t'would seem,
Of the Trader, that deep-water Dean,
Who put in the day in the usual way
And painted the privy light green.

February 3. Fine going in evening. A half moon & the Doc's
music box serving to increase, if possible, the air of general
satisfaction caused by the fact that it looks as though we might
possibly carry the mainsail tonight without tearing the vessel
apart. 8 P.M., always a critical hour, passing with a very decent,
if spasmodic, trade holding about east.

With the wind well astern on our long run west and south
across the meridians as I remember it, the squaresail and raffee
worked much to our advantage. To have carried the regular
schooner rig, even with the booms guyed forward, and to have
steered without jibing would have been nerve-wracking as well
as nearly impossible. There were spells when the wind hauled
round far enough on the quarter for us to carry the mainsail, but
these were for the most part brief opportunities. The squaresail,
which never slatted and required little attention, kept on pulling
day after day and night after night, and was by all odds the
favorite piece of canvas.

No untoward event occurred on the entire run, nor was its
pleasant monotony destroyed by any circumstance. To think of
one starlit night is to remember them all. Once in a while, a light
rain squall passed over with a *whish*, washing some of the salt off
the decks and the helmsman. Then it passed on and left the sky as
before, studded with stars. Here and there, one saw one of the
tidy little cumulus clouds characteristic of the trade winds blot
out the stars, then let them into view again.

With the quick disappearance of the glow in the western sky
at sunset, meteorites flashed and disappeared, and the sea awoke

The Chief taking a sight.

with phosphorescence. Each lunge and roll of the schooner spread softly gleaming streamers of light out from under the bow while the stern unrolled in a continuous wake of bubbling fire along the surface of the sea. For a long time, there would be no sound but the water, bubbling like a brook against the sides of the ship and the gentle creaking of gear. Then would come the familiar *ch-ch* as our nightly companions, the porpoises, found us and broke water alongside in their play about the ship — round the bow, under the keel, and up on the other side, every beautiful flashing movement written in the writhing phosphorescence.

✪ ✪ ✪

Although the *Pilgrim* had been designed with an eye to the ventilation so important in the tropics, there were times when the following wind moved so little faster than the schooner that scarcely a breath found its way down through the open hatches. Wind-chutes were rigged to funnel air into the galley and main cabin, but the result was worse than before. Entering by different hatches, the competing currents seemed to expend their feeble forces against each other and expire completely. The choice off watch was to suffocate in one's own bunk below or to sleep in the freer air on deck, wedged between a stanchion and a dory gripe, at the risk of being awakened rudely by a lop of sea or the pressure of a prowling foot.

From time to time, too, the hatches had to be completely closed in a rain squall. This produced a state of stuffiness hardly preferable to being drenched. This deficiency was improved when we reached Tahiti and a shipyard, where the flat hatch covers were replaced by sky lights. Our conditions still fell short of the comfort found in a regular South Seas schooner, with her raised deckhouse large enough for six to eight people. The heat, how-ever, was never intolerable — thermometer readings in the chart house ranged at night from seventy-four to seventy-eight degrees while in the day they seldom topped or even reached eighty-five degrees.

We carried no ice machine but did not notice the lack of ice except in the limitation of the variety of perishable foods. Our drinking water got pretty hot in the water tanks just beneath the deck. It was made pleasantly cool by leaving it for a short time in a canvas bottle Joe had made and hung in the sun. This was an old device in that large part of the world which had not yet bound itself to the expense, noise, and trouble of electric refrigeration.

A cotton hat provided our heads with plenty of protection from the sun, and our backs became thoroughly browned and inured to its rays. The only direct discomfort we had from it was stepping with bare feet on a well baked deck. Aside from the infrequent bursts of energy occasioned by such a circumstance and the regular but mild exertion called for by ordinary routine, there was little enough exercise for those used to it on land. The Skipper made up for this every afternoon by performing an energetic wand drill with a pump brake and climbing the weather main rigging hand over hand. This gave him a superior appetite for the evening's particular form of tinned beef.

Lovely day with bright sun out. The beach umbrella has been rigged up over the wheel & is great when you're steering.

As we drew near the Marquesas, there rose again the fervor to brighten ship that can seize a crew before entering a port, and which had moved us before in the last days of crossing the Caribbean to Cristóbal. Now, however, this incentive was lent a more particular cast.

February 7, 12-4.... Turned to getting the binnacle & portholes furbished up in preparation for the bevy of lovely Marquesans confidently expected to swarm aboard.

The life-rings were repainted, hatch coverings and beadings scraped, sandpapered, and varnished, and the *Pilgrim's* modest beauty was at last ready for a more critical inspection than it was soon to meet.

> I have been painting the engine room again & have given the whole thing two coats of gray & red trimming on the valves & fly wheels & top of diesel. On deck the boys have scraped & varnished all the bright work & it looks great. We only have about 200 miles to go to Nuku Hiva or wherever it is we are making our landfall. I guess we'll be there in a couple of days but I'm in no hurry as the going is so slick out here.

On the evening of February 7, nineteen days from Tagus Cove, a moderate breeze was bowling us along under squaresail and rafee at seven knots. A considerable swell, set up by the fresh trade during the day, added its force to the breeze as the great rollers passed successively under the schooner from stern to bow. We had rigged the anchor burton, oiled and tested the windlass, fished the anchor chains up through the pipes from the chain locker, and shackled them to the anchors.

A clear sky now offered the whole galaxy for contemplation and use: Aldebaran, Deneb Kaitos, Sirius, and the southern blazers, Canopus and Achernar, were all captured and brought down from their noble heights to the limits of a plotting sheet. The fix showed that, at seven o'clock in the evening, we were some sixty miles off the island of Hiva Oa, which Robert Louis Stevenson in his travel book, *In the South Seas,* called "the man-eating isle." The breeze moderated but shortly after three o'clock in the morning, a loom of high land appeared on the starboard bow in the light of a full moon. The raffee was taken in so we wouldn't come too close to it before daylight.

As the light increased, the loom expanded further and further to the west, taking in the precipitous slopes of the whole southern coast of the island. Gradually, I saw the coast blossom from a deep gray to the rich colors of sand beaches, black-brown rock cliffs, and luxuriant vegetation beyond. The slanting rays of early morning defined in clear every shade of green in the deep valleys and on the ridges rising between them, to the mountain peaks wreathed in clouds, in which they disappeared from sight. As we drew closer and sailed along the shore, the smell of moist rich humus, mingled with the freshness of leaves and flowers and the pungency of smoke from burning coconut shells, perfumed the trade wind.

After identifying to port the small island on the chart called Motane, and further along, Tahuata, we entered Vipihae, or Traitors Bay. We ran in past Hanake Islet for Taa Huku Bay, a smaller bight which made in from its northern shore. Joe saw that both anchors were ready to let go and the Chief started the engine. The *Pacific Islands Pilot* warns that sailing vessels in the Marquesas should not approach the land too closely, even with a fresh breeze, because the wind sometimes dies suddenly. Brailing in the squaresail and running the French tricolor up to the foremast truck, we ran into the smaller bay and, after several casts of the lead, dropped anchor in four fathoms at our first real South Sea island.

chapter 5

The Marquesas Islands

WHATEVER VISIONS THE SEA-WORN company of the *Pilgrim* may have entertained of a reception by laughing *vahines* swarming and dripping up the bobstay and climbing over the rail with flowers in their hair were not to be given substance. A half dozen iron-roofed shacks and a small knot of natives looked down on our arrival from the top of a bank. The southeast swell swept obliquely into the harbor, booming along its western shore. It sent water jets 70' into the air from a roaring blow-hole among the rocks and produced a condition at the low cement landing place reminiscent of old prints of William Tell's escape during a storm from the boat on Lake Geneva.

Above this spot on the bank appeared several more figures, one of them wearing white European dress. They waved their arms and seemed to beckon. We put the peapod dory over, and Joe rowed across the harbor. He backed into the landing on the crest of a roller and, picking up a passenger, pulled instantly away on its backwash. The passenger proved to be the administrator of the southeastern Marquesas. He also served as the health officer. I have described his dress as seen from a distance as European, and to be sure it was largely so, but the combination of silk pajama coat and ten-gallon straw hat encircled by a band of fine vari-colored snail shells was hardly what I had expected to find on a government officer either in Europe or on a tropical island.

Dr. Benoit, finding our Bill of Health in order, granted us pratique, welcomed us to the islands without enthusiasm, answered a few questions, and was off again before the sweat had time to cool on his brow. He was very busy, he said, being the only physician for five islands. When later we called at his house, we were told he was on the other side of Hiva Oa attending the delivery of a child.

The yellow quarantine flag was hauled down, and a party of us set out for the shore. Once the treacherous landing-place was negotiated, we climbed a steep bank under the stares of half a dozen pairs of eyes, one of which brightened with tentative friendliness as its owner said something that sounded like Ka-o-ha.

"Ka-o-ha," we said.

"*Kaoha,*" they all said. Then they pointed up the road saying "Atuona," and we set out for the port town a little uncertainly, for the ground seemed to heave like the schooner's deck we had just quitted. If there had been any doubt as to the right path after the concerted direction given by the natives, it was shortly removed by an oval sign on a post in a design familiar to travelers in France. Of black, white, yellow, and blue enamel, it read: "ATUONA 1 km. — *don de Citroën.*"

Further on, a lantern on a weathered pole served as the light which marked the port, and a figure in the blue and red uniform of the French gendarmerie lounged nearby on the bluff. The *Pilgrim* tossed down below us with the Stars and Stripes fluttering from her stern, but he, knowing nothing of our business, made no assumptions. His attitude and mien were those of a man both uninterested and unutterably sad. Perhaps he was thinking that there is sunlight in Provence as well as in Hiva Oa, that the best gardens are laid out by the hand of man and have geraniums and ageratum in them and that an almost deserted path strewn with trodden mangoes is no substitute for a concrete sidewalk complete with café and *dégustation*. If such were his thoughts, we apparently offered no diversion from them. His *bon jour* was as empty of cordiality as of surprise.

The road sloped down again, past overhanging bushes dotted with scarlet hibiscus flowers into a settlement of board shacks with corrugated iron roofs set in clearings among the coconut palms. Each trunk was circled by a band of zinc to prevent rats from climbing to the nuts. Here and there, a native, dressed in a red and white cotton waistcloth but more often in blue dungarees and undershirt, sat silent on his porch or tended a fire of coconut husks and shells left over from copra making.

"Kaoha."

"Ka-o-ha," I would say. We couldn't give the greeting quite the native values and intonation, but the smiles which followed indicated it was understood at least as a friendly effort.

A tattered, yellowing paper tacked to a tree gave notice in the French and Marquesan languages of a court hearing to be held at Papeete, Tahiti, some 850 miles away, on a date then past. Just beyond the tree we approached a store built of unfinished boarding that might have been found in a country village back in New England. Several natives stood and sat in a group on the edge of the store's broad verandah raised one step above the road. A painted sign indicated the proprietorship of the successor of Donald and Edinborough of New Zealand, familiar to readers of Robert Louis Stevenson, with the words *Établissements Donald Tahiti.*

A little brown boy ran out of the store, tugged at my arm, and said, "You come see my fada. He 'Mer'can too; Liv'pool." Bob McKettrick, while not an American, was a good Liverpool Irishman. For many years a trader among the French islands, he was now, his ramblings over for a time at least, the agent of "Donald's" at Atuona. The store presented an assortment of hardware, straw hats, rope, belts, cigarettes, perfume, canned food, jewelry, flour, and *pareus*. The latter is a wraparound skirt made of cotton, one meter by two, with floral designs in various color combinations. Made in Glasgow, it is the modern equivalent of the less colorful pareu made of tapa, the paperlike cloth made by pounding the inner bark of the paper mulberry tree, which used to be the universal material for this native dress.

Now, European trousers and shirts seem to be preferred by most natives and are even required by law within some town limits, as at Papeete; recently, however, newspaper pictures of American girls wearing pareus on Florida beaches stimulated such protests that the law was relaxed. We were all eager to acquire such a novel, convenient, and comfortable costume, and soon all but the Cook's portly figure were bound about the loins with gaily colored Glasgow cotton which at first, due to unfamiliarity with the rig, was constantly falling off.

From "Donald's," the main street, a path through uncut grass lined with flowering trees and bushes, continued past the inevitable Chinese-owned shops and more simple board houses, then climbed the promontory that encloses the western part of Traitors Bay. At the top, I looked down on the schooner far below and on the village. Atuona lies between two steep mountains, behind a crescent of white sand beach. The sea thunders continually there during the season of the southeast wind.

Viewed from that height where the outlines of palm trees lose themselves in the general greenness of the valley but where the threads of rising smoke remain distinct, the little settlement, clustered about the white wooden spire of the Catholic Mission Church, reminded me again of a small New England town. On our way up the hill, two little native boys appeared and followed along with us. They stopped from time to time to pick up a mango or flower and hand it to one of us, chattering in their soft language composed chiefly of vowels and the liquid and labial consonants.

Our canned ocean fare was replaced that night by fresh roast suckling pig. For an alternative to the schooner's tank water, which had turned a trifle cloudy, there was a bowl of coconut water, also a bit cloudy, with a dash of fresh lime juice added to it. This gave piquancy to its faintly leguminous taste.

From Hod Fuller's journal: Last night Joe had a fine time ashore with the natives & beat the village champion at their arm breaking game. He's a great pal of all the natives by now. Bob McKettrick came aboard for dinner & spun some fine yarns about the islands.

Early this morning, the Commander & Murph went up on horseback to the plateau, while the rest of us went ashore & walked around the town & saw the mission & Gauguin's grave in the little cemetery here.

Some boys appeared on the shore with horses — or ponies. We had requested the ponies the day before in order to give the boys time to catch them up in the hills where they roamed free. The animals were all of less than the usual size, their ancestors having been of a breed appropriate to transportation in sailing vessels. Quite ungroomed, they were fitted out with saddles carved from single blocks of wood, wooden stirrups, and rigging of sennet or braided leaves except for an occasional rein of very old hemp rope. They were tractable enough, for the most part, perhaps because the work of climbing took most of the ginger out of them.

My own mount, however, now and again uttered a wild unhorsely scream and sprang at one of the others, rearing and striking out with his front hooves. The attack was met in kind and things grew quite lively until both had enough. Miraculously, it seemed, neither man nor beast was injured by any of these set-to's. As we wound up a narrow path cut into the side of one of the foothills, the *Pilgrim* in the bay below became smaller and smaller and the palm groves in the valley diminished to the proportions of a garden in the woods. We attained the top of a plateau and came into the current of the trade wind. The vegetation became sparse and infrequent and provided an unobstructed view of the great peaks beyond and above which intercepted the clouds drifting in from the east. For many minutes, we stood there as the ponies panted and heaved with relief, watching the magnificent dark towered heights emerge and disappear again in the racing clouds like figures in a great cosmic kaleidoscope.

Further along, the trail turned and let us into the lee of a mountain; between this and the lower one on which we stood was an upland valley, on the floor of which were visible only the soft upper leaves of trees making a formless pattern in every shade of green. As we approached this valley, the hum of the breeze, cut off by the mountain, lessened and a great chorus of twittering, chirping, and trilling in every key blended together into a single harmonious song, welling up from below. Not a bird could be seen except two white bosun birds high above, soaring, wheeling, and diving, side by side and in perfect unison against the dark mountain side. Soon, the ridge dropped down and we found ourselves again walled in on both sides by broad-leaved banana trees, and by mango, orange, lemon, lime, papaya, and guava trees as well. The fei trees, which produce bright orange plantains, were remarkable for their roots arching from their trunks through the air several feet above the ground. The sun spotted the muddy path in bright patches, while on either side it reached us in softer tones through translucent foliage. There were no flowers here, and there was a smell of exuberant rankness. Then, suddenly, the downpouring light gave way to a drenching rain squall which washed away our sweat and that of the ponies and passed along, leaving the forest dripping and the mud underfoot even more boggy.

On these heights, as we proceeded up the climbing trail, we experienced a succession of squalls like this. At every turn, in the periods of glaring sunlight between the squalls, a new combination of magnificent slopes and precipices opened up below us with the blue Pacific beyond. Despite these numerous cool wettings, we were thoroughly baked by the mid-afternoon sun by the time the ponies had stumbled back down the long slopes. Relief, however, was near at hand. The bottom of the trail forked into the valley behind the bay and through a palm grove bordered by a stream. I tied my pony to one of the boles, undressed and lay on sand in a shallow part of the stream where it broadened into a pool. I looked up at the sky through the palm fronds while water still cold from the mountain tops ran over me and crayfish tickled my sides.

This was the quiet valley that used to ring with the shouts of cannibals, and where sometimes there was the crackling of faggots under a stew pot. But that had been many years before, in the latter days of the "long-pig" era, according to Bob McKettrick. Although the shouts were often fierce, the rival tribes usually remained on opposite sides of the valley at a safe distance from each other, calling insults and challenges back and forth over the heads of imported Annamese workmen, unperturbed and industrious in the valley plantation between. The pig in the stew pot, therefore, was usually of the short variety, and the stream in which I lay was seldom turgid with blood.

The natives of the Marquesas do not look like a race whose savage proclivities and practices have been curbed only within a few generations. It may not be true that the occasional eating of a freshly killed and dressed neighbor, done to a turn and served with island vegetables and fruits in season, is incompatible with handsome gentle faces. After all, before pigs, horses, and rats were brought to the islands, there was no non-human red meat, a condition which has everywhere been favorable to anthropophagic practices. Moreover, the flesh of their own kind, free from any admixture of alcohol, tobacco, or carbon monoxide, must have presented a more savory and tempting prospect than a steak from, for example, a twentieth century New Yorker. In addition, the islanders held a firm belief in the common theory that one assimilates the moral virtues of that which one eats. It is not surprising that simply to bury the body of a strong and courageous enemy killed in battle and still fresh seemed to them like unwarrantable waste.

Joe has heard that there is a queen & princess ashore who are both looking for husbands. They own many thousands of acres of land & have quite a house. He thinks he ought to hitch up with one of them & organize this place for yachtsmen & have it advertised in *Yachting* **as "Barnacle Joe's."**

After three days in Taa Huku Bay, we weighed anchor one evening and ran out through Bordelais Strait, skirting the southern coast of Hiva Oa to catch the nightly land breeze, and headed for Taiohae Bay on the neighboring island of Nuku Hiva. Sunrise the next morning revealed the shapes of Ua Pou and Ua Huka to port and starboard, while the dark heights of Nuku Hiva opened up directly ahead. Although Hiva Oa is the largest, most fertile and most populous of the group, Nuku Hiva has always been regarded as the principal island by the government. Its general appearance from sea is similar to that of Hiva Oa, but one of its peaks is nearly 400' higher.

Due to the greater steepness of the slopes rising from the south coast, the approach from that direction affords an even more striking view than we had seen on reaching Hiva Oa. All morning, with the four lowers and main topsail filling to a light breeze from the northeast, we drew up on Nuku Hiva. Its majestic silhouette gradually rose from the sea and resolved itself into color and the third dimension. The shore became a line of bare cliffs, here and there indented by a bay upon which the sea frothed itself white with each successive swell.

The mountain tops above, where not lost among the clouds, were scarred by the wind and rain which incessantly assault them but which, having lost the battle, condense into scores of silver threads of streams. These rushed down the valleys they had scored to dissolve here and there as they leaped from some precipice into white falls which vanished into thin air against the mat of foliage they nourished. The greenery on the heights seemed as immobile as a tufted carpet. Along the closer foreshore, it undulated under the soft trade wind in swells like the sea itself. The *Pilgrim* poked her headsails around the East Sentinel (just as Loudon Dodd's and Carthew's schooner in Robert Louis Stevenson's *The Wrecker* had appeared beyond the companion pinnacle islet at the west arm of the bay) and reached up to the anchorage now in the lee.

Taiohae Bay is large enough to accommodate several warships and has done so. Although there were already two sailing vessels at anchor before the settlement, there was plenty of room for us to cruise tentatively about, feel the bottom with the lead, drop anchor, and veer out an ample length of chain. The head of the bay was lined by a curving sand beach behind which, visible through coconut palms, was a row of neat white houses with, for the most part, red roofs. Threads of smoke streamed up from them, although the temperature ashore was very hot. Behind a little height off one end of the beach was a patch of flamboyant scarlet trees shading a larger house of European proportions and French dignity, further maintained by the tricolor spasmodically spreading and collapsing on a white pole above it.

Blanco of the *Evalu*, whom we had seen last at Balboa, was the first visitor aboard the *Pilgrim*, coming alongside with his small daughter. He reported that he had brought his little schooner from Panama in sixty-four days without making a stop, although their course took them right through the Galapagos Islands. With a limited water supply, he had no mind to subject an eleven-year-old girl to the chances of what might be found to replenish it among the Galapagos and had been content to wonder at the islands as they passed. His daughter was boarding temporarily at the residency, improving her French and being reminded of the amenities of life ashore.

> *From the ship's log: February 16. Anchored at Taiohae. Another lovely morning. After breakfast received a call from M. Quere who came aboard via outrigger canoe & arranged for us to take the mail to Tahiti…2 P.M. The mail was delivered by outrigger canoe but we found it is for Ua Huka & Ua Pou; our intention to visit these islands & also the Tuamotus apparently caused the consul to hold the Tahiti mail for Capt. Blanco who expects to sail there direct next week.*

The only convenient place to get water in the Marquesas — and the only source certainly not contaminated by lepers — was here. The next day, we scrubbed the inside of the peapod clean and repeatedly filled it with cool mountain stream water from a pipe on the end of the pier until the gunwales were not quite awash. We towed it out to the *Pilgrim* and there laboriously emptied it with buckets handed aboard and poured into the tanks. The day was a shimmering hot one with scarcely any air moving. After a morning of this work, the Chief, who had worn no hat, found himself with a rapidly rising fever. The Doc diagnosed it as sunstroke and brought it under control after some hours with rubbing alcohol. This was the only case during the entire voyage.

There was a radio station at Taiohae, manned by a native operator. I found he was perfectly capable of transmitting a message to Boston, but that there was a good deal of perplexity at the receiving end before the place of origin was identified.

The vale of Typee, or Taipi Vai, lay only a few miles up the coast. We had all read Herman Melville's description of the valley and of life in it, and this picture was the substance of some of my most lively anticipations of South Seas experience. Since the road (and Melville's route) lay over the hills, we again chartered island ponies and, guided by a signpost, set off up a grassy trail. The vegetation was generally what we had seen on the heights of Hiva Oa, but here was not the same pristine effect, for along the trail were many signs of dead men and their work.

At intervals, I saw flat low structures of stone whose black rectangular forms were only partially visible from under the mass of vegetation which had closed over them. These platforms, called *pae paes,* were raised only a few feet above the ground and varied in lateral dimensions from those of the shacks along the beach to many times their size. They were the foundations of abandoned native houses and outdoor living platforms. It has been estimated that two centuries ago, before the islands had been much visited or even all "discovered," the native population had been one hundred thousand. Now there are less than three thousand.

Diseases introduced by white explorers, settlers, and traders are supposed to have accounted for this tremendous loss of life, and among these vestiges of the dead, one is not unnaturally disposed to reflect on the fall of man from a state of nature. A happier thought that the scene inspired in me was that in these fertile valleys, where there once lived in plenty one hundred thousand people, as many could live again and with little greater effort than confining their desires to the simple necessaries of life which abound on every side.

Our laboring ponies finally brought us out on a ridgetop. The trail wound gradually down over intervening bare slopes toward Taipi Vai, which I could see only the far side rising almost perpendicularly before us. The sun was very hot, and against it and the small persistent biting black flies (*nau-naus*) which are characteristic of the island, we constructed headgear of handkerchiefs and pareus extending over the neck behind.

These made the expedition resemble somewhat, from a distance, a troop of Bedouins, although in other respects, such as the Skipper's patched trouser legs stuffed into the tops of plaid woolen socks, and the general sorriness of our mounts, we looked more like a group of unlucky prospectors. Of the spruce pith-helmet effect which is supposed to characterize shore parties landed from yachts on tropical islands, at least in the movies, there was nothing. Thus ill-recommended to whomever we might meet, we zig-zagged down the steep mountainside into the valley which seemed so near one could have thrown a mango onto one of its pandanus rooftops.

After cajoling and beating the ponies across a creek threading over a pebbly bottom, we came to a clearing just outside a group of leaf huts. Two natives, a strapping young man in cast-off trousers and a bland woman in a cotton dress, came forward to meet us. They smiled and motioned us to dismount. We made our horses fast to shady trees sufficiently far apart so that they could not attack each other, and the man set about taking off the saddles and bridles. He did this without any suggestion from us, nor would he allow us to help him. He indicated that we were to sit down under the trees where the woman pointed out a clear spot in the shade.

The husband appeared to speak no French whatever, but his wife had learned enough in school to carry on a conversation, although the finer shades of pronunciation were so far beyond her that she asked if we were Frenchmen. Finished with the animals, the young man disappeared into the hut of plaited leaves and then rejoined us with an old soccer ball which had been patched and repatched many times. He invited us to play with him. Barefooted as he was, he could out-kick any of us and was very skillful and quick dribbling the ball with his feet. Neither practiced in the game nor anxious to spend more time in Taipi Vai, especially under the broiling sun, we retired again to the shade with Boston's standing in the Association Football League of Nuku Hiva still at zero.

It was now past noon. We broke out our parcels of bread and canned tongue and offered some to our new acquaintances, but they refused it. We were their guests. The young man went into the bushes and reappeared with a large bunch of bananas. He broke off the best and gave them to us. The woman brought from the hut a basket of plaited leaves filled with papayas. After making deprecatory signs over Murph's Gordon gin bottle bound with reticulated marlin and full of water warm from his pony's steaming flank, the young man seized the bole of a coconut tree with both hands and knees and hitched himself up into the cluster of fruit and leaves at the top, where he detached about ten nuts, letting them fall to the ground.

Having climbed back down, he sharpened at both ends a stout stick about 3' long and stuck it into the ground. Squatting before it, he took a coconut firmly in both hands and brought it down sharply on the point of the stick several times. Each blow drove this wooden chisel into the thick fibrous husk, renting it apart and away from the shell, which was exposed and freed with a few deft motions. With his knife, he cut a hole at the soft end of the brown nut, and it was ready for drinking.

After this vegetarian repast, we went further into the village and met more descendants of Melville's hosts at Taipi. These others were, while friendly, less joyous and healthy in appearance. Scars left by yaws blotched the legs of many of them, while others were also disfigured by the swollen legs of elephantiasis. One old man had been attacked in such an inconvenient portion of his anatomy, and to such an extent, that he was unable to move about without assistance and sat on a porch, using the monstrous excrescence as a table for the materials of his cigarette rolling. He was friendly and alert, however, and asked eagerly for news of the world.

His first question was, "Has Charles Lindbergh's kidnaped baby been found yet?" Another asked how big the *Pilgrim* was, how many meters long, and upon being told seemed mildly scornful. William K. Vanderbilt's motor ship *Alva*, which had come right into Traitors Bay, he said, was at least a hundred meters long, and everyone had been invited onboard and given champagne — in other words, we were no competition for Vanderbilt. One of the women, in tribute to the Doc's charm, gave him a circular hat band, a thick rope made of hundreds of uniform tiny red and white snail shells, woven into a pattern.

I walked down toward the shore and found myself in an area of black mud caked thinly on the top by the sun, but underneath soft and treacherous. Crabs scuttled about under clumps of rushes and tiny flies and mosquitoes persistently attacked every part of exposed skin. The mosquitoes were particularly unpleasant in this place because they are one of the carriers of elephantiasis. While the Doc said many bites are necessary to produce a noticeable swelling, it was far from pleasant to think of being injected with any installment, however small. The unhealthiness of the place, combined with the attacks of insects, rather overpowered any impression I had of being in an earthly paradise induced by the magnificence and luxuriance of the valley. Perhaps if I had escaped from the salt-horse and lengthy confinement of a whaling vessel many months from home, these drawbacks would have had no weight.

Back in Taiohae, we took the opportunity of visiting the trading schooner *Tereora*, which lay near us, at the invitation of Captain Doom. Characteristic of her type, she was heavily constructed of kauri pine in New Zealand and rigged as a schooner with pole masts. She did most of her traveling under power, which was supplied by a huge diesel engine, and carried only the foresail and sometimes the fore-staysail. Most of the hull was taken up by the copra hold amidships. The native crew slept in the forecastle and on deck. Aft, and usually covered by an awning over the main boom even while under way, was a long deckhouse containing bunks for Captain and supercargo, when there was one, and a trade room.

Here against the bulkheads were shelves piled with bright pareus, blue dungarees, jewelry, cigarettes, soap, perfume, and other wares attractive to the natives who have little use for the money they receive for their copra except to buy such things. Sitting at the trade room table, with a soft breeze blowing the fragrance of the island in at the open ports and sunlight reflected from the ruffled harbor waters playing on the white deckhead above, we talked with Captain Doom.

The Captain combined the stout but muscular build of his whaling skipper father with the gentleness and dignity of his Polynesian mother. His build was quite evidently a size too large, even for his capacious khaki shorts, but his dignity was not in the least diminished by them. Hearing that we were to pass through the Tuamotus, he brought out his charts of the group and indicated the various passages which were favorable at that season; from his years of experience in those treacherous waters, he warned us to rely neither on charts nor our reckonings.

Not only is the velocity of the Equatorial current most irregular, but the low atolls are often nearly invisible due to atmospheric conditions until a ship is close to them or piled up on an outlying reef. His best advice for us was, "Use your eyes," which he reinforced by tapping one of his own with a forefinger. His remarks had a faintly sinister flavor which confirmed the impression given by the *Pilot Book* that the scattered islands of the Low Archipelago constitute something of a gauntlet to be run.

Before leaving Nuku Hiva, we ran six miles to the west of

Taiohae to Tai Oa Bay. After passing between cliffs at its narrow entrance, we turned into a cove called Hakatea that is entirely cut off from the sight and motion of the sea. A small village of native huts is quite hidden by a point, so that the scene at the anchorage is one of perfect calm and untouched natural beauty. Sheer cliffs rise several thousand feet, almost as close at hand as if one were in a street below a skyscraper. It was an ideal spot for contemplation and for sand papering and varnishing, which we did with differing degrees of intensity, according to our temperaments.

After anchoring some of us went ashore in the outboard & landed in the surf on the black sand beach in front of the village. There are many fine *pae-paes* scattered all through the village, some of which are made of large blocks of stone perfectly polished & fitted together. One fellow took us a short way back into the bush & showed us the remains of an old war canoe which used to carry one hundred men. Both ends of it had been sawed off by souvenir hunters & only the part amidships remained.

February 17. Three of us started up the valley of Haka Vai, passing many long abandoned pae-paes & gradually getting up into the mountains. The usual native trail easy to follow... Considerable rain off & on. After lunch worked up into the famous (we heard of it at Atuona) waterfall. Grand precipices we estimate at 2000 ft & sheer walls & pinnacles of all sorts. The Doc & Skipper had a swim in the pool under the fall.

On our way from this spot to the island of Ua Huka, we sailed into Taiohae again and put a boat over for an author and adventurer bound also for Ua Huka. He came over the side providently equipped with his own mattress and a large jar of wine. He brought also a copy of a book he had written, which was mainly concerned with various island girls he had loved. It appeared that this lift to the next island was assisting in the collection of more material of the same nature.

After a daylight run of about 25 miles, close on a faltering tradewind from the northeast, we ran into Hanna Nai Bay in the lee of an islet of the shape often described as a sugar-loaf which protected the anchorage from the heft of the swell, and put our Lothario ashore through the breakers. The island appeared to offer the same abundant variety of partners as the others we had seen. The author returned a few hours later, after brief — but apparently unpromising — negotiations with the village chief to beg some of the *Pilgrim's* provisions; for some flour and tinned sardines he seemed very thankful. If the island was to provide material for a new chapter of conquest, this was an inauspicious beginning. I was told later that the islanders had seen and understood his book and did not care for it.

Fine day with occasional showers during the night. The Trader & I have our mattresses on deck on the chart house roof & a canvas over them so we can sleep through any weather now. This morning, Trader, Doc & I went ashore & after having some fruit & seeing some little TIKIS & models of native canoes at a native's house, we went up the valley & saw some old stone idols (or TIKIS) placed around a square of stones. Evidently this was a place of feasts or worship at one time as the images were arranged about a flat space on the hillside, many stone platforms were in the bushes & a big stone lined pit like a well was located nearby.

When we got back to the boat, we found it overrun with natives. The Commander had told two of them they might come aboard & the whole town showed up. We couldn't get rid of them until finally someone thought of loading them into the outboard for a ride & then

dumping them ashore. This worked great except on one or two trips ashore the boat was rushed by more who wanted to get aboard on the return trip.

Ua Huka offered less of the same kind of attraction we had already seen at the other islands. After an evening aboard spent enduring the administrator's son's singing of endless dismal Methodist hymn tunes with Polynesian words, we hove up for Ua Pou in plain sight to the west. This island is the most theatrical of all the Marquesas, volcanic action and erosion having produced in its center a cluster of rock columns rising over 4,000' into the clouds, and so precipitous that their sides are bare of soil or greenery. We anchored in a savage roll off the town of Hakahetau which lay behind a shingle beach so steep that landing on it with a boat was impossible.

The method for getting ashore was to pull the dory up to a great bud of cooled lava projecting from the beach and leap there, while a native simultaneously dropped into the dory and rowed it out beyond the breakers until we were ready to go off again. I visited one of the most honored citizens of this tidy town, an old gentleman named Samuel Kekela, whose father, a Hawaiian and a missionary, had received from President Lincoln in 1864 a watch and a telescope for preserving the mate of an American whale ship from the stew pot by swapping for him a whale-boat, a cutaway coat, and an old plug hat.

The swell in Hakahetau, driven by the northeast wind, was so violent (never before had I been rolled out of my bunk while at anchor), that we rounded a protecting promontory for the quieter and more beautiful shelter of Vaieo Bay. The *Tereora* came in here on her rounds of island bays to pick up copra, and Captain Doom brought several natives aboard for a visit. One old fellow was tattooed over his entire face, including his eyelids, with faded green geometrical designs which must at one time have lent him a most ferocious appearance.

To our requests for a cannibal song, translated by the Captain, he only chuckled with a tone that might have been either embarrassment or sinister reminiscence. He tottered about the main cabin turning the electric lights and fan on and off, repeating excitedly, "Ai! Ai! Ai!" The Trader put the radio earphones, humming with jazz from Los Angeles, on his head and his exclamations became an awed whisper. Then, with arm gestures and tears in his eyes, he made a speech which, if properly translated, said that now that he had seen the splendor of the *Pilgrim* and the scientific wonders with which she was equipped, he could die happy. When I recalled the incident to Captain Doom's supercargo some weeks later in Papeete, he said the old cannibal had been pulling our legs — no doubt about it. If so, he was a superb actor, if not very polite.

Spent the morning running the outboard while Murph hooked a couple of nice fish (name unknown) about 15 lbs. During the afternoon Doc & Murph caught ½ doz. nice big fish, some 30-35 lbs, & gave them to Capt. Doom for his crew. Did odd jobs about the boat during the afternoon & turned in early.

We left Vaieo Bay with our fore rigging hung with bunches of yellow and green bananas and bright orange plantain called *fei*. Mr. Kekela had sent his grandson out with a generous gift of fruit. Now coconuts, sugar cane, breadfruit, and papaya decorated the forward deck and the boats — more than enough to keep us in vitamins during the 420 mile run to Takaroa, our first stop in the Tuamotus, if we "used our eyes."

chapter 6

The Marquesas to the Tuamotus and Tahiti

ONCE OUT OF THE IMMEDIATE LEE of the abrupt shores of Vaieo Bay, the *Pilgrim* heeled to a smart breeze sweetened but undiminished by its passage over the heights of Ua Pou. The odors of the land gradually dissipated into the olfactory blankness of blue-water air as the island's black spires turned to hazy blue shapes and disappeared. For two days, the schooner raced along the hissing crests and silent hollows of a steady beam sea.

From Hod Fuller's journal: Fine day, clear sky & fresh trade bowling us along. What could be better? During our mid-watch a bit of a squall hit us & we took the flying jib off her. Next watch took off mains'l in preparation for a squall which never showed up & they had to get it on again!

From the ship's log: February 24. Forenoon blowing up fresh from about east & big trade sea. Weather fine. Good run to noon from noon yesterday: 202 miles.

On the morning of the third day, we came to that part of the Pacific where, according to a careful sun sight mixed with a pinch of dead reckoning, should have been the atoll of Takaroa. There was only the sparkling sea. Not even the faintest trace of a smoky streak against the horizon, often the mirage-like sign of an atoll, nor a significant clustering of clouds as if over land marked a break in the wet expanse. It seemed probable that an unpredictably powerful current had set us to the northwest, so we hauled up and ran south along the meridian of the atoll. Takaroa would be less difficult to spot than the ordinary atoll because the wreck of a large sailing vessel, according to the *Pilot Book*, "forms a conspicuous mark from seaward."

Several hours later, a high but indistinct blur appeared in the distance ahead, and might have been either a puff of smoke or a ship under full sail. As we drew closer to the blur, a thin gray streak on the horizon became visible to either side of it. The blur gradually condensed into the rusty hull and tangled spars of the wreck of a four-masted steel bark. The streak materialized into a blinding white beach, above which a line of coconut trees swayed their tawny, gangling trunks and tossed their verdant topknots in an offshore breeze.

We soon found ourselves in the lee of the atoll, as these low coral formations come into view suddenly and close aboard. We skimmed smoothly along close outside the fringing reef, between which and the beach the gently ruffled waters of the outer lagoon sparkled innocuously in sunlight. What a very different picture this shore must have presented when that great ship was overpowered by wind and seas and her thousands of tons of hull and cargo were driven clean over the reef to be flung down and broken upon the beach.

Takaroa is a typical atoll, as nearly all the Tuamotus are. To the eye, it presents a broken chain of small islets which, on the chart, are seen to join with submerged coral formations and make a great oval enclosing an inner lagoon. It was produced by the steady building of coral insects on the rim of a submerged

Deck view on the *Pilgrim* under weigh.

volcanic crater up to sea level and a subsequent accretion of sand, shells, and vegetable matter a few feet higher. The coral-building polyps cannot live above sea level. The ring which constitutes

Takaroa is some fifteen miles long and five miles wide, and is surrounded by a narrow outer lagoon protected from the open sea by another reef awash at high tide. It was over this so-called fringing reef that the *County of Roxburgh* was carried in the great hurricane of February 1906. As it was now the month of February, we kept a careful watch of the weather signs for a possible repetition of the blow.

Here and there in the reef, the sea had broken through into the inner lagoon, cutting the atoll into several separate islands. One of these breaks on the western side was large enough to admit ordinary vessels — this was the principal pass, and where it narrowed to cut through the principal reef was also the town. As we approached the entrance to this pass, we shortened sail and studied the problem of getting into our first atoll. The narrow gut off the town landing, being no more than 200' wide, was clearly no place for last-minute maneuvers.

Since the chart showed the inner lagoon studded with coral heads, our approach came down to the question of whether the tide was ebbing — only then could we venture under power to forge into the landing and hope to stop. While we were trying to settle this question by bare observation of the water's surface and by the more scientific but hasty and quite inconclusive reference to the phases of the moon, a small outrigger canoe put out from the shore.

The outrigger, paddled vigorously by two native boys, was soon alongside. A stalwart old brown man, barefooted and with a stubby gray beard, climbed over the rail. He introduced himself as "Rono," and in a mixture of execrable French and English said he was the local pilot. He also told us the tide was flooding but that he could take the *Pilgrim* in just the same. "Just leave it to me," he said in so many words. "I've been everywhere, including New York, including Coney Island, in sailing vessels, and I know my native Takaroa like the inside of my pocket."

Rono...has been to New York & says, "Hula, hula velly good at Coney Island."

Rono certainly looked as though he might have been a stout hand on many a vessel, with his wide sailor's stance and steady, though slightly unfocused, eye. Whether he had actually handled a schooner from the afterdeck or simply yearned to extend his experience of skippering beyond outrigger canoes was purely a matter of conjecture. However, he had no competition for the piloting job, and he was available.

"Well, Pete," I asked, "what do you think?"

"She's your ship, son" the Skipper replied as he sometimes did when things looked not quite good enough to receive his endorsement.

We decided to take a chance.

Rono walked out on the bowsprit, seized the headstay with one hand and motioned for full speed ahead with the other. We went in toward the gut very quickly then since the tide also was running in at a good three knots. The coral limestone quay lay just ahead to port while close to starboard was the jagged coral of the opposite shore, some of it clearly discernible as ugly patches a few feet below the surface. Fifty yards further off to starboard, the wreck of a schooner, a little smaller than the *Pilgrim* and with white paint peeling from her torn topsides, lay broken on one of these dangerous coral heads. It was into a nest of these heads that we were now charging, it appeared recklessly, led by the hand motions of a perfectly strange little man in torn trousers.

Suddenly, we were in the gut, rushing past the coral which it seemed we must at least be scraping. The quay was just abeam, on the port side, and our way further into the lagoon would soon be entirely blocked by coral heads. We had scarcely twice the length of the schooner to turn her in. I knew the engine in reverse, full speed, would be powerless to stop her in this tide, but Rono, in any case, hadn't asked for reverse. He hadn't, in fact, indicated any directions other than full speed ahead into the boneyard. Once we started, it would have been foolish not to follow his orders strictly — although it looked to me like a job for the underwriters in the next instant. Takaroa seemed about to acquire another "conspicuous landmark from seaward."

While I was briefly occupied with this melancholy reflection, Rono gestured with a quick and positive sweep of his arm, "Hard Over!" And just in time. Our stem barely missed the hazardous coral under the bowsprit as the schooner swung hard to port for the other side of the channel. I saw this side was now less than a length away, and the schooner was still at full speed ahead! In this new event, it seemed the *Pilgrim* was not even to continue her life as a useful landmark from seaward but was going to sink in the channel and be a menace to navigation. All these reasonable apprehensions were, however, unfounded. A powerful eddy caught the bow. The *Pilgrim* was spun as if on a pivot, shot forward parallel to the quay and into what was now a head tide, and brought up alongside the landing.

The edge of this structure was built of unfinished coral blocks. The maneuver that Rono's knowledge and skill had just brought off might still have its end, I was thinking, in a torn mess of copper and planking. However, the throng of natives who had collected at the spot with the intention of selling us copra lent their sturdy arms and backs, fending her off from the final shock, as Rono had undoubtedly known they would. Several took the lines and made them fast to an old anchor and other rusty fittings that had once sailed with the *County of Roxburgh* and were now embedded in the sand as integral parts of the landing-place.

Takaroa's town consisted of a wooden church, a few dozen neat pine board houses painted white, and rusty corrugated iron shacks. The general bleakness was relieved here and there by a patch of flowers rooted insecurely in a few handfuls of soil brought by schooner from Tahiti and partially protected from dissipation by the wind by a border of limestone blocks. Some-what over one hundred Polynesian inhabitants earned an intermittent and meager livelihood transforming coconut meat into copra and diving for pearls. They lived a subdued existence according to the doctrines of the Mormon Church as interpreted by a local missionary. Some of the more familiar of its injunctions are responsible for the European dress of the women and for the natives' abstinence from tobacco. These canons are apparently not confined in their application to the personal conduct of the faithful, since the designs of yachts belonging to non-believers also come within the Church's purview.

On the day following our arrival, the village chief, a white-bearded Polynesian wearing dungarees, a white high-collared tunic and a topi, looking like a photographic negative of a white man with a black beard, came aboard to pay an official call. After surveying the schooner from stem to stern, on deck and below, with an expression of pompous gravity, he made a pontifical pronouncement which Rono interpreted to mean that he found the *Pilgrim*, in design, construction, gear, and condition, in conformance with the principles of the Mormon religion. This observation was most unexpected and also gratifying.

The town is laid out in a coconut grove behind the pass & all the houses are modernized & made of boards. The damned Mormon missionaries have raised hell with the people here & none of them smoke, drink, sing their own old songs or dance their native dances. The missionaries have taken all the natives' pleasures away from them & now are slowly killing them off with all the clothes they make them wear.

In this community, there had been living for some weeks a British resident of Tahiti who had come to the atoll to paint. He exhausted the beauties of the lagoon as a subject for his watercolors and was beginning to long for the varied delicacy of Tahitian fare as a relief from the diet of fish, coconuts, and an occasional fowl or pig. Mr. W. Alister MacDonald accordingly became a member of the ship's company. This acquisition of a new source of information about many things in general and about the islands and Tahiti in particular, provided a lively leaven to the company's conversation.

Not that talk on board had by any means approached extinction. It had, however, in the many months since we had left Boston, gradually become confined to the serious and comic verbal currency of the daily routine and to a tolerant exchange of scraps of personal history which could hardly be called conversation. Since it seemed that every reflection on life, letters, the arts, and the sciences that might be elicited from us had already come forth, a new voice and a new audience were a relief and a stimulation.

Mr. MacDonald, for his part, appeared to enjoy the trip, although once we were underway, he was shocked at what he regarded as the barbarousness of the ship's rule which prevented our having a glass of his wine with him at dinner. We had the opportunity later on at Tahiti of demonstrating that the rule was truly one of nautical expediency and not an extension to other lands of the ideal of temperance which at that time was embodied in the United States Constitution.

> *February 26. Heavy squall from about East early in A.M. lasted some time with much rain. Tied alongside wharf at Takaroa together with four small copra sloops. Overcast & rainy A.M. All hands put in some swimming alongside the vessel. Lovely water & all kinds of queer shaped fish of various colors including yellow & blue. The Harpooner (Murph), the Doc & the Chief got some big fish just outside the passage in the dory.*

Before leaving Takaroa, we visited the wreck of the *County of*

Roxburgh. Crossing the inner lagoon in the motor dory, we had several close shaves with coral heads and soon became more familiar with the significance of strange light effects. We learned to distinguish, below the twinkling whitecaps and the metallic reflections of the sunlight on waves, the shades of green, brown, and yellow that denoted the various depths and bottoms we sped over. Wherever there was green, there was plenty of water; even over the darker brown patches of coral, there were three or four feet. But there was a peculiar shade of lighter brown which meant destruction to the soft pine bottom of a Swampscott dory and a spinning outboard propeller. We had close but brief views of many coral heads as we careened around and between them. When the motor was shut off in the still water and we waded ashore, we studied more carefully their strange shapes and beautiful designs.

What had appeared to be patches of yellowish-brown were really of many colors — blue, mauve, purple, green, yellow, gray, and white. Some of the coral growths I saw had taken the form of brain-folds, while others were like pebbly footballs. The brittle buff antlers from the staghorn coral crunched and broke under my feet as I walked along. All of these and many more I found made up a single head from 10' to 20' wide.

The surface of some of these heads was gashed by a pair of wavy turquoise blue lips, perhaps 12" long. They were parted innocently until the Trader put the very tip of an oar into one pair. They clamped so tightly shut with a horrid grip that squeezed the color out of them. The *tridacna*, or giant clam, abandons every hope of locomotion and allows its heavy crinkled shell to become completely embedded in the coral, retaining only enough freedom of action to open its beautiful deadly jaws and shut them on whatever little finny brother or sister may find its way between them. The larger *tridacnae* is said to hold divers below the surface by an arm or a leg and hold them until dead, thereafter presumably to assimilate them at leisure.

The atoll was about fifty yards wide at this point. Along its seaward side stretched a dazzling white sand beach strewn with streaked and spotted seashells, some of which, having been taken over as dwellings by hermit crabs, fled with awkward tumbles at my approach. Two large light green fish shot away from the shore and across the lagoon toward the reef where the black-tipped dorsal fin of a small green shark cruised back and forth. One hundred yards down the shore sat the hulk of the wrecked bark.

> *She is a 4 masted ship, yards on all 4 masts & most of the yards are still there. Hailed from Glasgow.*

We found convenient access into her through a large hole in the battered bilge. Most of her fittings and all of her cargo had been removed by wreckers through this hole, leaving nothing but a rusty skeleton still clearly marked "2090 net tons" for inspection these twenty-seven years later. When the vessel was driven ashore, ten of her crew, perhaps thinking she would strike the outer reef and slide off again into deep water, had tried to get ashore in a small boat but were lost in the attempt. Those who remained aboard were saved. It had been in that same 1906 blow that the father of Captain Palmer of the schooner *Suzanne* of Papeete, which had come in that morning and tied up astern the *Pilgrim,* had saved himself by climbing to the top of a well-rooted coconut tree as the seas washed completely over the neighboring island of Hikueru.

> **Got caught in the usual afternoon squall before leaving & took shelter in a fine thatched hut of palm leaves built on stilts in the coral about 10 yards off the shore & drank coconut water while the rain came down in sheets across the lagoon. In the evening Joe & I, under the guidance of Rono, our old pilot, went ashore. Had a couple of quarts of "Old Tom" with us & went to a**

"hula-hula" in a house belonging to two girls. I was on the harmonica & there were a couple of guitars. We filled the girls up with gin and away they went. They certainly could "hula-hula." After the crowd had left they put on a real dance. Some of the girls were fine looking. Fine features, good figures and lovely hair way down their backs, and very even white teeth. They just couldn't be still when the music played. We sure had a hell of a time all around.

During the two days we were tied up at Takaroa, two of the squalls for which the Tuamotus are famous had struck — one early in the morning and the other at about four in the afternoon. In these sudden vicious blasts, accompanied by blinding downpours, we received a vivid warning of what to expect on the rest of our course through the archipelago. The following afternoon, we put out through the pass under power with Rono again serving as pilot, then dropped him off into the outrigger paddled by two boys. We hoisted the four lowers, hauled up for the passage between Takaroa and Takapoto, and set the course for Aratika, some 62 miles away. Another squall passed over, this time with the sole effect of killing the wind entirely. It left us tossing and slatting in a short sea, subject to the mildly vexatious necessity of taking in all the canvas while a dinner of fresh mackerel cooled down below and sent its delicious odors up through the hatch.

February 27. 6:30 P.M. Started engine. Left foresail, jumbo & jib on to prevent rolling & got enough easterly breeze after the rain squall to keep these sails quiet. 8-12 P.M. Uneventful.

We hove-to early in the morning to avoid coming up on Aratika in the darkness and sighted the atoll off the starboard bow after daybreak. Since the breeze was very light, we decided not to await the fortunes of squalls and currents in such close proximity to land, and set about to start the engine. I have explained that the added ballast found necessary to bring the *Pilgrim* down to her proper lines brought the outlet of the engine's exhaust so close to the water line that a shut-off valve was necessary to keep the sea water from backing up into the engine when it was not running. This valve, of course, had to be opened before the engine was started — preferably only the instant before, if there were any sea — and someone would crouch in the lazarette to perform this office and report that he had done so to the Chief who, ready in the engine room, would then pull the starting lever.

On this morning, in an unfortunate access of exuberance, an impromptu relay system of communication between the valve operator and the Chief was substituted for the usual formal one. Although very spirited, the communication had the fatal defect of ambiguity. The result was that the air was turned on too soon and, with a dire explosive clank, the heavy cast steel top of the diesel engine blew off, barely missing the Chief's forehead on its way to the skylight. The expression "O.K.," while avoiding the pedantic flavor of more precise locutions, is at least responsible for some debasement of the English language. On this occasion, it put a heavy diesel engine out of commission and nearly killed a man.

It seemed wiser, with the power plant thus gone, to forego our projected excursion to the atoll of Fakarava and to get out of the dangerous archipelago as soon as the wind would allow. Leaving that atoll to windward, we set a course and a full spread of muslin for Tahiti.

February 28. 6-8 P.M. Fresh quartering breeze & sea making up a little as we got out from under the lee of Fakarava. Bowling along as if she smelled the waterfront bars of Papeete.

March 1. 4-8 A.M. Shortly before 6, set balloon jib & took in

jumbo. Then set main gaff topsail & fisherman, the latter
requiring the assistance of the Cook who was almost carried
away clinging to the halyard & looking less dignified than usual.

We cleared the archipelago, and by four of the following
afternoon, sighted off the port bow the loom of Taiarapu Peninsula which extends to the southeast of Tahiti's main land mass. In
the dying light of day, I saw the higher parts of Tahiti fade from
blue to black while the peaks of its satellite island, Moorea, spread
a purple silhouette across the copper sunset ahead.

March 1. Powerful supper of creamed chicken, potatoes, spinach,
hot muffins & egg plums. Evening the same. Clouds over Tahiti
gradually dispersing & leaving a beautiful night. 9:10 picked up
Pt. Venus Light, the Chief sighting it from the foremast head a
point on the port bow. Ran down keeping off a bit from the land
& at 9:45 took in raffee to slow vessel down.

March 2. At midnight took in squaresail & set foresail & hove to
on starboard tack until about 1:15, when wore 'round to port
tack. 2:30. Stood in again, heading SE, Point Venus Light
bearing E by N 1/4 N. Continued jogging under the land until
daylight.

With daylight and a fresh breeze, we sailed past the broad
mouth of Matavai Bay, the anchorage of Wallis, Cook, and Bligh
but now seldom used and held on for Papeete. The valleys among
the magnificent heights of the Diadem and towering Orohena
were still in partial darkness. The rising sun touched their eastern
slopes with a golden green and distilled from their foliage a sweet
smell of early morning which blended with the familiar, smoky
fumes rising from the galley stove through the Charley Noble.
Moorea, the playground of early Tahitian deities, lay only ten
miles to starboard, but Tahiti had no rival for our attention as we
studied her famous glory now unfolding close at hand. I entertained a medley of lively but vague anticipations that sprung from

all I'd read about the island in the past. Cook, Melville, Stevenson, Pierre Loti, George Calderon, Frederick O'Brien — how much, I wondered, of what they had seen of aboriginal Tahiti in its successive stages of decline remained to be found by an American yachtsman in the third decade of the twentieth century?

As we skirted Fareute Point, the easterly limit of Papeete Harbor, a sparse forest of masts and spars that had seemed concentrated at a distance became apparent as parts of a dozen or so individual vessels at Walker's Shipyard. The schooner *Moana* was up on the ways having a new stern put in before making another trading trip to the Marquesas, and a large schooner yacht, the *White Shadow* of Marseilles, lay at anchor in the quiet lagoon.

Some distance along the shore beyond the shipyard was a long concrete wharf which served an equally long, iron-roofed warehouse, or copra shed, and a coalyard. Further to the west, the shorefront gradually became less baldly commercial and stretched away past a thinning line of schooners and cutters moored to the quay along which ran the shore road under a row of luxuriant scarlet-flowered flamboyant trees. From under the trees, a line of low wooden stores and government buildings — white, red, and yellow — fronting the town behind it which, horned with scattered church spires, turned a wide expressionless face on our approach.

The harbor of Papeete (which means "basket of water") is enclosed by a reef over which the sea continually breaks. The pass, somewhat over one hundred yards wide, is toward the western end of the reef. The *Pilot Book* warns: "The danger to sailing vessels entering the pass at Papeete is that the wind may fail them suddenly, and the current, which is nearly always setting out, may set them on the reef. Sailing vessels need the pilot to enter the harbor, as he will know about the wind." Findlay's advice is similar: "It is evident that a pilot is advisable for this port, and that the boats should be in readiness to tow or run out kedges as required." The modern paraphrase of this counsel is, of course, that you either have the engine turning over in readiness or else rely on it altogether.

The *Pilgrim*, however, since the accident to our power plant in the Tuamotus, was again purely a sailing craft and in no better position than the earliest fore-and-aft'ers that sailed into Papeete since it was first surveyed. However, there was no reason to apprehend even any appreciable delay, much less danger, since Mr. MacDonald assured us that a pilot would be forced on us, and a tow would be simply a matter of price. As we came abeam the islet called Motu Uta, which sits on the reef opposite the center of town and bears the old holiday pavilion of Queen Pomare, I saw a small power boat cross the harbor. It emerged from the pass into the swell of the open sea bucking and rolling, with two figures dressed in the high-collared white uniform of the French colonial, keeping to their feet handily.

In order to prepare for negotiations, I asked Mr. MacDonald, "What's the French word for 'tow'?"

"Oh, you won't need any French with Lucas," he replied. "Lucas speaks English perfectly. He used to be the pilot here, but they put him out for some political reason and appointed that little fellow there," he said, pointing to the smaller of the two in the boat. "Lucas has to come along with him to do the actual piloting."

The little "pickle boat," as the Skipper called it, was hardly up to the job, so after I struck a bargain at one hundred francs with Lucas, he set off for the town and sent out a larger motor boat which took a line from Joe and drew the *Pilgrim* in through the pass. Like breaching whales, the broad black reefs on both hands seemed to raise their tops ominously from the water between each crash of the swell on them. Inside the pass, we found ourselves immediately in calm water, sliding along in line with two white range towers on the hillside at the west end of town.

We gave a good berth to three iron cannon snouts that protruded from the water and marked coral heads clustered about Motu Uta to port. As we approached the quay, the mountains sank behind the waterfront treetops, and on the iron roof of the warehouse on the steamship wharf, a beer advertisement and the words there became legible, "Societè de Tourisme de l'Océanie." We had left Tahiti and entered Papeete.

A large schooner, the *Zeleé,* constituting the full naval force of French Oceania, half-a-dozen copra schooners, some island cutters, and the British ketch *Vanora* were moored, according to regulation, sterns to the quay like elephants in a circus menagerie. At the pilot's command, we let go the port bower at about three boat lengths from the quay opposite a vacant berth and swung on twenty-five fathoms of chain into position. At the same time, Joe ran a stern line to the bank in the peapod. It was made fast by a ready native to another iron cannon, this one and many others embedded perpendicularly along the shore, doing duty as bollards. The schooner's other quarter was then made fast and an idle gangplank lying on the bank was hauled aboard to rest on the taffrail. The mooring lines, once parceled with burlap chafing pads, gave no further concern as the rise and fall of the tide, high between noon and two o'clock every day, is no more than a foot.

A small group of early risers standing around or leaning on their bicycles had, until now, been watching these proceedings with undemonstrative calm. As soon as the connection with the schooner was made, and greatly to my inconvenience as I finished securing the gangplank to the stern, they pushed their way on board with all the insistence of a mob fleeing from a burning theater, flourishing the business cards of laundries, grocery stores, and taxicab stands. I attempted to check the assault by plucking at the sleeve of one of the moneychangers as he boarded, but he jostled me aside. He cast a contemptuous look at my full but untrimmed beard and worn undershirt and continued firmly on, saying he wished to speak with the "capitaine." The capitaine, however, was dressed in his usual harbor rig of very old gray trousers, patched across the seat with sail-cloth, and a white cotton cap bearing the inscription across the front in red letters, "Tarr & Wonson's Racing Compound — a Liquid Copper Paint," and was therefore as unimpressive and as helpless as I.

It was the Cook, John, to whom all addresses were being made, and to whom alone I could appeal for some restoration of order. The Cook, who, with white yachting cap, cigar and decently covered torso, was the sole symbol of authority. With a mouthful of promises and threats, he soon had the deck cleared. Since we intended to spend several weeks in this spot, we set to unbending all the sails and setting the awnings. I did not want whatever pleasures lay ahead interfered with by the thought of work left undone. The main and foresail lacelines buzzed as they were whipped out of their grommets, the water around the hull was sprinkled by a shower of marlin from cut jib hank seizings, and the khaki awnings soon stretched from foremast to boom-gallows.

When the deck was thus transformed into a great shaded piazza, the Trader selected the elevated top of the charthouse as suitable to his comfort and ventilation, brought his mattress up from below, and extended his giant bulk there with a luxurious sigh. His recumbent figure, dressed in varying costumes — shirts, pajamas, or pareus, according to the weather or the state of his laundry — became a familiar sight to the passersby along the main street as well as to the permanent occupants of the bench in front of Maxwell's store some 40' or 50' distant across the thoroughfare.

The Cook went ashore immediately, as usual, to get the lay of the land and a glass of beer. He returned, smoking a cigar he'd gotten free from a grocer who promised to sell us groceries. He also brought a great deal of mail since Papeete was the first steamship port we had sailed into since leaving Panama. Confident that there would be plenty of opportunity later on for further inspection and judgment, the crowd which assisted at our arrival dispersed. For a time, there was no sound above the roar of the galley range but that of ripping envelopes and an occasional sympathetic or derisive comment on some news item from home. It was 2 March 1933, and aside from the interest of purely personal messages, the letters conveyed considerable uneasiness about the economic and political structure of the country.

> We have a fine view of the waterfront & on either side of us are moored copra & trading schooners. We are getting a mechanic to grind the valves on the engine & will be able to have new studs made here & after this job she should go better than ever.

chapter 7

Tahiti

TAHITI, ON THE CHART, resembles a fat tadpole headed in a northwesterly direction for a triangular meal, which is the neighboring island of Moorea. The body of the tadpole is a cluster of lofty peaks of volcanic origin, some over 7,000' in height. Their common base flattens out into a coastal shelf encircling the island. The tail crosses the narrow peninsula of Taiarapu and diminishes to nothing at the tip of the tail, where its mountains descend directly into the sea.

It is often said that the island was discovered by the great Spanish explorer Pedro Fernández de Quirós in 1606, but this is more than doubtful. The reference in his account to the island, which is supposed to have been Tahiti, suggests a neighboring island which is low and partly covered with water. It was seen, moreover, in about latitude fourteen degrees south, whereas Tahiti lies between the seventeenth and eighteenth parallels. Allowing for considerable inaccuracy in the navigational instruments and methods of those days, there is still a total absence of even suggestive evidence in his offshore glimpse of the discovery of one of such striking and majestic loftiness as the "Queen of the Pacific." Clouds often cluster about her crown, the multiple jagged peak called the Diadem, but they seldom, if ever, obscure all of her except the hem of her skirt.

The Spaniard did not land on the island, whatever it was, or pass closer than fifteen miles to it, and that in rainy weather. Even if there remains room for the supposition that he saw Tahiti from a distance of five or six leagues, it is most unlikely that the Tahitians saw him. The debated event is, in any case, without the significance of the real discovery of inhabited land typically marked by the captain, attired in the full panoply of his time, planting his nation's flag in the beach sand, after which representatives of the two peoples meet face to face for the first time in history and exchange gifts or blows.

If any such meeting had occurred in Tahiti before the arrival of Samuel Wallis, island lore presumably would tell of it. According to that body of oral history, an ancient prophet called Maui told the people there would at some time come a canoe without an outrigger. This prediction, while not at the time understood, was apparently not forgotten; later, another seer, Paue, revived the promise, saying that in the canoe would come the children of the Glorious Princess.

These people would differ from and yet be the same as themselves, they would be covered from head to foot, and they would possess the land and cause the end to native customs. A short time later, in 1767, the British ship H.M.S. *Dolphin* arrived with Captain Wallis, who had James Cook as a lieutenant, and they were not unnaturally taken to be the children of the Glorious Princess. They were certainly covered from head to foot, and it would become true that from that time forward neither the land nor the customs of the Tahitians were ever the same again.

The immediate change was not extensive, since Wallis left behind him but a looking glass, some turkeys, a pair of geese, and a cat. From the time of Louis Antoine De Bougainville's visit eight months later in the frigate *La Boudeuse*, accompanied by the store ship *L'Étoile*, the scene changed rapidly. The Frenchman found a people inhabiting what seemed to him a paradise, a people of beauty, grace, and joy, dancing and singing with flowers in their hair. He formally annexed the island and called it *la Nouvelle Cythère*. The people were, to be sure, in what I believe is called the Neolithic stage of culture, having no metals with which to make tools and ornaments.

For nearly fifteen hundred years, since some long forgotten and amazing voyage from Asia in an outrigger canoe, they multiplied and thrived in a state of nature which seems rather stuffy to deplore. The French captain knew that he carried in his ships the germs of destruction of this community. To his credit, he "took measures" to prevent their dissemination among the natives. His vigilance was ineffective against generous native hospitality and his crew's shameful abuse of it. Over the next several decades, nearly nine-tenths of the people died after awful and pathetic suffering due to venereal and other European diseases. What desolation this must have caused among the remaining tenth can be imagined.

Far from receiving apology or commiseration for this outrageous visitation from Western civilization which had inflicted it, the Tahitians were further abused, this time verbally. In the grog shops and parish churches of Europe, they were called a shamefully immoral people. If, the reasoning went, it was too late to save their pathetically corroded and destroyed carcasses, wasn't there still time to save the souls of those who remained?

Early in 1797, the thirty awful years since the arrival of white men seemed to reach a kind of cosmic climax in a combined earthquake and storm. Three shocks were felt, the first in the peoples' history. Tremendous seas vaulted the reefs and a great wind brought the palm trees low and flattened the pandanus houses. The people cried to their gods. Indeed, it might have seemed to them that their old protectors had abandoned them or were no longer potent in this world of new influences — an earth

that shook, ships that sailed without outriggers, men who killed
with cannons and embraces.

Perhaps some new, more sophisticated gods were needed to
match them. On the following day, the tremors stopped. As the
sun rose over the now abated seas, the missionary ship *Duff*
approached the relieved and wondering multitude and dropped
anchor. Aboard were thirty missionaries and their families, the
first permanent European settlers, all sent out by the Protestant
London Missionary Society.

If the central figure of the New Testament disdained the
dramatic support of a factitious display of supernatural phenomena, the company of the *Duff* permitted themselves to depart from
that precedent and to make the most of the connection which the
natives imagined to exist between the cessation of the earthquake
and the arrival of the missionary ship. Playing upon the supersti-
tions of the natives, they convinced many of them that they were
the lieutenants of powerful and touchy gods, all the while
consolidating their position politically by supplying arms and
ammunition to the nearest local chief and setting up a corps of
secret police.

The chief was an outlander from the Tuamotus and by no
means of great importance in Tahiti. Due to the fact that Cook,
Wallis, and Bligh had all landed in his district (Matavai) and
thought he must be the high chief of the island because he was
nearest and their friend, the missionaries supported him as such
in many bloody revolutions. The house of Pomare was finally
established as the one royal house. By the time Pomare had
become a confirmed Christian and died of drink, the ancient
traditions and taboos which were a part of the Tahitian culture
had been abandoned for a hodgepodge of church observances,
Calvinistic morality, and gun-running opportunism.

It would be misleading to characterize the pre-discovery state
of the Tahitians as purely paradisiacal. To do so lends added

flavor to the game of disparaging the missionaries, but it leads away from the truth. They engaged in inter-tribal wars, made human sacrifices, and ate one another at times. Without European assistance, they had discovered at least some of the vices. From an account of the *Pandora*, the ship sent to arrest the *Bounty's* mutineers in 1791, comes this ethnographic description written by the ship's captain and surgeon: "Their houses are well adapted to the temperate climate they inhabit, and generally consist of three chambers, the interior one of which the chief retires to, after he has drank his cava. A profound silence is observed during his repose; for should he be suddenly awaked, it (the cava) produces violent vomiting, and a train of uneasy sensations; but otherwise, if undisturbed, it proves a safe anodyne, creates amorous dreams, and a powerful excitement to venery."

Cava, or *kava*, made from the dried roots of a shrub, *Piper methysticum*, was regarded as sacred to the chiefs who cultivated the white skin blotches that it produced when drunk to excess with the same pride a German duelist takes in his saber scars. It was not regarded as fitting that these distinguished blemishes be affected by the common people, who therefore had to be content with fermented coconut milk and skins as smooth and unspotted at the *tiare maohi*, or native wild gardenia. On the other hand, although the fruit of the Tree of Knowledge had long since been sampled in this island Eden when the Children of the Princess arrived in the great canoe without an outrigger, the apple had not upset their digestion. That several thousand people lived on the island in a state described by Bougainville and others in the eighteenth century as near to Paradise is sufficient evidence that their present depleted numbers and cultural bewilderment are far from an improvement.

❂ ❂ ❂

There is no way to see the world, to my taste, that approaches in satisfaction a cruise in a sailing vessel, not too large. Instead of speeding over the earth's surface in a series of jumps from port to port in an ocean liner, one progresses in a leisurely fashion through the sea, never more than a few feet distant from the water. One's life is for the time being wholly occupied in adapting the ship and oneself to the forces of air and water, and in contemplating these in all their variety. To cross the ocean in a few days or weeks of bridge, pool swimming, and deck tennis aboard a steamer is to remain nearly unconscious of the element of which three-fourths of the earth's surface is composed.

On the other hand, the small sailing vessel has its disadvantages when land is reached, for the center of one's living is a spot on a waterfront which exercises the constant centripetal force of a hundred and one concerns of repairs, maintenance, supplies, and curiosities. Our observations of Tahiti, for example, as of every other place we went in the *Pilgrim,* were largely confined to the life of the main port. One can imagine the picture of Boston that would be received by a foreigner who spent a few weeks tied up to the city's main wharf in a schooner. *The Seaman's Handbook for Shore Leave* would have informed him of the chief cultural and historical spots in the city. Even if the most hospitable citizens did not set about entertaining the voyager intensively in a social way, as they seem to do in most of the ports of the world, it is unlikely that his account of the city and its people would be comprehensive.

To be sure, the quay at Papeete, due to its proximity to the Broom Road, gives a better opportunity for observing Tahitians than does Boston's T-Wharf for observing Bostonians. The Broom Road makes a complete circuit of the main island, running along the coastal shelf where nearly all of the natives and all of the white residents live. When any of these wishes to go to town, he has only to step out to the road, lay a coconut frond across the way, and return to sharpening his fish spear or playing his hand

Tahiti waterfront scene.

of bridge. When the next bus comes along — it may be ten minutes or half a day later — the driver, seeing the signal, stops. He sounds his horn and waits — and this may be ten minutes or longer, too — until the new passenger emerges from the grove and is hailed with friendly greetings. The safari then resumes.

The Broom Road is a relatively modern innovation. Before the discovery of Tahiti by Westerners, there was for a highway only the shallow water of the lagoons inside the reef which encircles most of the island, and all travel of any distance was done by canoe. With the revelation of sin and crime came the prescription of expiation and punishment, and the standard treatment for everything from adultery to lobbing a ripe breadfruit at a government informer was a few months' duty building the coastal road. Like the naughty proclivities of the human heart, of which it is thus the monument, the road is endless. It sweeps out through the districts and back again: Hitiaa, Mahaena, Tiarei, Papenu, and Arue; Papeari, Mataiea, Papara, Paea, Punaavia, Faaa, Papeete. It runs over the wide pebbly bottoms of streams where naked women bathe and wash their clothes, and marshy pools bright with purple water hyacinth, past grassy plains and around rocky shoulders covered with moss and hanging ferns.

Each valley mouth makes up a vast proscenium, topped by the central peaks and framed by walls of green, in which the action of the play is the pouring, tumbling, and foaming into misty tongues of many waterfalls. Here and there along the road is a settlement: a Chinese store, a limestone church, and a dozen whitewashed board huts. A few canoes (*vaas*) are pulled up on the beach or resting on short stilts with bamboo fish lockers drying beside them. As the road approaches Papeete from both directions, the informality of the landscape fades, first with the clipped lawns and dagger-plants of foreigners' country estates, then with the planted avenues of flamboyant trees and acacias, hedges of yellow and red hibiscus, white picket fences, gardens, and the wide verandaed houses of French government officials. Reaching the *Quai des Subsistances Militaires* from the west side of Papeete, the road takes an abrupt right face to march like a good colonial thoroughfare past the blank stucco façade of the Old Magazine. It then passes the American consulate and a row of wooden residences screened by bougainvillea and yellow jasmine, and meets itself coming the other way in front of a four-story apartment house built of concrete simulated stone blocks.

Over the Broom Road and into Papeete come the natives: tall, flat-nosed, light tan, smooth-muscled Polynesians with dark brown hair, shorter and darker types with coarse black hair, the children of an admixture in the Tonga Islands, some with brown eyes, gray eyes, green, or blue. Others with the round fine-boned face of a Chinese grandfather, or the high-bridged nose of a Spanish ancestor from Peru, or the red hair from an Irish sailor, or the thin lips from perhaps a missionary who forswore his mandate and his frock.

They come on foot and on bicycles, in ancient surreys and Fords. They are piled, laughing, in open omnibuses which sway from side to side with their weight and that of their produce and small livestock. All the fruits of the earth, upon which ten times their number once lived happily, sprout and ripen in one continuous harvest season, but the natives are no longer free from the want of other things which only money can buy. So into town they come, to turn their superfluity of food into calico, gasoline, ukuleles, candy, and fleeting views of cowboys riding across the cinema screen.

The market opens exactly at 5:30 every morning of the week except the last, and the audience is never late for the curtain. At about half past four one morning, I was awakened by the ear-splitting shrieks of a hog as a boy from the old schooner *Manureva*, which had wallowed in the day before from Tubuai in the Austral Islands, dragged the frightened creature ashore by one leg, trussed it with coconut fiber, and then hung it by both pairs of legs over a carrying pole.

Across the road I saw a heap of older women from the same vessel who had escaped its crowded deck and spent the night under the arcade in front of Maxwell's stores. They were rousing and extricating themselves, straightening their long cotton dresses, and gathering together the homemade straw hats they hoped to sell to the Tahitians. I swung by the gallows frame, over the gangway and onto the dirt road along the quay. Ahead of me walked a stout legged woman and a little boy, both in bare feet and perhaps in from Punaavia, which is not far enough out to have warranted their taking a bus. The woman was carrying on each arm a basket of plaited rush-like leaves heaped with oranges, while the boy was carrying two strings of red and blue rock fish swinging from the opposite ends of a stick.

A bicycle passed me with a whish, topped by Jones, a retired chemical engineer, pedaling with dignified deliberation. He, like myself, was empty-handed. He, however, was not going to the market out of curiosity or in search of novelty. He went every morning to hear the news and see acquaintances who appear in Papeete at no other time of the day. He heard more news than most of his fellow white islanders because he knew the colloquial language. He told me that a thorough acquaintance with it protected him from being the subject of the constant personal and critical — though always good-humored — remarks with which young Tahitian girls amuse themselves in the presence of visiting white men. Jones also picks up mangoes and flowers because he keeps his professional talents alive by making a bit of chutney and perfume from time to time.

To return to our trip to the market: I passed the row of glass cabinet carts with their displays of popcorn, peanuts, cigarettes, and American candy bars. These carts were arranged along the little park where their Chinese proprietors dozed on wooden benches beneath the second story veranda of the *Cercle Bougainville*. I continued down the *Rue de Rivoli*, which debauches into the busy center of Tahiti's early morning life.

In the shade of the huge roof over two great concrete-floored "halles" and overflowing into the sunlight of adjoining streets, I saw a picture of the island's abundance — golden papayas, guavas, and mangoes that needed no printed legend saying, "kissed by the sun," of oranges, lemons, limes, bananas, pumpkins, and melons. On the slabs of the fish stall were round-bellied bonito fresh but lately guzzling small fry outside the reef. Also there to be bought were whole tuna, grouper, rock fish, sea centipedes, and prawns.

Live chickens tethered by one leg contributed mightily to the medley of sounds, as did the hog from Tubuai, unconsoled by finding others in the same plight. There were bamboo pipes containing coconut sauce, jars of honey from the mountains, and other jars of coconut cream. This last is not the stale white liquid which has stewed inside the dried shell of an old coconut one buys at home. This is the juice of the meat of a freshly plucked coconut, and it is not yielded willingly like the water which pours out of a pierced nut, but must be pressed from the meat after it has been removed and grated. This liquid is more than worth the trouble, and to the extent that a sensual memory can recreate the whole image of a place, the recollection of a cup of coffee made with this coconut elixir conjures up a complete nostalgic picture of Tahiti for me.

Speaking of coffee, I had some on that particular morning. Since I was too ignorant of the island tongue to learn what jest Mama Ruau was tossing to Turia, or in what terms young Tiurai was haggling for his fish with the proprietor of the Blue Lagoon, or what news Marotea was relating with such zest to lovely Tahiri, and since our gentle activity in the morning air and the proximity of so much food made me hungry, I crossed the street and went into Monsieur Drollet's shop for a cup of coffee and a croissant.

Returning to the quay and crossing the gangplank, I discovered the Skipper emerged from the doghouse still wearing his mosquito-proof night costume. His pajama legs were secured over the tops of his socks with lengths of marlin, his hands were encased in white cotton work gloves, and the upper half of his vulnerable skull was crowned with the invariable painter's cap. He laid his Flit gun on top of the house, and, after an appraising sniff of the general conditions, asked, "How about a swim out to the buoy and back, Commander?" (The crew had taken to calling me "Commander" back in Panama after the sham hearing we had in front of a real Commander as a result of damage to the schooner in a lock.)

"What? A swim in the city sewer on a nice morning like this?"

"Sewer!" he said, scornfully. "Think of L Street and its beach on Boston Harbor — that never hurt anybody."

The Trader on his lofty divan raised one eyelid without the slightest movement of any other part of his body and looked at me.

"Where'n'hell have you been? Just getting home?"

"I've been to market."

"To market? Wha's matter, can't you sleep?"

From somewhere below and forward came the Cook's morning bellow at the Doc, trying to get him out of his bunk in time for a more or less common breakfast.

There was a sewer outlet not far from the *Pilgrim's* mooring, but there was no indication of it in the freshness of the morning air. I looked overboard. A red hibiscus flower, only recently fallen, was floating on the water. The Skipper and I dove off the bow and swam out for the steamer mooring buoy in the lagoon.

Later that morning, and on many others, we had a longer swim off the end of Motu Uta, just inside the passage through the reef. There, the water is as clean as the sea can be and full of tropical sunlight both from above and reflected from the white coral below. Wearing a pair of fisherman's goggles so that each eye had its water telescope, I dove down and swam among the fish that move in little processions in and out of the crevices in the reef.

I saw yellow and black striped angel fish, little minnows as bright as indigo birds, and larger fish which were like carp and colored green. They were wary but they kept no great distance, and after a while seemed to know that we were there only to observe and that soon we would have to surface for air. A man named Lucas told us a giant grouper lurked in the reef and once had swallowed a boy, so we always kept a sharp lookout. He said sharks had been seen in the lagoon, but they were timorous and frightened away by the sound of a loud slap on the surface of the water. We saw none, however, and were not put to verify this statement.

❂ ❂ ❂

As a social organism, Tahiti has progressed far since the

aboriginal days, at least in the Spencerian sense of becoming more heterogeneous. The Tahitians themselves are multifariously stratified by inherited nobility, connections with other races, and individual merits and tastes. The Chinese, who in Papeete live in a separate quarter (a jerry-built fire trap of tortuous passages and hidden doors), keep to themselves as do the petty merchants and eating-house keepers of their race in other countries.

The French colony is composed for the most part of officials of the French government, from the Governor General of French Oceania down to the customs officials and the police and gendarmerie of the island. The French, as is well known, practice no distinctions of race, and in Papeete entertain their native mistresses with Pernod and beer at the *Cercle Coloniale*. They drink on the back veranda there, not because of their mistresses' blood but to preserve the piquancy of the relationship. Our Gallic brothers, however, take little advantage of the opportunity to mix with the island's Americans, of whom there are some hundreds, or with those objects of their traditional antipathy, the British.

The English-speaking residents divide themselves into fairly miscible groups according to their pursuits which, on the whole, entail very little concentrated attention or physical effort. For a few, such as the writers Charles Nordhoff and James Norman Hall who wrote, among other books, *Mutiny On the Bounty*, work was important and demanding. Others kept various commercial enterprises alive by attending them before the eleven o'clock rum and lime hour at Bohler's Bar, and between siesta time and cocktails in the afternoon. Some of these businesses, such as copra and vanilla exporting, were at a low level of activity when I was there in 1933. Others, like store-keeping and bar-keeping, were fairly constant.

One American I met was making a good thing out of transshipping Canadian whiskey in the direction of the United States, then under Prohibition. In general practice, customs officials did not permit liquor to leave a port of origin unless it was consigned to and unloaded in a "wet" port. However, the *douane* at Papeete asked few questions and raked in customs duties, the local stevedores made good wages unloading and reloading the cases, and the American was becoming comfortably rich.

The great majority of the English-speaking population, as I have said, had no regular obligations. Some of these escaped disintegration by pursuing the marlin offshore with great energy, but most were showing obvious signs of having found no satisfactory substitutes or alternatives for the lives they had left behind them. There were the bridge players, for example. Each bright morning, as the mists burned from the valleys and sun sparkled from the falls of Fautaua and the waters of the lagoon, the bridge players congregated on the second floor of a wooden building behind the quay which formerly housed the *Cercle Bougainville* and was now the quarters of the Tahiti Yacht Club. Millet would be the first, sometimes arriving as early as eight o'clock, so as to have an eye-opener as soon as Alex arrived to set the club in order for the day.

One by one, recent graduates of several of America's leading eastern universities would join him, and by ten o'clock there might be two tables going — eight brows furrowed in earnest competition, the silence broken only by the flutter and slap of the cards and the occasional tinkle of ice in a glass. Had they come to the Pearl of the Pacific to play bridge? Perhaps, where else, even in those days of unemployment, would they have been always sure of a fourth player and, at the same time, safe from public opinion which, at least in America, frowned on dealing a card before lunch?

It was not that the foreign colony in Papeete did not care what one another did, quite on the contrary: report and discussion of their fellows' doings and the fabrication of spicy variations on those reports consumed a large part of their waking moments. It was rather that so few were invulnerable that any concerted program of ostracism would have torn the fabric of their expatriate society into tatters. It was "live and let live." However, the bridge players were discontent. Some, like Millet, drank heavily, and four of them finally chartered a schooner and disappeared over the western horizon, still playing bridge.

Then there was poor Strong. He had left an active life as editor of a national magazine and a wife in order to be alone with Muriel. Strong had been used to the society of what he regarded as "high-powered" people, and the lack of tension on the island plainly irked him. Muriel herself was quite without tension.

"There's nothing to *do* here, man," he told me. "I've sent for my guns and a skeet trap. I can throw the clay pigeons out over the lagoon, just *there*."

I learned later that Strong shot himself.

The permanent and semi-permanent residents of Tahiti, like those of other places, had long since discovered the various predilections of their neighbors and settled into their respective strata. Alister MacDonald, for example, whom we had brought from Takaroa, led the simple life of a painter, which in his case radiated from a cottage on the beach near Point Venus to the scenes of his work in Tahiti and other islands. Tea, not rum, was the lubricant of thought in his studio.

Like his friend Bolton, Alister was as unknown to the group which issued annual invitations, under the name *La Jeunesse Tahitienne*, to balls in the *Garage Citroën* as they were to him. Bolton, a retired British colonial administrator, had crossed the island alone at the age of seventy by climbing the central peaks of Orohena and swimming across eel-infested Lake Vaihiria, a feat which few of any age ever accomplished. The event of the year among *La Jeunesse* was a projected trip around the island by bicycle, but this never came off.

From Hod Fuller's journal: The country & scenery is

**great here but one would soon become bored with
nothing to do. We've met many people and some of the
more socially inclined members of the crew were kept
busy wining and dining.... We met Norman Hall &
Charles Nordhoff. All my friends here have been
natives & half-castes who are far more interesting than
the crowd of Americans that hang around the yacht club
& booze all day.**

The *Pilgrim* became a kind of conduit through which passed
at one time or another, and at all times of the day and night, most
of the characters who washed and backwashed through the town
of Papeete. The ship's company, being neither settled into their
habits of life nor faced with the problem of selecting the associates
of a long voyage and, being fired with both the curiosity and
catholicity of youth, had made contacts with virtually the entire
life of the island. As a result, the main cabin became the scene of
very nearly a twenty-four-hour continuous show. Murph soon
discovered that it was not necessary to go anywhere to see a great
variety of people and spent an entire week sitting on the main
cabin transom or settee and conversing, leaving it only for
occasional snatches of sleep in the bunk above.

To return to the ship late was seldom to sleep. There might be
a debate in progress, for example, on whether to heave a schooner
to under staysail and trysail (Captain Vigo Rasmussen of the *Tiare
Taporo*) or under her foresail alone (Captain Peters of the *Pilgrim*),
or the cabin might be filled with laughing and singing vahines
playing guitars. At the same time Mrs. T. might be telling Murph
the story of her life. When finally the asseverations, squeals, or
drone died away and one had laid down upon one's pillow, there
would be a rush of feet on deck overhead and a chorus of
invitations to drive out to the Moana Hotel.

chapter 8

Tahitian Days and Nights

From the ship's log: We were close neighbors of the Mouette, an old Government schooner manned by prisoners, which cruises occasionally in the Tuamotus, and the Zelée, the French gunboat for Oceana. The Zelée is an old schooner which in her halcyon days with no engine & topsails established the sailing record of 17 days from 'Frisco to Papeete.

Among numerous trading or copra schooners, a few deserve special mention due to the fact that we became more or less friendly with their commanders. Captain Doom arrived from the Marquesas in the Tereora & went on Icky Walker's yard railway for repairs. Captain Andy Thompson of the Tagua was also in for an annual overhaul. A particularly good sort of a convivial nature, he hails from Rarotonga. We also saw something of Captain Viggo Rasmussen of the Tiare Taporo, who was in twice during our stay. He is a short round genial bird, "terrible slick." Then there is Captain Winnie Brander of the Moana and Tahitienne, a fine old bird & very interesting but difficult to know as he is invariably quite unintelligible after 10 A.M. We also met his brother, Arthur Brander, equally genial, who is in business in Papeete. The family once owned Easter Island.

Other vessels of interest are the Aratapu of Callao, taken by Icky

Walker for a bad debt. She arrived early in April from Mexican waters after delivering a load of whiskey. The Pro Patria, which returned with a leaky stuffing box after reaching the Marquesas with a load of the same liquid bound for Mexico, was another interesting old hooker. Then there was the Vaite, a slick little bit of a schooner commanded by old Captain Larsen who came out with Robert Louis Stevenson in the Casco in 1888.

In those days of 1933, there were only dim recollections of the First World War and no premonition of the Second. When the French cruiser *Savorgnan de Brazza* slid in through the reef and backed up to the quay beyond the naval schooner *Zelée* on a routine voyage through the French possessions, she brought no associations of armed conflict and awoke instead only thoughts of revelry. A five day *fête* was declared. In no time at all, the shore front sprouted a solid row of canvas *baraques* which extended from the *Pilgrim's* backyard all the way to the Old Magazine and offered all the treats of a street fair, from a merry-go-round to a ring-toss, with bright new pareus for prizes.

The island administrator and his wife came into town from the districts, and what with Americans and Englishmen, tourists, French residents, and visiting yachtsmen, in addition to the natives, all trying to move about at once, the most passionately gregarious nightclubber would have had his fill of company. The giant hum of voices shouting, singing, and laughing was punctuated here and there by a lively singing orchestra of "native" music. The music had attracted to the island's particular *boîte* an even denser mass of revelers, hopping and shoving about with the grim determination of people dancing in couples.

In such a group, I often saw the Skipper, who for the time being had changed his patched gray flannel trousers and painter's cap for white ducks, shirtsleeves, and panama hat, its brim sagging and bobbing with the weight of flowers piled on it. Every morning of the *fête*, the Skipper's first act after breakfast was to scrub his hat and sneakers to comparative whiteness with soap and water, then to set them in the sun to dry. Each evening, he stepped off the schooner in clothes clean and fresh from top to toe, his newly laundered white duck trousers fairly crackling with respectability.

One evening, a heavy rain squall swept the carnival and its effect on the Skipper's carefully prepared outfit was particularly striking. Some time after the tumult had died away, there came slowly down the companionway a pair of legs covered with black mud up to the knees. Above these, two soaking wet trouser legs appeared, followed by an equally wet silk shirt, through which most of his extensive tattooing was clearly visible — then a great mound of tiare Tahiti, the favorite island lei flower, its weight having pushed a wet and expended straw hat well down to the ears and over a face of which I could see little but what was in the circumstances an amazingly beatific smile.

"That was a slick hog-rassle," remarked the Skipper.

From Hod Fuller's journal: The Skipper and I took in the *fête* every night along with our girls Tuara & Tere. We gave it the big jib on the dance floor for several hours straight every evening to music supplied by accordions & guitars. Also went on a fine picnic around the whole island accompanied by a full piece orchestra.... The fun lasted steadily all day long and far into the night.

Not long after, the sailors aboard the *de Brazza* had been sped on their way by the copious but brief tears of their temporary sweethearts, and the canvass baraques had been folded and stored away. While confetti still littered the streets, a new diversion appeared in the shape of a wedding which was to take place on Moorea. As we had decided only the evening before to take a party of guests across to the festivities in the *Pilgrim,* and as the sails were all stowed on deck under tarpaulins, we powered out of Papeete's lagoon and into the full swell of the Pacific under bare poles, rolling like a barrel.

The motion soon put an effective damper on the spirits of most of the guests, who sat about on the deckhouses and rail, gradually assuming expressions of apathy. The chief musician, who had begun "fortifying" himself at once, alternately played and danced the dance of the spirit of creativity and fertility with unflagging enthusiasm on the forward deck. One by one, his assistants laid aside their instruments and curled up in the scuppers. The smiles on the faces of his audience became more and more automatic and then died away, whereafter one after another gave up completely. Lunch for some forty people was a very simple affair.

Moorea is ten miles away from Papeete, and before long its central mountains were almost above us as we skirted the reef marked by the wreck of the French gunboat *Kearsaint* and ran up Papetoai Bay. Peaks several thousand feet high rose sheer from the head of the inlet and seemed to command the silence that increased as we drew in under them, away from the thundering reef. One of the peaks is marked by a great hole which has been there for many years, ever since a man named Hiro brought a band of thieves with him from Raiatea and attempted to steal the whole range of mountains.

When they had almost succeeded in detaching the range by pulling on long vines which they had fastened to the peaks, a hero named Pai was awakened and told of the attempt. Pai was ten miles away at Pauaavia on Tahiti, but he had a spear made of a long hibiscus shoot tipped with bone from the arm of a witch. He climbed to the top of a hill and hurled the spear across the intervening sea. The spear pierced the peak. While it did no direct damage to the thieves, its passage set up such a commotion among the fowls that the thieves were forced to hurry away to escape capture, taking with them only a small hill from the end of the range. The evidence is there in the form of a hole, a nick out of another mountain over on Raiatea where the spear landed, and, some distance off, the stolen hill as well.

The merrymakers had by now revived, and we all trooped ashore to attend a short and dignified wedding ceremony in a whitewashed church. The bride, who was American, wore a picture hat and gown of the latest models from San Francisco, and the male principals and guests, many for the first time in months, sported neckties and coats. The party maintained some sort of order during a tremendous banquet, at which many toasts were drunk, while Mr. Phillips (whose father was English and mother of Moorea) and Mrs. Phillips (so recently Miss Gump of San Francisco) received their new Tahitian names and were thus properly and finally shackled. Soon afterwards, however, the party began to proliferate like tropical foliage and lost all signs of organization.

People separated into groups for dancing, arguing, lovemaking, and just plain drinking. They bulged out over the verandas, halted temporarily under the breadfruit trees, and eventually arrived in slow and irregular stages at the only hotel on the island. This was nominally managed by an English expatriate who had decided to join the party and let the hotel run itself that day. Since he had not locked up the bar, this worked well enough in a rough way. There were not enough beds to go around, of course, so the available ones were naturally occupied by those who were first exhausted or overcome, leaving for the rest only the floors and a few narrow settees on the veranda.

The rays of the next morning's sun bathed the old battleground of the gods in glory, then lit up alike the outlines and recesses of the Papetoai Hotel. The little hostelry, a haven for travelers and the world-weary, was a terrible sight. The straw matting on the veranda lay in a crumpled heap to one side as if withdrawing itself from the litter of crushed cigarette stubs, empty bottles, stale heeltaps, and overturned chairs which decorated the hotel entrance.

From within came voices: "My God! Is this the only can in this place?"

"How about ringing the bell for some breakfast?"

"Trader, where do you think you are? There isn't any bell, and there isn't a damn thing in the kitchen!"

"Call the manager," the Doc said.

"Don't be silly. He's passed out like everyone else."

"There's a native woman padding around out there. I said *'petit dejeuner'* to her and she just laughed."

"I've got to get some coffee."

A few yards over the roof hung bunches of ripe coconuts. On the slopes beyond the little settlement was every fruit tree characteristic of the region. Nearby there was a cool stream, the condensed bounty of the clouds above. Here was plenty, but it was not the kind of plenty the company was used to, and everybody was starving. One by one, we struggled out to the *Vanora* and the *Pilgrim* and had coffee grown in Brazil, wheat grown in Minnesota, and eggs cooked on a stove fabricated in Connecticut.

❂ ❂ ❂

One afternoon, on my way to the bicycle repair shop near the marketplace, I found an abnormal press of traffic — several dozen people — converging on the gate to a usually vacant lot. A sheet spread between two bamboo poles over the gate announced in French and Tahitian that a spectacle of walking through fire, or *umu-ti*, was to take place. It seemed worth the ticket price of five francs to see someone pass through fire and either burn or not burn, so I joined the crowd and walked to the center of the field.

In a pit perhaps 18' long, 8' wide, and several feet deep, was a mass of rounded, water-worn stones as large as footballs. These were black near the edge of the pit, while the others were in various stages of red and white heat. Flames licked up between them. The air for several yards above was visibly distorted by the heat to a quivering atmosphere. The crowd moved to within 20' of the oven on all sides, this distance being the result of their curiosity on one hand and the discomfort from the fiery pit on the other. There was no question about the reality of the fire, and it seemed incredible that any human being, unless clothed in asbestos, would attempt to pass through it.

However, preparations were going forward for the ordeal among six tender, *café au lait*-skinned girls wearing cotton dresses, and who were wreathed and girdled with leaves and flowers. Except for their entirely bare feet, they resembled young ladies at the graduating exercises of a seminary. The girls stood in a single line, each holding erect a green frond, the leaf of a *ti* plant, and listened to an invocation chanted by a young man similarly garbed and furnished. He walked slowly around the pit, holding his wand ahead of him, and chanted: *E na ta'ata e tahutahu i the umu e, a ta pohe na!* ("O spirits who enchant the oven, let it die out for a while") and much more.

The fire did not die out, however, not in the slightest perceptible degree. Nevertheless, the young man stepped onto the nearest stones, placing a bare instep squarely on the top of each one, and walked slowly the length of the pit. The girls followed him in an unbroken procession, some calmly and boldly, several it seemed with some trepidation, but all without faltering. Then they turned and walked back the way they had come, repeated the round-trip journey several times, and then stood aside to be examined and marveled at. I saw no sign on any of them of any burning or scorching. Sweat had gathered on their brows, but that was the only apparent effect.

Emboldened by this, a young American wearing sneakers dashed to the pit and crossed its length in a series of frenzied steps, as if playing hop-scotch on a giant hot stove. Several others did likewise, each with diminishing speed, but none with bare feet. I was not moved to emulate the rubber-shod scotch-hoppers, if only because their experiment seemed to throw no light on what had preceded it. Considering the toughness of the native sole and the possibility of a hypnotic state accounting for the native's immunity, I was unwilling to walk the stones with relatively tender bare feet and unhypnotized. I did find a clue to the performance in its parody, however, as one of the tourists turned out to have suffered an uncomfortable burn.

The fire-walking ceremony, or sideshow performance, apparently is not uncommon in certain parts of the world. It is performed, with local variations, not only in the Society Islands (where its chief priests have been on the island of Raiatea) but also in Fiji, Mauritius, Bulgaria, and Trinidad. By the end of the nineteenth century, the phenomenon had been credibly attested beyond a doubt. At that point, Professor Samuel Langley visited Tahiti, arranged to see an *umu-ti,* and went to work. Langley, then serving as Secretary of the Smithsonian Institution and known to history as the inventor of the bolometer and the first heavier-than-air flying machine, had many scientific interests, one of which was heat and its sources of radiation.

Whereas previous witnesses had made scattered observations and such inconclusive experiments as putting a cambric handker-chief on the shoulder of one of the walkers, Professor Langley took along a stoker from his ship, a thermometer, a bucket, and the trained observation of a physicist. He observed, first of all, several operations in the preparation of the fiery furnace. They seemed designed to create an impression of greater danger than was actually present, such as the use of 15' poles to arrange the stones and the insertion of their ends into the burning embers so that they caught fire. He noticed also that, although many of the stones were indeed red and white with heat, the tops of those walked on were black.

By having the stoker remove one of the stones and place it in a bucket of water, he found its average temperature was well over one thousand degrees Fahrenheit. By this and other tests, he found the most distinctive feature of the stone, a vesicular basalt, was its porosity and non-conductibility, which was such that it could be heated red-hot on one side and yet remain comparatively cool on the other. Langley's observations suggest that the secret of the ceremony lies in the peculiar character of the stones used, their judicious arrangement, and the performer's exercise of care in placing his feet. When the professor asked the priest why he did not step between the stones, the priest said, "My fathers did not tell me to do it that way."

The regions where fire-walking is performed seem to confirm Professor Langley's conclusions: several are of volcanic origin, and it is most probable that all contain basalt rock. There may well be other regions where the show could be staged (I suppose even in America), but the secret seems to have been held only by peoples having their origin in Asia — even on Trinidad the population is nearly one-half Hindu. There also is no doubt that although the delicate feet of white commissioners and even of their European wives have passed through the fire unscathed, it must at least be reassuring to have the leathery sole of the Polynesian. Professor Langley's stoker remarked that he had seen a Kanaka place a bare instep on an uncovered steam pipe of at least three hundred degrees.

✪ ✪ ✪

A connection which had done much to keep the expatriate group of Tahiti in an interesting state of flux was the monthly arrival of a large modern ocean liner, first from San Francisco en route to Sydney, and then from Sydney back to San Francisco. For a few days after each of these occasions, one could vary one's diet with not very old steaks or mutton, the cinema would change its film, and a large part of the island population enjoyed that state of torpor which may be supposed to have followed the old Roman saturnalia

One of the arrivals from Australia was Wilfrid O. White of Boston. We had corresponded in the hope that he might extend an absence, which he had taken to visit the land of his birth, from his well-known emporium on State Street in order to see how his spherical compass worked among the reefs of the South Pacific. "Kelvin," as we usually called him, referring to the Kelvin instruments he sold, cast a politely interested eye at the more obvious attractions of the island, then went on a busman's holiday among the navigational equipment of the vessels in the port. The little cutters from the Tuamotus were the only sea-going vessels in the harbor which did not receive his ministrations.

These little craft normally are guided not by a magnetic needle but by mental dead reckoning verified by the actions of clouds and sea-birds. They also are usually so loaded with copra that the crew and their friends (who are going to town to help spend the proceeds of the cargo) must sleep, cook, eat, and take their exercise on the tiny deck, which is usually no more than 3" above the water. To a sailor without confidence in these primitive methods, a voyage over the broad Pacific that relies on them is something to marvel at. Even with chronometer, sextant, nautical almanac, and *Bowditch,* it is possible to miss an island as large as Bermuda (as has been done more than once). The consequent feeling of helplessness for those on board a big, well-found vessel must be nothing compared to what it would be on an overloaded copra cutter with its sole water supply in a jug, and with only the signs of nature to go by.

The yawl *Inyala* received Kelvin's particular attention. She was a middle-aged, if not elderly, craft of the English plank-on-edge type with plumb stem, deep draft, and narrow beam. She had been brought out from England by Dr. Temple Utley, to whom I referred in connection with the Galapagos Islands. He had for crew what fortune had brought him along the way. His account of the 3,000-mile run from Isabela Island to the Marquesas, accompanied only by a Polynesian boy who continually saw visions and mistook them for actuality, made me question the malevolence of the sea. Utley had met a young lady in Barbados a year or so previously, and she eventually joined him in the Marquesas, where they were married. They lived in a small wooden house which was officially an infirmary on Papeete's main street. There, Dr. Utley dispensed useful but illegal (since, not being a French citizen, he was unqualified to practice) medical treatment, and intermittently thought about getting on west.

At about this time, his plans to sail west were crystallized by the appearance of Harold Mapes and his daughter, who had come out from Panama in the *Coquet* and who undertook to defray some of the doctor's expenses as far as Suva, in the Fiji Islands. The *Inyala*, during her long inaction in the harbor, had begun to show the effects of alternate rains and tropical sun: her paint was cracked, her spars were white, her decks were black and her running rigging slatted limply in the breeze. She was a challenge to Kelvin, and his holiday was made. For some days, we saw him only at meals, except occasionally as he hurried ashore for a piece of brass, a shackle, or a pot of paint at *L'Établissement Donald Tahiti*.

Another craft which came under Kelvin's friendly eye was a 54' schooner built in Auckland to the amateur design of her owner, who had an eye for a good high freeboard. It was said that his wife, on discovering he was holed up in Papeete, had pursued him from New Zealand, only to be denied permission to come aboard. The high freeboard had served as an added discouragement (perhaps according to plan). Since Captain G. had a fish line and plenty of flour and tea aboard, she finally gave up waiting for him to come ashore and returned to New Zealand.

The cabin of the schooner was unusually rich in appearance. It was finished in molded paneling of a deep brown wood which once formed the counters of a defunct Auckland bank, providentially being torn down just when Captain G. was building his dream ship. To Kelvin, however, she was just a floating coffin until he had brought his pelorus aboard, swung ship, and adjusted her compass to a hair on all points. The *Evalu*, which we also met in Balboa and Taiohae Bay, came in for a dose of the same gratuitous treatment. Blanco, the owner, never had the use of this service, however, because he sold the schooner to the French Government within the year.

> *Mr. C. B. G. Murphy, our able raffee man & Assistant Engineer, was unfortunately compelled to return to Detroit & in his place we were fortunate to ship Mr. Charles J. Lipscomb, of Easton, Maryland, on the Chesapeake Bay.*

One of the things that concerned me most at this time was the insurance on the *Pilgrim*. The first year's policy was soon to expire, and I had every reason to believe there might be difficulty in obtaining a renewal. The vessel had been pronounced unseaworthy and unfit to proceed on the voyage in the Canal Zone, but the inspectors who had so freely diverted our voyage into the slimy dry docks had not been correspondingly ready to give her a clean bill after the repairs were done. They wouldn't say she was still unseaworthy, but they wouldn't say she wasn't.

At the same time, there were their certificates — official and unqualified written condemnation. It was hard to see how underwriters, who had taken pains to satisfy themselves of the *Pilgrim's* soundness in the beginning, would be inclined to continue the risk without a thorough inspection. Immediately after arriving in Papeete, I went to see the local agent (who was also the manager of *L'Établissement Donald Tahiti*), reported our reassuring performance across some 5,000 miles of open water. I cabled to the home office a request for a policy renewal, stating that the vessel was available for inspection. For weeks, I waited anxiously, calling upon the agent from time to time. Finally, one day, without having received any request for information, I heard news that the policy was renewed.

I have learned since that the agent in Boston had heard quite unofficially of the schooner's tightening up through letters to our friends at home. The insurers wished for no further assurance that we were not going to the bottom than that we were all willing to risk our skins in her. Marine insurance carries a large element of moral risk due to the movability of its subject matter, both laterally and perpendicularly, beyond the range of *ex post facto* inspection. Bill Wainwright, the owner of the Blue Lagoon Hotel and of an old Barraud chronometer, told me a tale of an insured shipowner who made a faulty estimate of that range in the perpendicular plane.

The Blue Lagoon, where I heard the story, was a board building which served as a dining hall, dance hall, tap-room, and cook-house. It had a number of scattered cottages (one of them constructed chiefly of remnants of Zane Grey's old schooner, the *Fisherman I*) in which the guests had their living quarters. The evening meal in the main building was apt to be a patchy affair, due not to the cooking but to the fact that the guests would make frequent visits to the bar and the dance floor regardless of the stage of the meal and often forget which table they had started at. If you sat down to dinner with the girl from Oklahoma who was interested in the stage, you were as likely as not to find yourself, over the tapioca, sitting opposite "the Panther" and his mournful red beard, listening to a tale of hard luck, or in a whole group of expatriates listening to almost anything.

Sometimes a few guitar players dropped in, and by eleven o'clock the gaiety reached a fine pitch of frenzy. Unfortunately, the regulations said that at eleven o'clock on the dot the shutter over the bar must go up, and the lights and guests must go out. Even with the aid of the old Barraud chronometer, Wainwright had been found in contempt of the law several times by a few minutes and suffered fines. What he wanted, he told me, was a good full-faced ship's clock with a bell. Regardless of the greatly superior value of his chronometer over any ordinary ship's clock, he was more than anxious to make a trade. It was when I agreed to the trade that he told me the story of the chronometer and the perpendicular plane.

Several years before, the shipowner had embarked on an ostensible trading voyage in his schooner with an apparent cargo of an automobile, several phonographs, and many drums of fuel oil. The vessel departed for the Tuamotus, but before she arrived at a port where business might be done, she sank in about six fathoms. All hands saved themselves in the dories and eventually made their way back to Papeete. An insurance claim was made for the total loss of schooner and cargo, and the owner presented the company with a list made up in such detail that even the serial number of the ship's chronometer was included.

Through one of those odd mischances from which the wicked are never secure, a representative of the insurance company discovered that the listed chronometer, having been sold to Wainwright, was ticking away the hours of revelry at the Blue Lagoon. He immediately smelled fraud. An expedition was sent to the sunken schooner and native divers soon had her cargo on the shore. The automobile proved to be a mere shell without working parts, and the phonographs were shells too. The oil drums, though tightly sealed, were full of seawater. The shipowner was convicted and sentenced to the Broom Road gang.

Another matter of business which was more directly important than the insurance was remodeling the hatches for better ventilation below. As I discovered when running before the trade winds to the Marquesas, the lack of moving air in the cabins was a source of distinct discomfort. In spite of the fact that the financial situation had become extremely uncertain (the franc had fallen to twenty-two cents at the only bank in town), the remodeling expense seemed justified. The simplest solution seemed to be to substitute for the solid hatch covers hinged skylights. These would not only permit the leeward side of the hatch to be left open during rain or moderately heavy weather, but then would serve in fair and light conditions to catch any moving airs with their raised leaves and lead them below.

Mr. Isaac Walker, more commonly known as "Icky," had come aboard shortly after our arrival in his capacity as Commodore of the Yacht Club to invite us to make use of that versatile institution. Icky, besides being the British Vice Consul, was also the owner and manager of an excellent shipyard, which was up to any kind of work on a wooden vessel. The work on the skylights went forward at once under his supervision. However, it was considerably delayed by the arrival of special skylight glass from San Francisco in crates plastered with warnings that they contained glass which proved to be smashed to pieces.

My own cabin was also remodeled in order to bring the bunk closer to the skylight. New lockers of native *tamanu*, a teak-colored wood with a close grain which works easily and hardens with time, were installed with perfect accuracy and finish by a Czech joiner. An improvement of more general utility was a pair of stout catheads, also of *tamanu*, which, when fitted by Joe with pointed ringstoppers and finished with red, white, and blue manrope knots, made the handling of the four-hundred-pound anchors a pleasure.

✪ ✪ ✪

A letter of introduction to Harrison W. Smith, who luckily was not away on his annual visit to his dentist in Boston, led to an excursion to his estate at Papeari. Mr. Smith once had taught a science course at MIT and later spent some years in Borneo for the sake of his health. It was there that he had taken the opportunity to indulge his taste for horticulture. When he subsequently moved to Tahiti, he took with him many of the strange plants of Borneo to cultivate in his new home. The story of his arrival, as wonderfully sketched in Charles B. Nordhoff's poem, "Saved By the Durian!" (its central theme is the alleged youth-recreating power of the foul-smelling fruit), is that by the time his steamer reached Tahiti, the many plants on the upper deck had grown and luxuriated to such a degree that the natives were astonished to see a green island approaching the pass with a stream of smoke trailing from its midst.

Mr. Smith's most recent point of origin gave rise to the nickname of "Borneo" to distinguish him from two other Smiths, "Five Kilometer" Smith and "Whiskey" Smith, respectively, but a moniker could hardly be found more incongruous with the bearded, professional dignity of its bearer. ("Five Kilometer" Smith was so named because he traveled that distance from his house each evening into Papeete, where he spent the night away from the presence of *tupapaus,* or spirits, which the natives persuaded him entered the house regularly at dusk.)

Borneo Smith's house at Papeari was surrounded by an immense tropical garden. At its entrance was a tall fan-shaped tree called a traveler's palm which, like many other trees, shrubs, and flowers visible from the drive, were a part of the floating island from the East Indies. Jasmine, mimosas, and the wild convolvulus bordered the long avenue, and a half acre was set apart for individual pineapple plants, each in a separate protective cage, safe from rats and crabs. The coconut crab, with a claw spread of sometimes 16", is so powerful that it can tear the outer husk from the coconuts. It climbs the palm trees to detach them, an operation which a strong man can perform only with a tool and some skill, as we had seen in the Marquesas.

Mr. Smith's one-story house was only as tidy as could be expected of a bachelor's dwelling. It was crammed with books, papers, and scientific apparatus, and had an atmosphere of *laissez-faire* about it which was also due somewhat to the hens and chickens that wandered freely in and out. Our host interrupted the conversation at one point with a low clucking noise in the direction of a pullet which was studying one of the Skipper's sneakers. It is my distinct impression that the bird immediately abandoned its study and went over to Mr. Smith, who picked it up and performed a slight operation on one of its eyes with a pair of tweezers. The tweezers came into play again a short time later when Mr. Smith, who was no idler, caught a mosquito, again during the conversation, and popped it into a bottle of cyanic gas. He then placed it carefully in cotton in a little box for shipment to a biologist interested in elephantiasis with whom he was in correspondence.

A mid-day feast had been ordered by Mr. Smith at the establishment of a *restaurateur* named Mauu in Taravao, a short distance away, where, in a clearing surrounded on three sides by little cottages, sat a structure consisting only of a pandanus roof on supporting poles. It was not difficult to believe the report that Mauu's cooking was the best on the island, although we were not in a critical mood as soft hands placed coronets of wild gardenias on our heads and kept our glasses filled with perfectly good wine.

What the exact order and combination is for eating Tahitian dishes was hard to discover, since the table was covered simultaneously with pickled fish, prawns, curried shrimps, sea centipedes or *varo*, chicken, young pig, yam, coconut and sea water sauce, taro shoots, and *poi*, a pasty pudding like tapioca. The wealth of food had the same confusing effect as the steam tables of a cafeteria, but since the food was all extremely digestible and no one seemed to give a damn about orderly procedure, we hungry mariners ranged the board as our fancies dictated.

Another delicacy of the island rarely tasted is heart of palm —
the fresh bud at the top of a growing tree. Its removal means the
death of the tree, a fact which has given it the name of "million-
aire's salad." It enhances the nutty, celery-like taste of the bud
itself to any slave of the theory of conspicuous waste.

chapter 9

The Islands Under The Wind

AFTER TEN WEEKS OF HOLIDAY LIFE along the Papeete waterfront, most of the ship's company would have been content to remain there indefinitely. The legend of the immobilizing quality of the lotus finds its parallel in the islands in the *fei*, the wild banana also known as plantain. We had eaten a large quantity of that bland vegetable, deliciously baked in sugar in surroundings of which it is an apt symbol. Somewhere down under our spiritual lethargy, however, were faint vestiges of our native wills-to-accomplish. Did our experience of Tahiti not reflect a disproportionate emphasis on the life of Papeete? Should we not strike further afield and sample the more wholesome life of the districts, or even go up into the mountains?

While I shared these fruitless misgivings with the crew, of more moment to me personally was the question of money. The continuing expense of the expedition, in proportion to what the economic unsettlement at home was doing to my investments, was assuming an aspect of prodigality. However, the controlling element in the formation of future plans was not personal inclination. Instead, it was the necessity of getting the *Pilgrim* past Australia and somewhere near the Malay peninsula before the northwest monsoon began in November to roar down from the

Asiatic mainland. We should be reaching that area in time to utilize the main and northeasterly branch of that same seasonal wind in crossing the Indian Ocean.

Many cruises have ended in Tahiti because of crew disintegration or explosion. Others that have extended further have done so only after a number of false starts. With this in mind, I set a time for departure, not only to the day but to the hour, and my doing so was viewed in a manner appropriate to something at once impossible, unnecessary, and somewhat impolite. The French authorities were sufficiently convinced of my determination, however, to send aboard three dirty mail sacks, all very limp, addressed respectively to the islands of Raiatea, Bora Bora, and Tubuai. Within less than an hour of the appointed time, the gangplank was hauled ashore and our stern lines were cast off the cannon bollards of the Papeete waterfront.

All islands were alike to the Cook, as they had been to the Surgeon in Nordhoff and Hall's *Mutiny on the Bounty,* and our departure left him unmoved. The rest of the ship's company, in varying degrees, took it harder. There was far more evidence of genuine sorrow at leaving Tahiti and its people than there had been of mild regret at leaving Boston and its people. We knew that probably we would never return to the island. Those nibbles at the *fei* had been stolen during a truancy, and we felt as if we were being driven back to school. There would be a few more frolics on the way, but we knew then that the doors would close on us again.

> From the ship's log: May 11, 1933. Outfit feeling a bit shaky in spots after two months of Papeete, but able to do justice to the Cook's lunch of pork chops, potatoes & carrots.

Since the trade wind was well up into the east and blowing fresh, we did not have to motor far beyond the pass before we were out of the lee of the island and riding the rollers to the west.

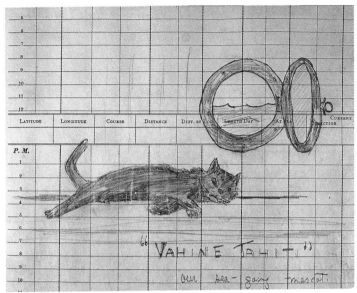

Vahine Tahiti, our sea-going mascot.

Under the mainsail and squaresail, we sailed past the north coast of Moorea headed for the *Isles Sous le Vent*, otherwise known as the Leeward Society Islands. Since these were less than a day's run away, we took off the mainsail during the evening. A little after two o'clock in the morning, by the light of the stars, we sighted the shape of Huahine Island to starboard; soon after, the loom of the more lofty Raiatea appeared on the port bow, outlined against the sunrise.

> **From Hod Fuller's journal: We have another new member of our crew now, *Vahine*, a small coal black cat brought aboard by Lipscomb. She has spent most of her time below in the lazarette so far and doesn't seem very partial to going to sea.**

A description of Raiatea must include Tahaa. The islands are both sprouts of the same submarine formation and only two miles apart. The upper rim of their common sunken volcanic base shows above the sea's surface in the form of a single great ellipse of barrier reef. Over twenty miles from end to end and running roughly north and south, it encloses within it the two islands. Raiatea, at the southern end, is separated from Tahaa in the north by a stretch of shoal water. With the eastern side of the barrier reef breaking the seas but letting the easterly wind pass over undisturbed, the lagoon between the islands is an ideal place for sailing outrigger canoes. These canoes race back and forth between the islands with generally a spanking wind which is thus abeam when one sails to either island from the other.

Avoiding Motu Tabu pass, which the *Pilot Book* warns should not be attempted without a good pilot, we identified Tahaa Pass in the north. Guided by two white range beacons, we swung into a channel which led to a pier of wood and coral blocks off the town of Uturoa. The inter-island schooner *Potii Raiatea* occupied the entire end of the pier, but her native captain shouted that the mooring buoy out in the channel was available. Joe and the Chief ran two lines to the iron can, and we all prepared to rest comfortably.

A boat soon put out from the shore bringing a determined looking *gendarme*, his *képi* pulled firmly down to his eyebrows. He climbed aboard without asking leave and inquired for a "*Monsieur Fewlair.*" Upon the Chief's answering to that name (although he had been called "Cheemy" in Papeete), the *gendarme* drew a paper from his pocket. It was a confused report of the *Inyala's* departure from Papeete with somebody on board who didn't belong there, and with M. *Fewlair* suspiciously involved.

While we were still in Papeete, Temple Utley had been refused permission by the French authorities to take with him in the *Inyala* the boy, Haputu, who had joined him in the Marquesas. Unwilling to acquiesce in this prohibition, Utley had sent Haputu over to Moorea the night before his departure, with the plan to pick him up from a canoe as he sailed past the island. To help Utley get clear of the reef, the Skipper and the Chief had gone aboard the *Inyala*, then jumped into a launch just beyond the pass and returned.

To complicate things further, Utley had also taken Haputu's cousin, just for the ride, and dropped him off beyond Moorea at the island of Huahine. The Chief had no connection with the smuggling of Haputu, but it was no wonder that the port officials were confused. Moreover, he knew nothing about what Utley had done after jumping into the launch and could only give an account of his own doings. After a glass or two of *vin blanc* laced with brandy, the *gendarme* agreed that whatever swangdanglings might have taken place, the Chief belonged where he was and that somebody had gotten his signals mixed (that fact alone was perfectly clear). The *gendarme* went ashore with his *képi* at a magnanimous and jaunty angle.

Meanwhile, John delivered the mail.

I took the oil pump on the engine apart to replace a leaking gasket which was letting oil drip into the bilge. Meanwhile, the combination of wind & tide was making us chafe our topsides against the buoy so the boys ran a line ashore & warped the *Pilgrim* in next to the wharf, which makes a fine place to stay. I spent all day in the engine room trying to get the return pump on the oil line to work but with no luck.

Turned to again on the engine & hauled the oil pump off once more & on the suggestion of Mr. White I tried a thinner gasket & everything went perfectly again! Then scrubbed the whole engine room & got everything in order & back in its place.

Raiatea, though mountainous and covered with vegetation, is not on the grand scale of Tahiti and Moorea. The view from the

Pilgrim of the shacks and shops along the beach which comprise the town of Uturoa was not at all stimulating. The lagoon, however, is a rare spot for sailing, fishing, and swimming. A Frenchman named M. Bourcart had come to the islands chiefly to swim, coursing over the lagoon every morning for several hours at a time with an easy overhand stroke which left him breathing as easily as though he had covered the distance in a boat. Such a practice, even where an absence of reports of sharks and barracuda is reassuring, requires a mind not given to apprehensiveness. M. Bourcart appeared to feel secure from any such danger — except, as he told us, for the recurrence of a mishap that had overtaken a native swimmer in those waters. The man's skull had been pierced by the sharp and rigid snout of a heavy garfish leaping clear of the water.

I had been wanting to experience the speed with which Raiatean sailing canoes are credited — some twenty knots — and when, that afternoon, the champion team of the two islands came alongside to give us a taste of their sport, I jumped at the opportunity. The canoe was perhaps 20' long and about 18" wide. It had a solid pontoon made of a light wood attached to an outrigger on the port side and was rigged with a relatively large boomless sail supported by a heavy sprit which ran between the peak and a hole in the thwart alongside the mast.

A burly young man motioned me aboard, and we were off. He sat in the stern sheets where he handled a broad-bladed sweep, the sheet, and peak guy all at once, a feat he simplified by the skillful use of one of his broad feet. His equally husky wife, who was the other half of the team, provided the indispensable shifting ballast by perching at the proper distance from the hull on the outrigger. The rig did much better on one tack than the other, since on the port tack, with a nicely adjusted wife, the outrigger was carried out of the water so that the canoe's narrow hull offered the only resistance to the water. On this point of

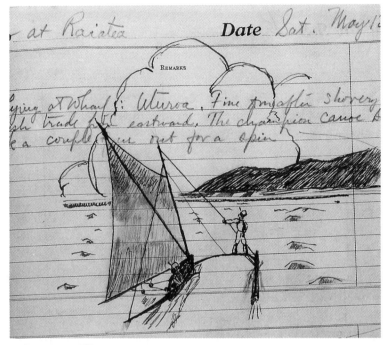

Ra'iatean sailing canoe.

sailing, the craft fairly shot across the lagoon.

There is no deck or wash board on these canoes. When the helmsman had handed me a small bailing scoop, I had an indication of the part I was to play on the sail. Spray dashed in over the bows as we tore across the wind, and the backwash from the lee rail, which now and then shoveled up a green bucketful just to make the bailing harder, poured into the little hull. My main impression was of bailing frantically, smothered in foam and spray, while the helmsman shrieked with exultation, apparently with the speed and amusement at the game he was playing with me.

After a while, I discovered that as I seemed to tire, he would ease the sheet just enough so I could keep pace with the water coming in. The faster I bailed, the more there was to bail. As soon as I caught on to this game, I stopped bailing altogether and sat up and wiped the brine from my eyes. Whatever the actual speed of the Raiatean outrigger canoe, it seems almost meteoric to the man with the coconut shell. Moreover, it is the only craft I have ever seen which inspires its helmsman to scream with such excitement that he can be heard half a mile away.

We were planning to leave today but the Doc was asked by the island administrator to stay & help with a birth of a child. Late this afternoon another doctor arrived by launch from Bora-Bora & they tried to remove the child which had died. The woman was in poor condition & also had elephantiasis & died just after the operation.

From Raiatea, we headed for Bora Bora, an island familiar to many through the movie *Tabu*, which was filmed there some years ago. Since this mountainous island was only 32 miles away, we saw it clearly in the distance to the northwest. We had no detailed chart of the lagoon toward Tahaa and of the passage out, but a friendly Raiatean gave us a sheaf of them, of which the Skipper remarked in the log:

The rats have eaten quite a bit of them, but fortunately the rats seem to prefer the mountains to the water, so that we could proceed confidently.

With a fresh breeze on the quarter, the *Pilgrim's* hermaphrodite rig of squaresail, rafee, and mainsail drove her at eight knots, and in four hours we were off the pass of Bora Bora. We sailed into the anchorage at Vaitape under a steep bluff in the midst of a fleet of *pirogues* engaged in a sailing race. Before the last of fifty fathoms of chain had veered out, the *Pilgrim* was surrounded by natives in canoes, holding up for inspection grass hula skirts, head-dresses of grass decorated with shiny red and white seeds, and model canoes.

American white shirts with collars attached were the currency most in demand, with trousers second and soap a poor third. The tawdry nature of the dancing gear, the careless workmanship of the models, and the persistence with which the natives hung about displaying their goods and asking for offers were depressing signs of the passage, first of the movie crew and then of the stream of tourists who had come to see the "island paradise" advertised in the movie. In contrast with the emphasis on dancing in the predominance of its proper paraphernalia among the canoe-men's wares, it later appeared that the single *gendarme* on the island had the duty (and perhaps the pleasure) of enforcing fairly strict regulations over the practice of the art itself.

The Cook took the mail ashore & later the Commander, the Chief and the Skipper went in and called on the gendarme who seemed to be a very good egg. He swapped coats while we were in his office, putting on one with a lot of decorations & badges. Very lovely ashore. With the big peak of Bora Bora looming up close by, the whole place is certainly attractive.

In the evening, several of the outfit hit the beach in anticipation of a bit of guitar playing & possibly a dance. The guitar playing was entirely male & quite uninspiring & although the Chief organized a bit of dancing in a remote house, the necessity of smothering one guitar with his shirt at one point when we thought the gendarme approaching & the general air of caution & the lack of grog combined to produce only a very, very moderate evening.

No permit was required, however, for swimming in the lagoon, sailing among the islets scattered around it, and fishing. A fifty-pound barracuda caught by the Trader caused all but the Skipper to keep a sharp eye out while swimming, but no other was seen. The Trader gave the fish to the natives, who actually followed the principle of "trying it on the dog." The hound to

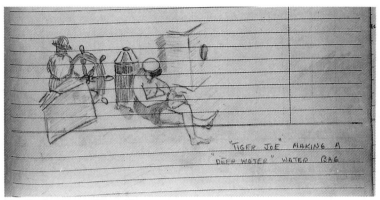

"TIGER JOE" MAKING A
"DEEP WATER" WATER BAG

Deck chores at Bora Bora.

which a bit of the flesh was fed was quite hale the next day, and the natives ate the rest of the fish confidently. It is well known that the same species of fish found harmless in one place can be poisonous in another only a few miles away. It is generally supposed that these differences in the fish are constant and that the natives of each place are acquainted with them. The dog incident suggested otherwise.

Before supper we took an unsuccessful turn through the lagoon and pass in search of fish. After dinner we loaded three *vahines*, three guitar players, the Trader, the Doc, Lipscomb & myself & a couple of native boys into the power dory & headed out for Motu Tabu, a little island near the pass where the film *Tabu* was taken. On arriving, we lit a fire under a fine coconut frond thatch, uncorked three gallons of white wine & gin punch and started the party off. Soon the girls were hulaing in grass skirts accompanied by the Trader & myself, while the boys went wide open on the guitars. The party continued until about 12:30 when one of the boys set the island on fire while trying to get some coconuts for drinking. We all rushed in and beat it out with palm leaves but, for awhile, it looked as though the whole little island was going up in smoke. This was the climax for the evening & we all piled into the launch & headed home leaving the guests off on a little point far from the inquisitive *gendarme's* observation. One of the boys whom I've had out fishing a great deal seemed quite disappointed because I wouldn't go back to his house & turn in with his sister who was along on the party with us!

"Kelvin" White had come this far with us from Papeete and returned there on the first leg of his return to Boston in the Schooner *Potii Raiatea*. On the day after their departure, the schooner *Vahine Tahiti* pulled up at the dock, carrying a crew of Tahitians and Tuamotuans. She was commanded jointly by our friends Winnie Brander and Pedro Miller, both of whom had chartered the vessel for a trip to the latter's plantation on Mopihaa, farther to the west in the same group.

Captain Miller was part Maori and part French. He exhibited the characteristics of both racial strains by managing plantations on at least three islands with efficiency and success as well as navigating schooners over several thousand miles of sometimes dangerous waters for both business and pleasure, at the same time thoroughly enjoying himself. He had brought along several crew members simply because they played guitars and sang. They were playing and singing in the dark of the forward deck one evening, while around a bottle of rum on the table under the after awning some of us listened to Pedro's talk of Mopihaa.

You may remember that it was on the reef of that island that Count Graf Felix von Luckner's famous square-rigged warship *Seeadler* ended her predatory career in 1917 after sinking fourteen Allied merchant vessels. It was not a tidal wave that delivered the *coup de grâce*, Pedro said, but an ordinary ocean swell. One of the prisoners aboard had disingenuously advised the Count that the reef was a nice natural dock where he could tie up the schooner with perfect safety. A short time after, Pedro had arrived in a schooner on one of his periodic visits to the plantation; von Luckner and some of his crew seized the schooner and sailed away.

Pedro and five of his crew eluded the guard left behind by the Count and set off in a 16' rowboat for Raiatea, 120 miles dead into the teeth of the fresh trade wind. After the better part of a week, they were only ten miles away from Raiatea which was, of course, then in full sight. However, they were exhausted and, confronted by a storm, dropped off downwind. They arrived back at Mopihaa eleven days later, having made the whole round-trip without the aid of a compass. Pedro escaped again in the same boat and rowed with his crew downwind some 900 miles to Samoa in the space of ten days.

Those who have read in James Norman Hall's *Tale of a Shipwreck* an account of the wreck of the *Pro Patria* on the reef off Timoe in 1933 will remember that it was Pedro Miller who, after the schooner struck, put off to leeward in one of the boats despite a big sea running in the dead of night, to learn whether they were stranded off an island or whether there was nothing but open sea beyond. There was land there, and although the schooner broke up, the whole ship's company was saved.

Bora Bora was to have been our last stop in the Society Islands. Maupiti lay 23 miles away and on our course, but the difficulty of entering its narrow pass seemed a risk unwarranted by the prospect of visiting one more tropical island. Again, to quote our omniscient Hydrographic Office: "In bad weather the sea breaks right across the entrance, and it is only fit for small craft in fine weather; great care is even then necessary on account of rollers. A strong current always sets out at the entrance and is, as usual, strongest when the surf is heaviest."

The plan of the *Vahine Tahiti's* to put into Maupiti and Pedro's offer to pilot the *Pilgrim*, however, changed the situation, and we decided to make the call. A short, sail-drying run under power brought us off the long reef which encircles the island, and Pedro, squinting, waved toward an indistinguishable point where we should find the pass. Motoring apprehensively up on the backs of the breakers, we suddenly found a gap before us, almost directly under the schooner's forefoot. With Pedro gesturing directions from the bowsprit, we slowly edged the *Pilgrim* against the outgoing current and into the lagoon.

Ugly brown coral heads lay awash to either side. Although the sea had been moderately calm and the breakers lazy, the abrupt transition from the turbulence at the pass to the utter quiet of the lagoon immediately inside created a sense of isolation and

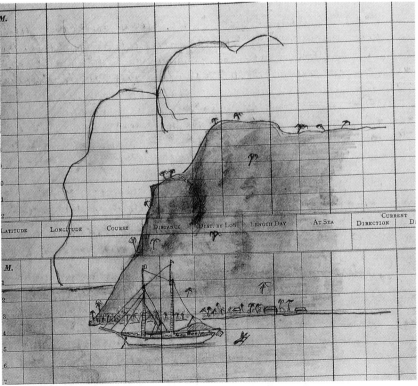

The *Pilgrim* at Maupiti.

security which pervaded all my impressions of the island. The channel was tortuous, and Pedro's directions often indicated the necessity of turning the wheel very fast — so fast that the Skipper and I both had to put our backs into it. There was still time between these exercises to observe that we were entering the gem of all the islands we had visited. We had seen transparent turquoise waters, white beaches, coconut palms, flowering trees above lawn-like undergrowth, and mountains far higher than these we were approaching.

Although in smaller scale, all these combined here into a picture of such intimacy and dramatic value that the others paled. This is what we had come for! The nearest of the heights was but a hill rising vertically about 800' from the lagoon, with ribbed gray rock formations suggesting the battlements and turrets of an old castle. In its shadow, in three fathoms of water, Joe let the anchor go a quarter of a mile from the wharf to which the *Vahine* was presently tied up.

We passed two canoe-loads of natives fishing outside the surf. As they came into the town, they paused to examine us with a gentle curiosity which was very far from the insistent commercialism that had welcomed us at Bora Bora.

Even Maupiti had its *gendarme* and school master in addition to its native chief, and these gentlemen paid us a visit that afternoon. The chief said the *Pilgrim* was the biggest and finest ship that had ever entered the harbor, but the school master, in a more matter-of-fact tone, said the larger *Zeleé* once worked her way in and that the *Chance* had visited the island two years before. It was six months, however, since any vessel whatsoever had been there, and they were genuinely glad to see us. Our prestige was considerably heightened by our friendship with Captain Brander, whose descent from "Sovereign-who-Settled-the-Sky" and the rest of the royal house of Tahiti, as well as from John Brander of Scotland, was well known to them all.

We were invited to visit the community *himine* house, or singing place, the next evening. After a dinner with Captains Brander and Miller of rum, roast chicken, yams, and more rum, we went to the structure that stood in a clearing behind the wharf. Seen in the dusk, it was a windowless house about 50' long and 20' wide, with sides of weathered boards and a peaked roof of plaited pandanus leaves. On arriving, we found the sand floor almost entirely occupied by men, women, and children all dressed up in trousers and dresses. Talking and twittering with excitement, they were sitting in rows facing one of the side walls like an audience waiting for the curtain to go up. We were herded by the reception committee to a plain wooden bench that represented the stage. We arranged ourselves on both sides of Captain Brander, the guest of honor, and sat blinking into the lights of two kerosene lanterns which threw confused shadow enlargements of the proceedings on the walls.

An exchange of speeches followed, all in the Tahitian language in which vowels predominate to such an extent that we, even after several months exposure, could scarcely understand a word. Captain Brander filled us in on the substance of the talk. In addition to expressions of hospitality, there was a kind of verbal and temporary coronation of Winnie as King of Maupiti for as long as he remained there. This royalist utterance did not appear to disturb the representative of the French Republic, in the person of the school master, nor did the coronation itself, which saw wreaths of wild gardenias and tuberoses placed not only on the new king's head, but on the heads of his friends, the crew of the schooner yacht *Pilgrim* included.

The natives then began to sing by degrees, without direction or instruction, somewhat as the Undertaker's Song develops from the stands at a college football game. Soon, the first scattered rumbles and trills were taken up by all of them in a four-part Polynesian version of some now unrecognizable missionary hymn

Frigate bird.

that filled the house. One woman distinguished herself and lent an exotic flavor to the song by fixing first on one high note and then another, prolonging each with a piercing, wavering shriek while the others moved on to the following bars. Guitars struck up, and one girl after another rose from the floor to rotate her hips in the familiar fashion characteristic of the Eastern Pacific Islands.

Amateur night was now in full swing and there were cries for favorite performers. Six Tuamotuans from the *Vahine Tahiti* took the floor and, in three rows of two abreast, performed a dance announced as that of the frigate bird. This soaring sea bird has a deeply forked tail and narrow, angled wings that have a normal span of 6'. It is reputed to be unable to rise from the water when away from high land from which alone it can take off to soar aloft for days at a time. Although a fisher, it gets waterlogged quickly. While in mid-air, it plucks flying fish out of the air or raids others of its kind and boobies for fish they have caught, causing them to disgorge their meals, which it then takes.

The dancers extended their arms and hands horizontally to represent the wings and swooped and dipped from side to side, flapping their arms in a remarkably impressionistic imitation of the bird, considering that they were, for the most part, upright on two legs. As the dancers' excitement increased, they seemed to forget about the frigate bird and hopped up and down, and kicked stiff-legged with such spirit that the air was soon thick with flying sand. The dance ended abruptly with a six-fold simultaneous shout. This performance seemed to give the most pleasure to the Maupitians, to whom it was like something imported from a relatively metropolitan area of culture.

Joe & I took a couple of *vahines* out for a ride in the outboard during the morning & in the afternoon took a walk about half way around the island. All the houses are made of coconut thatch over wooden frames. The furniture consists of mats on the floor for sleeping and usually a large brass bed which is never used except by guests. The cooking is done in little cook houses next door to the living houses, while numerous pigs are moored to palm trees all about the houses. This spot is by far the most interesting and least spoiled of any we have visited.... The people here are only French subjects and consequently do their own governing & have

their own court & judge. They all work together building houses or gathering food & have a fine time of it,
singing & laughing all the time. Dogs & pigs wander
about everywhere and at night often set up one hell of
a row. Pig is the only meat available here & suckling
pig is a favorite dish.... Many of the girls here are fine
examples of the pure Polynesian type with lovely big
dark eyes, full well-formed hips, and long wavy hair
down their backs. There is very little outside blood in
the people here. The men are very well built, with large
shoulders and narrow hips and fine white teeth. They
usually dress only in a *pareu* and spend much of their
time fishing on the reef and in the water.

Considering that few of the older natives spoke French and
none of them any English, the tirelessness with which they invited
us to feasts, along with the two captains of the *Vahine*, was
amazing. Since we did not wish to talk among ourselves and leave
our hosts out of the conversation, our contribution to these affairs
was made by beaming foolishly over our food, bowing a great
deal in acknowledgment of every favor or service, and extending,
through one of the interpreters, invitations to come aboard.

One meal I remember in particular was at the house of an old
fellow whose wife, from Samoa, was half German. A large grass
mat was laid on the floor as a table cloth. We sat around it cross-
legged. In front of each of us was a perfect green banana leaf for
a plate on which we put whatever we chose. In the coconut-shell
bowls were pickled fish, roast pig, taro, coconut sauce — the same
dishes we had eaten at Mauu's, plus a peculiarly piquant cheese
made from coconut milk.

In the center of this floor-table was a little potted bush, and
from its branches were suspended, by cotton threads, cigarettes
made of a mild herb wrapped in dried leaves. None of the family
members joined us at the meal. Two sat behind us in chairs (the

only furniture in the room) and others waited on us. At the end of the meal, as each of us pulled a cigarette off the bush, a son of the house appeared at our elbows with two fire-making rubbing sticks. One was grooved so that the point of the other could rub up and down it. The boy, sitting by my side, held the grooved stick against his stomach and extended out to his feet. He grabbed the pointed stick with both hands and pushed it up and down the grooved stick with increasing speed until the dust created by the friction collected at the lower end of the groove and ignited.

The gaiety of the occasion was considerably heightened by our all attempting to make the sticks work, wholly without success. Later, on board the *Pilgrim*, I tried to interest the fire-maker by burning a piece of paper with the sun's rays using a magnifying glass kept for reading charts. He was quite unimpressed, however, and scornfully pointed out that his system was not dependent on having the glass.

As we took our leave of our hostess, another son, this one with freckles and wavy blond hair, appeared from somewhere and said: "My mammy, she want wash your clothes. I come get all clothes. My mammy, she want wash for you." It was plain that she was by no means soliciting the job of doing our laundry for money. The dear old creature's generosity had not been exhausted by setting out a feast for us, and her imagination had suggested an additional favor she might do. I protested that we could not accept such a favor. I was afraid that the refusal might be a grave offense against politeness, particularly since I could not communicate our appreciation for the idea of it in her language, but we left on excellent terms.

Our broadcast invitations soon bore fruit, and one day we were visited by a sort of Women's Club, of which the chief's wife was president. With the assistance of the *Vahine Tahiti's* whaleboat, some seventy ladies were ferried across a choppy lagoon and brought aboard to swarm over the schooner on a tour of inspection. On second thought, "swarm" is hardly the verb to convey the modest and even timorous manner in which they moved about, peering into cabins and cupboards with nearly expressionless faces. While the business parts of the *Pilgrim* had engaged the attention of their men, there really was nothing to compare in appeal for the women. For example, since the *Pilgrim* was furnished in the simplest manner below, there was nothing like the red plush cushions on Robert Louis Stevenson's *Casco* which, he wrote in *In the South Seas*, had moved one native lady to raise her skirts to try its blushing texture with her bare behind.

A schooner, to a Polynesian woman, is an unmitigatedly disagreeable means of getting from one island to another, and there was nothing about the *Pilgrim* in particular to distinguish her from the rest of the species. The Cook brought out jars of candy sticks and, with the Skipper, passed them around with careful regard for seniority and social position, but the rows of ladies who sat stiffly along the transoms in the main cabin rightly regarded this pathetic attempt as a poor substitute for, at the very least, conversation.

While Joe had separated two or three of the fairest of the flock on the foredeck and was entertaining them with characteristic success by means of sign language, the situation below was one of complete social stagnation. The Doc tried his harmonium and tenor repertoire for a time, causing a little flutter among those whom he addressed with his songs, but it was, after all, high noon of a bright and sunny day, and music seems, if not immoral, at least inappropriate at such an hour. This did little to excite the Club as a whole. Finally, the guests were ferried ashore, and they laughed and screamed with relief and gaiety as the fresh chop in the lagoon drenched their party dresses.

Since our arrival in Maupiti, the wind had veered south and raised a sea that broke continually across the mouth of the pass, blocking any entrance or departure. On the third day, the Skipper

The Chief reading in the Doghouse.

and I sailed the dory across the lagoon, beached it on the sand of Motu Titi Ahe on the west shore of the passage, and climbed over the wet volcanic rocks on the seaward side for a closer look at conditions. The swift current rushing out of the pass spread fanwise from its jaws and tripped the great rollers as they came in, causing them to stop in their tracks, rise to a height of 8' or 10' of green water, totter for an instant, and then fall upon the coral heads with roars that filled the air. Under a smother of spray, we could see a tumbling mass of white water — the broken seas, the backwash, and the current struggling together through which no vessel or boat could have picked and forced her way.

We returned to our lotus gathering, assured that we were not being seduced from an immediate departure to the west, but that we were imprisoned in the lagoon by the forces of nature. Tolstoy wrote that the most agreeable sensation possible to man is that which accompanies enforced idleness, and that sensation was certainly what the crew of the *Pilgrim* knew in Maupiti.

Three days later, the dual command of the *Vahine Tahiti* announced that the wind and seas had shifted sufficiently to allow departure. We decided to trail their schooner through the pass. The seas outside were still too rough to carry one of the captains as pilot and then attempt to transfer him at sea. Having spent six days at Maupiti, we determined also to forego the call to Tubuai, some distance to the south, and handed the mailbag for that island over to Winnie.

The *Vahine Tahiti*, properly a motorsailer with a diesel as tall as a man, got under way first. Just as she steamed by the *Pilgrim*, a canoe-load of natives, one of whom was of really venerable appearance, came aboard to say good-bye. We could not turn them away. By the time they were all aboard, the other schooner was so far ahead we could no longer follow her for pilotage. Four big natives seized the windlass brakes from unreluctant hands and the anchor fairly leaped to the cathead. As we came up to the pass, some of the natives who had stayed aboard for the ride down the lagoon dropped into canoes paddled by their friends, while others simply dove overboard, to be picked up later.

Turning from hurried farewells, we found the situation ahead by no means reassuring. The conditions of three days earlier had abated, but the current, which was now carrying us, had been increased by the southerly winds of the last few days to almost torrential proportions. We had no pilot now, only oral instructions, and I was sure a crack-up in this place would be final. Moreover, steerageway in the confused waters and the power to claw clear of the coral and go over the rollers at the point where they were just short of breaking required plenty of engine thrust.

The diesel's horsepower, together with a small, two-bladed propeller, delivered only five knots when wide-open in smooth water and gave me no reassurance here. However, neither Pedro nor Winnie had expressed any doubt of our ability to negotiate the passage, so the Skipper and I, in a very brief conference, decided to keep going for it.

"What was it Miller said?" the Skipper asked.

"Keep the easterly reef six feet from the port side."

It was not difficult to pick out with the eye a course so malignantly buoyed with water that it churned white over sunken coral. The channel was by no means straight, however. As we tore by on the racing flood and under full power, the Skipper did some lively wheel handling. Just beyond the narrow entrance, I saw the first line of rollers, well off the port bow. I saw that to meet them head on and not be tossed back onto the coral off to starboard would require a quick turn. When the time came, the Skipper and I together heaved the wheel hard over. I felt the schooner swing, rise high on a great wall of water, almost stop, then drop far down into the trough on the other side. The swell was breaking with a roar to either hand; still in the current, the *Pilgrim* crept slowly ahead, out of trouble.

We soon set some canvas to steady the schooner, and by the time the fisherman staysail was up, we had overtaken our friends in the *Vahine Tahiti*.

The *Pilgrim* must have been a lovely sight to them with some of her light canvas on & slipping right by them under sail alone.

The *Vahine Tahiti* was still under power and rolling so badly that the natives aboard were reduced to apathetic recumbency. Our last farewells were returned from the crowded deck by waves of varying degrees of enthusiasm, and we were soon alone on our course for Tongatapu, nearly 1,400 miles away.

chapter 10

The Kingdom of Tonga

IT WAS NEAR THE END OF MAY. The winter season of the southern hemisphere, when the trade wind blows more steadily than in summer, was not far off. According to meteorologists, the trades are stronger then because the sun, being farthest north and heating the sands and waters of the Tuamotuan atolls, causes less interruption in the air currents. The wind roses on the Pilot Chart indicated a great preponderance of southeasterly winds of Force 4 to 5 on the Beaufort Scale.

For the benefit of those unfamiliar with that standard, Force 4 is characterized as a "moderate breeze," sufficient to drive a full-rigged ship, full and by, at a speed of five to six knots, while for "smacks" it is a good working breeze. Force 5 is a "fresh breeze" in which a ship can just carry her topgallants, while on land, "small trees in leaf begin to sway and crested wavelets form on inland waters."

Our course for Tongatabu was in a general west-southwesterly direction. The wind of the roses came in over our port quarter on schedule all afternoon of our first day out, causing us to haul up somewhat to be sure of not running into Mopelia in the dark. However, it then confounded our unreasonable expectations of an average performance by wafting capriciously at Force 2 ("fishing smacks with topsails and light canvas, full and by, make up to two knots. Wind felt on face; leaves rustle; ordinary vane moved by wind"), or Force 1 ("full-rigged ship, all sails set, no headway...smoke rises vertically"), when smoke from the Skipper's pipe drifted with the wind, and even at times Force 0, when the pipe smoke rose straight up.

At the same time, the breeze backed northward just enough to make it impossible to head off for the course under fore and aft sails, which had, into the bargain, been slatting a good deal due to a long roll coming up from the south. Here, again, the square rig paid its way as we poked along in silence under raffee and squaresail, with the main boom snug in the gallows frame and our topmasts describing long arcs across the sun and starlit skies. This was flying fish weather. Catching the fish kept not only our little black cat Vahine Tahiti, our only pet for the time being, bursting with vitamins, but also the bosun birds and the bonito, which harried the poor creatures from above and below in dramatic skirmishes.

From Hod Fuller's journal: Vahine, the ship's cat, has turned out to be very able. She climbs everywhere possible and yesterday tried to make her way out along the main boom, from which she was dragged inboard before falling into the deep six.

Everything is lovely at present with nothing to do but sit back and let her run dead before it under the square rig and give the wheel a spoke or two now and then. Am turning in early this evening after putting in most of the morning, all afternoon & some time this evening working problems from Bowditch. My head is one mass of figures & formulas at present.

Early in the morning of the fourth day, the Trader sighted the loom of the sugar loaf shape off to port called Aitutaki, northernmost island in the Cook group. Since no anchorage there is safe for a vessel with less power than a steamer, we had no intention of stopping by. However, Aitutaki was discovered by the *Bounty* in April 1798, a few days before the mutiny, and because of the universal desire to visualize history by setting eyes on any event of the past scene, we ran in toward the reef for a closer view. The reward for this maneuver, which involved but a turn of the wheel, was not great. I saw a line of breakers and beyond a collection of red board warehouses on the beach of a low hilly island, suggesting nothing but an efficient British copra depot.

As we bore off again and onto our course, I saw a boat putting out through the barrier reef passage off Arutunga, propelled vigorously in our direction by eight oarsmen. There was, at first, no reason to think the boat was headed for us, but it continued to follow in our wake with a speed which would not have been necessary on any other imaginable errand. As we discerned a hail from the stern sheets, we saw that they wanted to speak with us, so we hauled-to. We were a good three miles off the mouth of the pass. The swift boat pulled alongside, and two white men in the stern answered my invitation to come aboard.

One proved to be the Administrator, a sad-looking man with a face as white as his clay-colored pith helmet. He tendered his engraved visiting card, then left the talking to his more articulate companion, the local trader. I gathered they comprised nearly all of the island's white population and would welcome new company, no matter how temporary and, we could suppose also, no matter who it might be.

Mr. Low, the trader, reported that the *Tagua*, Captain Andy Thompson, was in the Hervey Islands, fifty miles to the east. He said that the chief bridge player on the *Inyala* had felt the call of the Papeete Yacht Club tables and transshipped there in the *Tiare Taporo*, Captain Vigo Rasmussen. Trader Low reiterated the invitation to visit for a few days, and the gloomy-looking Administrator seconded it with the information that there were some extremely interesting graves on the other side of the island, but we resisted these solicitations.

The bottle and glass are as necessary an appurtenance to receiving guests in a ship's cabin as any social amenity that I can think of. The Skipper and I joined our visitors in a glass of sherry, and said I hoped our declining their invitation would not seem unfriendly. This was the only occasion on the entire trip, to my knowledge, when any of the ship's company departed from the standing rule of no alcohol at sea. This minor exception did not strain the rule, and it never came up among us as it seemed to work no hardship whatsoever.

She was a fine kauri planked whale boat named *Lady Alice*.

These fellows stayed aboard about one and a half hours & then we started up the engine & headed back toward the pass with their boat in tow as it would have been a long difficult pull to windward for them.

The Chief and I had the midnight watch that night. After I took over the wheel from the Skipper, who had stayed up to admire the evening, he shambled forward out of the glow of the binnacle light. "I'm going to take a little kink," he said. "Let me know if any bunnies or frogs come aboard, will you?"

Nothing of the sort appeared on that or any other night during the passage, nor did any other incident which would have justified disturbing the rest of those not standing their peaceful four-hour watch. The few minutes of dusk, when horizon and stars are both clearly visible, were marked by a busy sighting of heavenly bodies, followed by hours spent with pencil and paper working out the sights under the cabin lamp. This mathematical labor was usually accompanied by cracks from the Trader in his bunk: "Jesus, boys, are we lost again?"

Our famous leak has in time reduced itself to about thirty to thirty-six clips per day on the pump, which is nothing. As yet the vessel has never been pushed into a head sea, so it remains to be seen how she will act under these conditions. The weather continues lovely & we wear a *pareu* for clothing aboard now.

The days passed with the leisurely scraping, sandpapering, and painting of skylights and deckhouse. This was preceded on the part of many hands by the unobtrusive — but determined — seizure of a paint brush, the possession of which was felt to excuse the holder from the necessary but disagreeable monotony of the preliminary abrasive processes. Laziness was rife.

From the ship's log: June 1. 8-12 A.M. The Skipper was considering setting the light mainsail, but as he unwisely gave voice to his reflections, his purpose was thwarted by a coat of paint hurriedly slapped on the roof of the chart house by the crew. Afterwards, all feelings were soothed by the wind (which had hitherto been distinctly well off the port quarter) hauling chock aft again. Continued running dead before it under squaresail & raffee.

P.M. Continued painting. Weather the same: absolutely ideal except for lightness of wind & a considerable roll from south'ard catching us abeam. Particularly powerful supper of cold tongue, boiled onions, cream sauce, baked bananas, chocolate cake, tea.

Running lights lit at 5:40.

June 4. 4-8 A.M. Continues moderate. Finest kind of day. Very cool & our light southerly still abeam. Big roll from SW, but enough wind to ease the vessel over it in good shape. After breakfast set topsail, fisherman's staysail & jib topsail. Against the doubts of the Skipper, the peapod was put over & the Trader & the Doc got several pictures of the vessel with all her finery on and incidentally got a good workout for themselves at the oars. Proceedings were completed in 45 minutes & we filled away on our course of SW by W, with the light southerly giving us a good clip.

As we drew further to the south, near to what is reported as the southern limit of the southeast trade wind, the temperature perceptibly declined. Although it did not go below seventy degrees, there were many complaints of cold. At the same time, the roll from the south came more from the southwest and increased in volume, indicating a disturbance of some intensity many hundreds of miles to the south, in the area of the westerlies. On one midnight watch, when rain clouds surrounded but did not obscure a bright half-moon, I observed a full rainbow with colors just barely discernible and about a quarter of a second rainbow above one end of the first. I believe neither a moon rainbow nor a double rainbow is uncommon, but a combination of the two is rare indeed.

About 5:30 or 6 a fine squall struck us coming out of the NW with plenty of rain & breeze & we tore along in the rain for a few minutes. This rain gave all hands an opportunity to get a fresh water bath on deck, while Vahine, the ship's cat, tore into the main cabin & waltzed around during the thunder. This evening the rain has stopped but there still is a nice little breeze & a bit of a sea running & it's fine below sitting here in my bunk, after a big dinner, & listening to the wind & water on deck. We go on watch in about 1 hr. & the weather looks a bit drier although you can't tell much with these squalls down here that come up from no-where & smack you.

The growing infrequency of the soundings on the chart showed that the region over which we were now sailing had not been surveyed as thoroughly as the waters more used by shipping. At noon of the ninth day from Maupiti, for instance, the nearest sounding to our position was about a hundred miles away. While this showed a reassuring depth of over twenty-four hundred fathoms, there were other marks less definite and more ominous. Sixty miles ahead on the port bow, for example, was marked "Dickinson Reef, Position Doubtful," while almost directly on course was Buffon Reef, also bearing the initials "P. D."

A little over thirty miles to the southwest of that spot is a little ring of dots marked "Discolored water, reported 1926." The latter reef was sighted by the French bark *Buffon* in 1880, whose officers reported seeing the breakers in time to escape being wrecked. Several vessels have since passed over the position without seeing any danger. Clearly, either mistakes were made in getting a position, or else Buffon Reef had subsided below the surface. If it had done that, it might, like Falcon Island, which lies some sixty miles north of Tongatabu, have resurfaced again. In any case, we ran about ten miles north of the reported latitude of Buffon Reef and saw nothing. The next day we ran south of our course to avoid another bit of territory marked "Rep. 1911, P. D." and then had clear white paper between us and Tongatabu.

Some years later, I found interesting the accusation by followers of Charles Fort, as reported in the newspapers, that when Amelia Earhart presumably crashed on a Pacific island, she was "murdered" by the pretensions of Science to accuracy in charting the earth's surface. Unfortunately, the Forteans chose one of the least vulnerable branches of Science to attack, as was indeed suggested by their own complaint that the charts of the South Pacific are dotted with "Position Doubtfuls."

The Introduction to the *Pacific Islands Pilot* published by the Hydrographic Office of the Navy Department, which also publishes the official charts of nearly all waters, contains the following statement which should be self-evident: "Many of the earlier surveys were incomplete and inaccurate, and charts based only upon them carry the resulting errors until later information or a resurvey furnishes the necessary corrections, so charts based on old surveys should be used with caution." Nearly all charts of the South Pacific are based on old surveys and are so marked.

Using our charts with caution, then, and vainly trying to break the somnolent watch habits of some of our less apprehensive shipmates, the Skipper and I brought the *Pilgrim* to within sight of Eua, the southernmost of the Tongas, and hove-to for the night.

At dusk a fine breeze & quite a sea came up. That's always the way: when you don't need the breeze, there's always a fine one blowing.

June 7. 5:30 P.M. Vessel lies lovely under foresail, on port tack, heading about SSE. Moon nearly full & although sky pretty well overcast, there is good light.

At half-past three on the morning (or seven bells of the midwatch), it was light enough to take bearings on Eua and then run off for the passage into Nuku'alofa, the capital and port of Tongatabu. The ten miles of Biha, or eastern, Passage ran through a vast lagoon broken everywhere by patches of reef awash and tiny islets. This made it difficult to determine just which islet bore the name of Makahaa, short of which we must turn to go through The Narrows. A beacon and two floating buoys finally provided the key. Soon after breakfast, we brought up opposite a town which justified none of the expectations naturally aroused in us by the mark of a cross on the chart accompanied by the word, "Palace."

There are no high points of land on the island. It sprawls indeterminately over a wide area of soil, coral patches, *motus*, quicksands, and tidal flats, and a fresh trade wind that was blowing in from the northeast passed over the island undiminished. The anchorage was so exposed that the low shore seemed to fall away from sea level to leeward, and the convexity of the earth's surface was a very real and immediate impression.

On arriving, our log read Thursday, 8 June 1933, while on shore it was Friday, 9 June. As one may well forget until one comes out here, it is necessary for a "date line" running north and south to mark the point where vessels sailing west or east can compensate their calendars. In sailing "with the sun" — to the west — each apparent day (or the period *between* two successive turns of the earth before the sun as marked at the opposite meridian in Greenwich, England) is a little longer than twenty-four hours. In one circumnavigation, the sum of these daily surpluses (which, of course, vary in length according to the speed of the vessel) will add up exactly to one extra day. If no adjustment in the ship's calendar is made, it is obvious that a whole day would have disappeared unobtrusively during the voyage, and the ship's log accordingly would count one less day than would have appeared in the diary of one who stayed home.

Most of the date line coincides with the 180th meridian. It curves east to include all of Siberia in the eastern calendar, to the west again to avoid confusion in the Aleutian Islands, and, much further south, takes a jog over to 173 degrees west to include Fiji, the Kingdom of Tonga, Kermadec, and a few other islands in the same calendar with New Zealand and Australia.

We were now in the western part of the South Pacific among people of a different culture, both native and superimposed, than in the Society Islands. The Tongans themselves have always been more active and vigorous than other Polynesians farther to the east, although their appearance, except for a tendency toward kinks in their hair, is very similar.

We saw comparatively few natives in this place, however, and these few were subdued by the national mourning which had been decreed for Queen Salote's sister, who had recently died. They went quietly about their business dressed in black shirts and

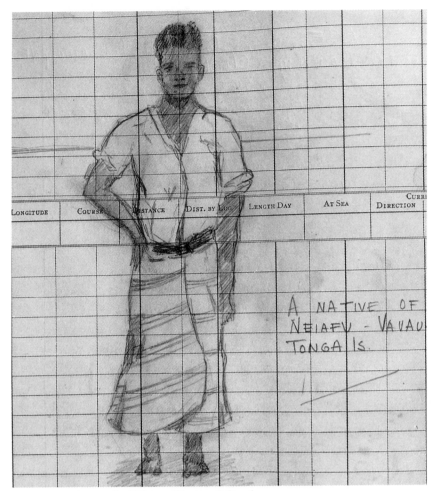

Longitude	Course	Distance	Dist. by Log	Length Day	At Sea	Current Direction

A NATIVE OF NEIAFU - VAVAU TONGA Is.

A Native of Neiafu, Vavau, Tonga Islands.

lava-lavas. *Lava-lava* is the name for the Tongan loin cloth which is worn longer than the Tahitian *pareu*, reaching nearly to the ankles at all times. Each window and door of the house which proved to be the palace of the Queen of Tonga was also draped with black cloth, so we did not pay a call on her.

In the afternoon I had a lot to do on the engine after its long run. I cleaned all the injection valves and adjusted

the inlet & exhaust valves which were badly in need of it after being run for such a long time. Also the electric system for lighting on the boat has gone haywire. Apparently it is grounded somewhere, as the lights were low as hell this morning and the battery way down for no reason at all. I have been trying to locate the trouble all day but have had no luck... We hear that Utley & the *Inyala* left here about ten days ago for Suva.

A British flag was flying from the palace rooftop, sharing the breeze with the red cross of the kingdom's own standard. The copra depots and stores were owned by Burns, Philip & Co. or by Morris, Hedstrom & Co. — we had seen the last of the successors of *L'Établissements Donald.* The currency was the Australian pound, and the local club was the exclusive retreat of men from the white community. A drink in this place, as I soon discovered, was a whiskey and soda, not a rum punch. The club had no back veranda for the entertainment of the members' local favorites — indeed, I doubt they had any favorites outside their lawful spouses.

The whites in Nuku'alofa, unlike those in the French island towns, seemed to be in the preponderance and were more particularly evident since, unlike Frenchmen but like British empire-builders everywhere, they were constantly striding about, going to and from tennis courts, the cricket grounds, and the bowling green. We were soon enmeshed in the cordial tentacles of the social octopus. The Skipper dug his 1912 model square-headed tennis racket out from under the mass of hula skirts and canoe models in his cabin. The Trader effected a magical metamorphosis from a disreputable *déshabillé* to a truly imposing respectability — and white sport coats were recovered from the provision lockers for all hands.

One evening at the house of the British Consul, we made the acquaintance of a handsome Amazon named Pamela Bourne. She told the Skipper that she arranged for passage around Cape Horn in the grain ship *Herzogin Cecilie* at ten shillings a day, but was determined to have the fare lowered to five shillings in return for her undertaking to chip iron work. Nearly three years later, the *New York Times* for 26 April 1936 printed a report from London, which reads in part:

> One of the finest sailing ships, the Finnish four-masted barque *Herzogin Cecilie*, 3,111 tons, which had just won the annual grain race from Australia for the eighth time, is now lying fast on the rocks of Devon Coast, badly holed and being pounded to pieces by heavy seas.
>
> For ten hours her young captain, Sven Eriksson, and his bride stuck to the doomed ship, striving vainly to save her after a lifeboat had taken ashore the crew of twenty-three...
>
> Although the windjammer was manned by young men training for the sea before the mast, there was no panic when she grounded. The captain's wife, formerly Pamela Bourne, daughter of the late Sir Ronald Bourne, a South African Minister of Defense, worked with the rest of the crew in hauling in the sails for the last time. Then she went to the charthouse, where the lamps were still burning, and remarked sadly:
>
> "We might as well put them out for all is over now."
>
> She was married to the captain just before the ship sailed to Australia.

I sent a copy of this to the Skipper, asking him to put it in the ship's log at the Nuku'alofa page. He responded, "Apparently, the young lady didn't have to chip much rust."

After luncheon, I went ashore to see my friend Kuli who is the son of the magistrate of police & nephew of the last premier. He is very hospitable & proud of his island & people & wants to show me all the customs of

his people. I had some native hop beer & then went out for a drive in the country to see the flying foxes. These animals live in the tree-tops in a certain small area from which they seldom move. They are like bats hanging by their feet when they sleep & often flap lazily about from one tree to another. Their wingspread must be about 3-3&1/2 feet and small bony hooks grow out of the wing tips with which they climb about the trees. They eat fruit & have a foxlike muzzle and ears. I tried to get one to bring back to the boat but had no luck as they all fly away if you climb in the trees after them.

The country is very fertile with all kinds of vegetables flourishing in well-kept gardens. The villages are located along the road and are made up of fine pandanus thatched huts built on a beautifully green lawn under the palm trees with avenues extending through the trees and bush down to the ocean. We stopped at the village of which Kuli is chief, and he loaded the car up with coconuts and sugarcane as a present to me.

When my friend Kuli left me at the dock after being aboard in the evening he told me that the girl he had introduced me to go around with here was his wife! She is an exceptionally pretty girl, about 26, and is lots of fun & very jolly. I'm afraid any other husband might have taken offense because we were a bit familiar, but he thought it was all fine & was greatly pleased because I liked his wife. Apparently that's the custom here: if you like a person you put your entire household including your wife at his disposal.

After two days of dining out, bridge, tennis, and snooker, most of the ship's company wanted to drop over the other anchor and stay indefinitely. I had dreams of fairer lands, braver deeds, and so, for once, I overrode the will of the majority and on the third day, the *Pilgrim* headed north for the Vavau Group of the Tongas, which lay on the course for Samoa.

The waters stretching along the western border of the Tonga Group have been well surveyed. The chart bears no "P. D." notations, and a number of buoys and a few lights mark important positions. Aside from the multitude of known hazards, we had a new cause of concern in the unreliable character of the ocean bottom. The region is apparently one where the crust over the earth's tempestuous vitals is at its thinnest, so that from time to time great volcanic bubbles spring to the surface, heaving up quantities of ash which remain as uncharted shoals. Earth tremors are said to be frequent, although none occurred during our short stay in Tongatabu.

As we emerged from Egeria Channel through the northwest reef of the island and took departure from the wreck of a steamer no doubt tossed up during one of the hurricanes that sometimes rage here, we were but fifteen miles away from two submarine volcanoes. One of these was reported active in 1911 and the other was seen emitting steam in 1923. During the afternoon, we passed about five miles from the islands of Honga Hapai and Honga Tonga, the first flat topped and the second peaked, and both very near to another submarine volcano which was seen in 1912 "emitting steam and smoke continuously, with intermittent volumes of water," according to the *Pacific Pilot*.

A few hours later, the Chief saw from the masthead the island of Fonuafoo, or Falcon Island, which has the most extraordinary history of all. It was first seen, both Findlay and the Hydrographic Office agree, as nothing more than a breaking reef by the British naval vessel *Falcon* in 1865. In 1877, smoke was seen issuing from the sea around it. Some ten years later, an island appeared at the spot, over a mile long and 130' high, made of volcanic ash and cinders. Interestingly, no growing coral was found by the surveyors. The island washed away gradually until it was only a low streak on the water which could not be seen at night.

Eight months later, in December 1894, the island had a new crater and had risen to a height of 50 . It was now some three miles long and a mile and a half wide, and the surface was "still quite hot." In 1913, the island was reported to have disappeared entirely. When we passed in the *Pilgrim* on 12 June 1933, it was again high enough to be seen distinctly from the masthead ten miles distant, but as it was so far off and in line with the setting sun, we received no impression of its color or size.

In the vicinity of these phenomena, we naturally heeded the injunction in the *Pacific Pilot* to keep a good lookout for any new shoal, particularly since the sea was calm and would not have broken readily, but we saw no unmarked dangers. We passed within two miles of the active volcano, Tofua, during the night and got good bearings on it and the 3,400' high cone of Kao just to the north of it.

June 12. 12-4 A.M. Smoke issuing ominously from Tofua turned out to be cloud.

After a two days' run, mostly under power in baffling winds, we spent the night jogging outside Vavau, the principal island of the group. There is a fixed green light on a spit near the pass, but it is only turned on when a steamer is expected. In the morning, we ran in through a deep sound bordered with steep cliffs and caves, then rounded a sharp corner and entered the completely landlocked harbor of Neiafu. The minimum depth is reported to be twenty-five fathoms, but a man on board the little island steamer *Hifofua*, which was tied up at the dock, waved us to a spot with only thirteen fathoms, about a cable's length south-southeast of the dock.

For breakfast we had the bonito that the Trader hooked last evening with a pearl shell lure & bamboo pole such

as the natives use. The hook has no barb and is made of a piece of brass rod bent & sharpened, with a piece of pearl shell fastened to it and shaped like a fish & with a pig's bristle tail. It skips over the water like a flying fish & the bonito take it & you have to swing them aboard very quickly before they get a chance to throw the hook out of their mouths.

This little town also had its men's club, and we were at once invited there to meet the local merchants, traders, and officials. The roof of the club was made of arched rafters held together only by an intricate lacing of long tough pandanus leaves. It was thatched with what appeared to be the same and housed a billiard table, library, and tap-room. Not a great deal of commerce passed through the port of Neiafu, and the inhabitants did not perhaps represent the most enterprising and potent of the empire's representatives, but they appeared to be respectable citizens doing their duty in the state to which it had pleased God to call them. They seemed justly resentful of having been libeled collectively in a recent world voyager's book as a "drink-sodden clique of white traders." This was not the first port we found from which some traveler had barred himself from a comfortable, or even safe, second visit by coloring a book of travel with a bit of defamation.

Poured rain most of the morning, clearing about noon. Have a couple of good books from the club to read at present, Conrad's *Victory* and *Chance*. After luncheon part of the crew went ashore for tennis, while Joe & a younger chap from ashore & I took a trip around the harbor in the outboard & looked for the remains of a 5,000 ton tramp that burned & sank with the captain and chief here in the harbor about five years ago. All you can see now is bits of oil bubbling up to the surface

from her oil tanks.

As I have no money, I can't even go to the club to read as there is always someone there who asks you to have a beer and you feel like hell not being able to reciprocate.

After dinner, the boys headed for the local cinema to see the wild west thriller. The natives are crazy about the cowboy pictures & thrillers. Have been reading a book called *Epistles from Deep Seas* by Patterson which I also got from the club. It's been 6 months since we've had a new book aboard & often we've been reduced to reading our small encyclopedia!

Although we were still in the Queen's dominions, the sympathy with her mourning seemed to have decreased as distance from Nuku'alofa, some 150 miles away, increased, and not a night passed that a troop of guitar players and dancers did not climb over the sides and perform for us. The dancing ran more to the spirit of Mars than Ceres or Venus and was of a very vigorous character. One youth specialized in a number in which he leaped as high as the roof of the cabin allowed, kicking and glaring ferociously, while accompanied by a crescendo of shouts from the rest. The young native ladies were much more modest in appearance than Tahitian girls. They wore long dresses and carried parasols, like the English ladies they presumably had seen pictured in old magazines.

The Skipper and I turned in to the doghouse about 12:30 and about 4 this morning they all headed ashore. The natives have gotten to be one hell of a nuisance on the boat. They have been coming aboard any time and make themselves at home & are always in the way & staring down through the hatches at you. We are now

keeping them off the boat altogether.

Mr. Spicer, of the trading concern Morris, Hedstrom & Co., took us down the sound one day in a power boat to a natural cave in the low cliffs. The boat ran in, out of the sunlight, through a low arch in the rocks. After adjusting my eyes to the comparative darkness, I saw a clammy dome of rock about 30' overhead, and a long passageway on one side of it led gradually upward among what looked like stalagmites. I could see the sea bottom below with perfect clarity, although a sounding showed fifteen fathoms. On the walls were the painted and chipped names of men and ships, with dates as far back as the later eighteenth century.

On the return trip, Mr. Spicer pointed out a spot on the same shore below which is the entrance to a cave that only one man has ever penetrated. The orifice is about 10' below the water, and one has to swim some distance at that depth before coming up to the surface inside the cave. "The man who repeats this feat will be a hero here in Tonga," the Englishman said, and added, "*if* he can get back to the outside surface again and report it."

Our excursion was cut short when the inter-island steamer, *Waipahi*, was sighted. We went promptly ashore, where Mr. Spicer had business to conduct with her First Officer. Most of the town had come down to the wharf to greet the boat, including a number of nuns from the Roman Catholic Mission. I fell into conversation with two of them and learned that one was a native of Lawrence, Massachusetts, and the other was from a little town in Brittany where I had once spent a week. They were the only nuns I had ever happened to speak with.

A youthful missionary, of a denomination which need not be divulged, invited some of the crew on a picnic, for which they set out in one of the Swampscott dories. A short time later, the dory passed the *Pilgrim* loaded down with the missionary, the Skipper, the Chief, Joe, and eight Tongans. They had found a stirrup cup at a native house and were making a most uncanonical lot of noise. Another boat was in tow, containing two dead pigs, some chickens. In all, about the merrymakers' weight in edibles. The next day, the Chief had a fever of 102 degrees. The local doctor ascribed it to the pig, although the missionary, who from all accounts had been no more moderate than the Chief, was in perfect health.

Due to the effect of this indirect contact with the church, we stayed two additional days in Neifau and saw the British naval vessel *Veronica* steam into the lake-like harbor. She was a lightly armored craft, less formidable than either a destroyer or a light cruiser, and classed as a "sloop." Her function was to pay periodic visits to British territory and protectorates, observe conditions and phenomena of interest to the hydrographic office, such as soundings and the current elevation of Falcon island, and to keep the natives impressed with the majesty of the Crown.

We were shown over the ship one evening by Captain Jackson and the officers, who were leading a life hardly distinguishable from that on board a large steam yacht, except that there was more punctiliousness in the crew's manners and the afterguard was being paid for being along. The Captain told me that the only factor determining the direction of their travels was the necessity of always heading so that the wind would not blow soot from the funnels on their white uniforms.

June 20, 1933. ONE YEAR OUT OF BOSTON TODAY!

On the day after the *Veronica* left for Pago Pago, the *Pilgrim* followed her out the sound, jibed over, and heeled to a smart beam wind coming off the northwest shore of Vavau. The islands of Samoa lay to the east of north, and with the wind coming from the southeast, we allowed an extra point to the east to compensate for the usual westerly set of the current across the Pacific in those latitudes and as a precaution against the possibility of the wind backing toward the northeast and heading us. With all plain sail set and her lee scuppers nearly awash, the *Pilgrim* drove ahead.

June 23. From 6 to 8 she made 17 miles, an 8.5 average. Five lowers & topsail.

8-12 P.M. Same conditions: fresh SSE with occasional puffs more easterly. Sheeted in a bit the mainsail and foresail. Tearing along at a fine rate most of the time, with some lighter spells. Partly cloudy (trade clouds) through which the Southern Cross shows occasionally astern — a melancholy spectacle. It looked much more cheerful over the bowsprit.

June 24. 12-4 A.M. A-roaring. Bit of a sea climbs aboard now and then. 35.75 miles for the watch!

The Skipper is standing my watch & in the evening I spelled Lipscomb at the wheel as he has been laid low with *mal de mer* since leaving…. A fine day but wet sailing with plenty of spray coming aboard. This is the first time since Panama we've been on the starboard tack for any distance & the schooner doesn't seem to leak a bit more — about a half a gallon an hour now.

These two days of reaching in the fresh breeze gave us as good sailing as we ever had in the schooner. When we picked up one of the two lights on Tutuila Island and a few hours later boiled into its principal harbor, it seemed a pity to all of us that the run had to be cut short so soon, even for a new island.

Took in fore and aft sails and ran into Pago harbor under squaresail. Did this while rolling around in the damned sea outside. You head for the entrance to the harbor, a little break in the high coastline, and come in through an entrance with a beach lined with palms to port and a high rocky bluff to starboard.

A gray navy tug flying the Stars and Stripes came out to meet us and put aboard two white-ducked naval officers, the port doctor, and the port captain. The captain delivered crisp directions for entering Pago Pago and mooring at a buoy in the upper part of the harbor, and promptly departed.

chapter 11

Tutuila

WE HAD ONCE BEFORE MADE ANCHORAGE in the inundated crater of an extinct volcano, at Tagus Cove in the Galapagos islands, and we found ourselves again in that situation at Pago Pago on Tutuila, the principal island of American Samoa. Whereas at Tagus Cove the inner fires of the earth seemed to have forever sterilized their hardened effluvium and made it unfit to nourish life, fit only to provide the architecture for basking iguanas and roosting boobies, here in the Samoan Islands they rather had activated the flesh of the earth, mixed the heaved-up sea-bottom with other elements from down below, and ground the whole into a rich bed of propagation from which pushed a thick crop of trunks, stalks, and creepers. The leaves and fronds and fruit of this growth ran up to the highest parts of the surrounding crater rim to disappear among the tempestuous clouds racing around the peak of "the Rainmaker" on our starboard hand.

As we proceeded along the dog's-leg channel, gradually opening up the rest of the inner face of the crater as it diminished in height, its natural covering yielded more and more to the hand of man. Along the northern side of the harbor, the steep slope afforded only the width of a narrow road which ran past several little white houses shaded by coconut palms. On the opposite side, a wider shelf, which the United States Navy in 1878 had thought would make a coaling station, had given foothold eventually to an army of carpenters, tinsmiths, and plasterers who had quite transformed it. The most conspicuous of the Navy's works were three steel-trellised, wireless masts, each some 300' high, and behind them two huge cylindrical fuel tanks which reflected a blazing sun, all the while remaining uselessly empty — monuments to the optimism of the original plans for the island formulated at the Washington Conference.

From Hod Fuller's journal: Got a couple of letters from home today, the first any of us have had in four months. As usual, there isn't any excitement around there & things go on just the same. I'm certainly in no hurry to get back there & stuck in a damned office behind a cage on State Street for the rest of my life.

The pilot tug was tied up near the *H.M.S. Veronica* at a wharf at the outer edge of the settlement. This was a straight row of almost identical gray clapboard houses with screened front porches, each bearing a painted sign with the name and rank of its occupant in black letters. A six-hole golf course ran across the back yards of these dreary structures, so that it was not unusual, as I was soon to see first hand, for a sliced drive to carom off a pantry window-screen or come to rest in the shade of a garbage can. Cement walks crossed clipped lawns, ran past two cement tennis courts, and connected the naval residences and the enlisted men's commissary and pool-room with a broad cement road which ran along the inner edge of the coastal shelf. This stopped abruptly after disappearing from sight around the first bend toward the sea.

In the opposite direction, this main and only artery rigidly passed the parade ground of the native guards and the Administration Building and Court House, whereafter it curved informally as the neighborhood degenerated into the equivalent of the other side of the railroad tracks in an American town. Here the show place of Pago Pago was pointed out to me by a companionable officer with much excitement and awe. I saw a poorly built frame building which, on the first floor, was a grocery store. I was informed that the original of the immortal Sadie Thompson, the reformed prostitute of Somerset Maugham's play "Rain," lived in the rooms above the store. (In 1922, the story became a successful play. In 1928 and 1932, the first and second movies based on the play appeared.) Here, then, was Pago Pago, referred to in a shirt advertisement as a "tropical heaven," where you can live upon lotus and no one cares whether there are wrinkles in your collar or not.

> Left our mooring buoy & moved alongside the dock this morning.... Now we are handy to things ashore and next door to a fine shower bath. I had my first hot shower in over a year the other day here.

> In the evening went ashore to see a review of the native *fita-fita* regiment. They looked damn snappy in their dress *lava-lava* uniforms (a *lava-lava* is a wrap-around skirt) & drilled very well. Pago Pago isn't much of a place to be in after all the slick islands we've been to. No decent swimming, no beach, too big a sea outside for fishing from our motor-dory, & cloudy & showery weather the whole time. However, there's not a thing to complain about... & we are taking things easy. Joe & I are aboard alone this evening & it's fine in the cabin with the wind whistling through the rigging. Am spending the evening working on a few navigation problems. Finished reading Alan Villiers' *By Way of Cape Horn.* He certainly can describe the sea in all its

A Samoan boy.

forms, in fair & foul weather.

Wrinkles or no wrinkles, not only is a shirt a sartorial necessity to a yachtsman visiting the American colony at Pago Pago, but a necktie and a coat as well are absolutely *de rigeur* on many occasions, including dinner parties. This seemed surprising, since it is hardly the case at most of the summer colonies along the east coast of the United States where yachtsmen visit on summer cruises. The naval colony, however, dressed up to the formality of the high-collared and brass-buttoned white tunics of the officers and saluted its own splendor when the Commandant-Governor entered the movie theater of an evening (always late) and stood while a trumpeter blew a few high resounding notes which drowned out almost entirely the Bronx cheers of the enlisted men in the rear rows. I was told that this ceremony (except for the part about the cheers) had been instituted after a recent visit of the Governor's to Suva, where he had observed with admiration and envy the pomp surrounding the comings and goings of His Majesty's High Commissioner of the Western Pacific. I was later told that the entire ceremony had been abandoned.

> *From the ship's log: July 2. Tied to the wharf, Pago Pago. After breakfast, the Commander & the Skipper went up the hill on the south side of the bay & down into a very slick little hole in the rocks called the "Virgin's Pool," guided by Captain Mercer of the Ontario. Got back in time to welcome the fat village virgin of Pago Pago with 3 female relatives who had a spot of lime juice & sugar in the cabin. Some rain showers. Governor Landenberger & Mrs. L. & Lt. Comdr. Douglass (the Captain of the yard) & Mrs. D. aboard for a splendid dinner of caviar, soup, broiled chicken, potatoes, green beans, ice cream with strawberries, coffee.*

I have finished another book by Captain Marryatt, *Masterman Ready*, & a book called *The Last Paradise* by Powell about Bali to which we hope to go. Also finished *Hot Countries* by Alec Waugh. He slings a lot of hot air about Tahiti and is almost but not quite as bad as most of the South Sea writers.

No less conventional in the American naval way of dress was the wedding party of a niece of old Chief Maunga, the senior of the three native Governors ruling under American supervision. The Skipper and I had been included on the list of guests by official suggestion and were advised to bring appropriate presents. We covered ourselves suitably in wiltless white collars and white suits. Bearing some perfumed soap from the commissary store (no offense meant and none taken) and a flashlight, we approached Chief Maunga's house at the homely end of a train of gold braid, brass buttons, and picture hats.

A Samoan house, or *fale*, is simply a steep conical thatched roof supported by a circle or oval of smooth tree trunks, which in fine weather are the only obstacle to the free movement of air across the clean pebble floor where the family eat, sleep, and sit while working or talking. In foul weather, mats are let down from under the eaves so that the *fale* has temporary flimsy walls; by the same device, the interior can be divided into separate apartments. The floor of Chief Maunga's *fale* was a slightly raised oval platform of greater than usual size. On one side of it, the seventy-eight-year-old chief, looking like an angry mandrill, sat cross-legged with his wife while other members of the family ranged to either side of them. Further along, in deference to different postural habits, a row of benches had been placed for the white party, who filed in and took seats strictly in order of rank.

The ceremony of the *kava* followed. You will recall this drink, made of vegetable abstract, so favored by the Tahitian chiefs of old. I myself had sampled the beverage only here when, during a call on one of the American administrative officials at his office, he drew from under his desk a chipped enamel wash basin containing a murky yellowish fluid and offered it to me in a tin cup with every evidence of enthusiasm. The taste was faintly soapy, perhaps redeemed by a touch of licorice, and the effect was imperceptible. We were now about to partake of the same brew, but under more portentous circumstances and certainly with more style.

Kava is made from the powdered root of a tropical tree, which is reputed at some stage to be reduced to pulp by mastication — mastication by a specially selected young girl, to be sure, but mastication none the less. Whether this process or a substitute had been used on this day, I can not say. I observed only the stage at which a young girl, sitting in the center of the *fale* floor, stirred the powder in water in a wooden basin with a handful of the shredded root mixed in, and wrung it out. Now and again she threw the mass over her shoulder to a young man outside who manipulated it mysteriously and threw it back again, the girl putting up her hand and catching it without looking around, warned of the throw by a single sharp cry.

When enough of the essence had been dissolved in the water, Chief Maunga made a speech and spun across the floor to the Governor a small individual bowl half-filled with *kava* by a waiting handmaiden. The Governor raised the bowl toward the Chief and said, *"Skål,"* but in the Samoan language, drained the bowl, and spun it back again. This was repeated with each of us guests. We were at a disadvantage in spinning the bowl from the greater height of our bench seat, and we all in turn felt faintly embarrassed at being the sole performer before a large company in a totally unfamiliar act.

After these civilities, some girls performed a decorous form of a Polynesian dance in a group, a few of them swaying their hips and twisting their arms in a manner similar to what we had seen to the eastward. It seemed a dull show, performed in mid-afternoon more from duty than from enthusiasm, but presently it was livened up by an old, old lady, white of hair and scrawny of leg and arm, who left the Maunga family group and circled about the dancers, imitating their movements in a broad and skillful burlesque. She stole the show, but when it was whispered to me that she was Chief Maunga's mother, I noticed he did not join in the merriment, but looked angrier than ever.

After the *kava* ceremony, we left the *fale* and gathered around a feast laid out on leaves spread on the open ground. Due to the time of day and the predominance of cold and burnt — but underdone — whole pigs (minus only their bristles), only the minimum of respect was paid to the repast by us of the *Pilgrim*.

❂ ❂ ❂

July 10. Tremendous activity by all hands, the paint fairly flying through the air. And when the smoke of battle cleared at 5:30 P.M., it was found that a substantial part of the waterways, bulwarks, kerosene boxes & fittings had received a coat of green paint, as had the big dory & the skylight gratings, and the outside of the dory was painted white & the bottom of the peapod green. Joe completed a fine new boom tackle pennant, parceled & covered with canvas.

The protection of the fine natural harbor, together with the availability of ship's stores, indicated a comfortable sojourn for cleaning, painting, and stocking up, and all these wholesome businesses went forward until there was nothing left to do. The most Herculean of the labors was represented by a year's deposit of grime and grease on the striped duck cushions of the main cabin transom, about fifteen square yards of them. Laid out on the wharf, they presented a monumental task which we preferred to contemplate rather than to begin. At that moment the Chief's eye lit upon four of the village belles who were watching us with amusement and interest, and giggling good-humoredly.

"Girls!" the Chief called. "How about washing these?"

"Fifty cents, eh?" I threw in.

"Sure, sure! Give us soap. We do 'em."

Brushes in strong brown arms made the soapsuds fly, and the Navy hose rinsed the lot. A bowl of sweetened lime juice fattened the slim wages and everybody was happy.

Later in the evening the Commander came aboard with an old fellow, Captain Stephanie, one of the real old time trading skippers of the islands. He has been down here 33 years & is married to a Samoan girl & has several grown children, all of whom he had educated in Germany, his home. In 1922 he went up to Boston and brought the ketch, *Ajax*, down here to use trading. It

was his first time back to civilization in 22 years & he
had some funny stories about it. Later he sold the *Ajax*
in the Philippines & I guess he couldn't make a go of
trading in her down around here when the U.S. Government started hauling freight and cargo with the *Ontario*,
the sea-going tug.

Just as we were preparing for sea, the Trader turned yellow
with jaundice and ran a fever. For two weeks he lay in the Navy
hospital ashore, achieving a phenomenally deep saffron color and
boasting about his urine, while we repeated the now familiar
pleasures of dining out with the hospitable Navy families and
seeing fairly recent moving pictures.

It has been raining steadily the last two days here. The
Trader has returned from the hospital & looks a lot
better. He lost about 20 pounds during his stay there &
all his clothes go around him several times now.

I went down to Pago at the head of the bay & saw them
bring in a big fish seine. The whole village was helping
in the fishing but they only landed a couple of hundred
fish, mostly skip-jacks & some stinger rays & a little
hammerhead shark. Last year in one haul with this big
seine they got 87,000 fish, but this time their seine
broke in half & they lost most of the haul. The head
fishermen wear little hats made of banana leaves & the
rest of the village people dash about in the shallow
water after the fish & have a great time laughing &
yelling at each other.

The Americans were good, friendly people, but somehow they
and their predecessors had suppressed the charm of Tutuila
completely, just as the French have enhanced that on Tahiti — for
the Europeans and Americans, at least: Both islands had much the

same elements to begin with, the same style of natural beauty, and the same race of inhabitants, but only one of them now troubled my traveler's sleep with dreams of return. This is not a surprising result. The French colonizers of the *Établissements de l'Océanie* are chiefly concerned with making life agreeable at their posts, and they not only have centuries of experience in the art but are respectful toward its observances.

The American administrators of Samoa have conscientiously sought to run an efficient naval base, set up model schools, improve hygiene, and clean up yaws. The contrast was especially marked during our visit to Tutuila by the enforcement of the prohibition amendment, but the difference was not to be accounted for by the absence or presence of alcohol. Who would not prefer a bottle of sarsaparilla on the rickety veranda of the Tiare Hotel in Papeete to a shot of the best cognac at the soda fountain of the Commissary at Tutuila?

chapter 12

Fiji to Port Moresby

WHEN FINALLY THE TRADER had turned as nearly white as his twelve-month tan permitted and was discharged from the hospital, I paid to the representative of our own Government by far the largest sum for harbor dues, pilotage, wharfage, and other port charges that any sovereign ever exacted from the *Pilgrim*. We swung away from the dock under the three lowers — main, fore, and staysail — before a large crowd of Navy steamboat men, and started to beat out the harbor. But the wind fell very light, and we were forced to abandon this bit of bravado. We had to start the engine before we were far enough off for its resonant putts to be inaudible from the shore.

> **From Hod Fuller's journal: This port seems to be the only spot in the world where a vessel is charged port charges in her own port & especially a yacht. There are all kinds of charges here to support the Samoan natives. We left the Doc here to catch the next boat to the States, as he must be back in Harvard Medical School in September. After beating out of Pago Pago Harbor we shaped our course SW by W for the Fiji Islands. There was a nice little breeze outside which freshened up and brought rain while I was on watch, 8-10.**

From the ship's log: July 28, Noon. Very decent run of 162 miles from Pago Pago. Excellent clam chowder for lunch.

There were now six of the original crew on board, and Lipscomb had begun to feel out of sorts and was keeping to his bunk. Short-handed as we were, we devised a new system of watches among the four of us — the Trader, the Chief, Joe, and I — with the Cook as always confined to the galley and the Skipper, having no watch, liable to be on deck at all hours. The system was to stand one-man watches of two hours each, with the precaution that the man with the two o'clock in the morning watch would bunk in the charthouse for the first half of the night, so as to turn out quickly if necessary, while the mid-watch man would take his place during the second half. In reality, this arrangement merely recognized the practice of leaving only one man on deck which had grown up under the previous plan of two-man watches. For the rest of the voyage this system proved entirely adequate, except that the extra vigilance required of the Skipper sometimes left him a little sleepy in the morning.

July 29, 2–4 P.M. Boisterous beam sea coming aboard now & then in small quantities. Clouds gradually breaking... Rough & windy all P.M. Vessel tearing along at a great rate. She doesn't seem to strain at all & takes everything very easy. Only 10 clips on the pump for 9 hours.

We made fine time, carrying the fisherman staysail and main topsail until it blew so hard that the schooner was forced down past her bearings, when she behaved better with only her working canvas. One of the most exhilarating operations on a gaff-headed schooner is the smothering of a clewed up topsail that is streaking horizontally out to leeward, with one's legs round its recalcitrant folds, with one's weight and one free hand to bring it down, to lash it snug to the topmast as one slides down its length. This game is best played in daylight, in not too rough a sea, and in warm weather as otherwise it can be quite disagreeable, if not somewhat hazardous.

The westerly set we had found most of the way across the Pacific carried us still further to leeward than our reckoning, despite the allowance we had made for it. Just before dawn of our third day, the loom of an island unexpectedly appeared dead ahead. This circular extinct volcano, now called Niuafou, or Tin Can Island, was discovered by Captain Edwards of the *Pandora* in 1791. The name of the island refers to the receptacle in which for many years a swimming native had received the mail from a passing steamer from Samoa.

I read in a news item some time later that the native most recently performing the service was killed by a shark and the tin can practice had been discontinued. In view of the great number of sharks in the Fiji group, which is not many miles away, I find it strange that this had not happened before. At any event, it is an incident to be called to mind when one is reassured of any particular spot, that "no one has ever been attacked by a shark in these waters." That is said of Niuafou until some time in the 1930's.

Our cat has been having a fine time this morning mauling a flying fish that came aboard last night. She finally pulled it all to bits & ate all but the tail which she still carries proudly about deck in her mouth.

On Sunday, 30 July 1933, shortly after six o'clock in the evening, we crossed the dateline for the second time, this time recognizing it in the ship's log, and consequently woke up the next morning on Tuesday. This mildly fantastic sensation of dropping an entire day was quite subordinate, however, to the sensation of being now in east longitude. Although it did not mean we were in the homeward hemisphere with regard to our starting point, it marked a definite stage of our voyage, the more

significant because at this distance Greenwich and Boston seemed
to be in a general way in the same part of the world.

We spent this night, which swallowed a day, running down
the last stretch toward Fiji along the course of the undersea
telegraph cable from Vancouver to the island of Viti Levu, where
Suva lies. The large number of reefs and islands we sailed through
presented some worries, since the system of lights had been
improved after our chart and light list were published. Koro
Island light was blinking according to the book, but further along
to the southwest there were two lights where there formerly had
been one. We assumed — it turned out, correctly — these were on
different islands, and we sailed between them and finally left
them astern. By breakfast time, the tall white shaft of Nasilai Reef
lighthouse and a rusty wreck nearby were in plain view in the
foreground of the mountains of Fiji's principal island. A few
hours later we were beating into Suva Harbor, 688 miles and four
days out of Pago Pago.

The large black schooner yacht *Zaca* passed us bound out,
under power and flying her owner absent pennant. Out of San
Francisco, she was another vessel on her way around the world.
We tied up at the long steamship dock, just ahead of the Matson
liner *Monterey*, opposite a store and two corrugated iron warehouses, one of them apparently devoted to coconut products and
the other, slightly larger, to alcoholic beverages and liquors. A
customs officer soon came aboard and sealed up our own scanty
store of beverages and liquors, as well as of tobacco, with festoons
of pink cotton ribbon and lead deals, a decorative indignity to
which we were subjected in no other port.

At the same time, a representative of the Department of
Agriculture explained that the Samoan beetle, of which we had
never heard in Samoa, is supposed to be so ruinous to coconuts
that every precaution must be taken to prevents its getting a
foothold in Fiji. The beetle was supposed to be purely nocturnal

and the regulation consequently was that any vessel that had been recently tied up at Samoa overnight could not remain within three miles of the Fiji shore from dusk to daylight. The official imparted all this and then, as if to assure us of his impartiality in enforcing the rule, related with cruel amusement how he had sent a freighter offshore in half a gale for the night just as her captain was congratulating himself and his crew on reaching a haven.

While we were considering whether to attempt to jolly him out of a similar exercise of authority toward the *Pilgrim* or to induce in him by imperceptible degrees a state of unofficial intoxication, he concluded that if a thorough search confirmed our denial that we were host to any beetles, we could stay where we were. The investigation produced some anxious moments, due to the difficulty of ascertaining conclusively the nature of our resident insect life that would not stop and pose for inspection. The final result was a clean bill of beetle health and we remained tied up to the bollards for that and several ensuing nights.

August 2. Tied to wharf. Fine cool day. Doc Utley aboard & says C. Lipscomb has a touch of jaundice. He decided to take a room at a hotel for a few days.

August 3. We dressed ship in honor of the arrival this P.M. of the Governor. The Commander, the Chief, the Trader & the Skipper ashore for lunch with the Acting Governor, Mr. Seymour. 5 P.M. ashore for a few cocktails at the parsonage, which resulted in our taking the ladies to dinner at the Metropole. "A good time was had by all."

The Governor returned on the *Orangi* & the whole town turned out to greet him. All the British officials were draped in red coats & lots of gold braid & they had a red velvet carpet spread out for him to walk down the gangway on. They certainly know how to put on the dog & love a big display.

The waterfront at Suva is most interesting. There are many small auxiliary sloops & schooners busy loading & discharging cargo. Natives & Indians work the cargoes of bananas, copra, & foods, and are supervised by Chinese supercargoes. There is quite a bit of traffic leaving & entering the harbor. All the local craft make good use of sail, and their gear & rigging is in far better shape than on the trading schooners in Papeete.

However, due to the necessity of tending the mooring lines constantly, to the natural curiosity of the natives who sat in a solid row on the dock and stared at us for hours at a time, to the smoke from the funnels of *H.M.S. Laburnum,* and not least, to a wharfage charge of thirteen shillings and sixpence a day, we soon put out into the harbor and lay at anchor. There was no swimming in this harbor, not even by the Skipper. We had all seen an armless native in the streets who reputedly had been attacked by a shark, or by a fish which looked and acted exactly like a shark. The sight was too vivid a warning to disregard.

With the water separating us from the shore, I reflected how necessary it is, when tied up along the shore, to make an allowance for general dockside curiosity toward anything that floats and all that takes place on or in it. The degree of privacy to which you are accustomed on land and which you also enjoy at sea is not found on a boat tied up to a wharf. You learn soon enough, whether tied up at Commercial Wharf in Boston or to the coral limestone at Takaroa, that your life is not entirely your own.

People who would never be found standing openly outside the windows of your house watching you brush your teeth, eat, or simply walk from one spot to another will stand or sit for long lengths of time within a few feet of your boat — if indeed they do not climb aboard and peer down the hatch — to watch you performing these or no more intrinsically interesting operations. It is not that you may do any of these things well but that, as with

Dr. Johnson's performing dog, you do them at all as part of life on the water. It may be that this interest has its roots in some dim racial recollection of the ages when, covered with scales, we lived in the water all of the time, and in a faint and wistful protest at the choice made by those of our ancestors who abandoned their marine way of life and went to live on shore. However, whatever the reason, it keeps you dressed in at least a pareu.

One morning, I happened to look over the side to see a bright yellow and black banded snake, about 14" long. It was squirming along by the waterline, with its little head and neck exploring the topsides above as if for a belly hold. I pinched it against the side with the blade of an oar and dropped it on the deck, mortally wounded, where it engaged the attentions of little black Vahine Tahiti. She soon chewed the reptile's head to a pulp, but a short time later was taken with violent fits and then lay in a stupor for a full day before recovering. I noticed the snake was distinguished by a vertically flattened tail that is something like a rudder, but I gave it no more thought until later in the voyage when we met more of them in great numbers and learned of their deadly nature.

Near the *Pilgrim* lay the *Inyala*, arrived some weeks before from Tahiti and now stripped of her sails. Only Haputu, the solitary boy from the Marquesas, was aboard, and he moved mournfully about the deck, homesick and lonely. I learned from Temple Utley over dinner one night aboard the schooner that, having settled on shore with his wife, he had dropped providentially into the native practice of an English doctor who had become entirely absorbed in Hindus and their physical and political problems.

One of the facts which is surprising if your only idea of Fiji is that it is the place where the fuzzy Feejee islanders live, is that in addition to the 100,000 natives and about 4,000 whites, there are some 40,000 Hindus on Viti Levu alone. Their presence is resented by the natives. Although they have some representation in the local parliament, this is apparently by way of a crust of so little nourishment that at every convocation of that body, the Hindu representatives attend meetings only to walk immediately out in protest.

Large numbers of the East Indians work in the sugar cane fields and some of the tallest of them serve in the constabulary. Other avenues of peaceful penetration into the island life are attested by the following items from the *Fiji Times and Herald* of 2 August 1933:

SAMBULA FESTIVAL

It is notified for general information that the annual Fire Walking Celebration of Goddess Mariamman of Golf Links Temple will be held on Sunday, 6 August 1933, at 2:30 P.M. Public are cordially invited to attend.

Madras Maha Sangam, K.S.
Mudaliar, Secretary.

NOTICE

All accounts owing and due to Nagindas Gopalji Pow must be cleared within eight days.

Nagindas Gopalji Pow.

The influx apparently had not entirely ceased. The same paper carried the notices:

The *Ganges* is scheduled to leave Calcutta for Fiji on 31 July, and will leave Suva at the end of August for Calcutta.

Early booking is advisable.

Burns, Philp (South Sea) Co., Ltd., Local Agents.

The following passengers will land at Suva from R. M. S. *Niagara* on Thursday: Sir A. Murchison Fletcher, Mr. F. C. T. Lord, Miss C. J. McDonald, Hiramatsu, Shinpachi, Rammlla, Chumappa.

The presence of so many East Indians in Fiji undoubtedly accounts for there being many East Indian police, since serious race riots probably would occur if a native tried to restrain one of the resentful foreigners. There are no white police, on the other hand. If one of the conquering whites commits a breach of peace, he must submit to being escorted to the hoosegow either by a better than six-foot Sikh completely encased in khaki uniform, puttees, and cotton turban, or by an even more enormous barefooted black native in a brass-buttoned blue jacket and white skirt, bearing on top a natural growth as big as a Grenadier's busby. If the occasion had arisen in my own case, which it did not, I am sure that I would not have considered either alternative an indignity, but would have hoped a friend was on hand to record the scene with a camera. He would certainly have been ill-advised to attempt a rescue.

With the Commander & the Trader went up the Rewa River. Left about 8, seated on a bench on the roof of a motor launch with an old Hupmobile engine for power. Many natives & Hindus piled aboard bringing all kinds of gear with them. The top of the launch was piled high with sacks of flour, sugar, vegetables, bundles of mats, cans of milk, & engine oil. We had a fine seat as the whole front of the launch was a separate compartment for whites & we were the only ones aboard. The river is about one quarter of a mile wide and is most shallow so that the launch wanders all over from one bank to another to keep in the channel. Stops were made frequently along the way to leave off cargo & passengers. They landed the launch by running into the mud bank bow-on, & then poled her off.

The little Hindu women keep their faces partly covered & wear many bracelets & metal bands on their arms &

legs. Their fingers are covered with rings and some of them even wear rings on their toes. Many Brahma cattle graze on the edge of the banks tended by little Indian boys. Fields of sugar cane are planted all along the river & the Indians cut the cane & load it into steel barges which are towed to the refinery down stream by ancient steam tugs. The further up the river we got, the steeper became the banks which at times were high cliffs covered with luxuriant bamboo, coconut & date palm trees. About one o'clock we stopped at a village which was as far up as the launch went, a distance of about thirty miles from the coast. The village consisted of many thatched huts with only a couple of small doors in the thatched walls to serve as windows and give ventilation. They were built on a plateau about 100 feet above the river.

Newspaper notoriety did come my own way when one morning I chartered a Fiji Airways seaplane just for a change of perspective and saw, as the paper reported, "more of this district than most residents see in a number of years." I watched the *H.M.S. Laburnum* pass out through the entrance. The reefs stood out with startling sharpness, the brilliant white foam of the breaking surf contrasting vividly with the rich blue of the deep clear water surrounding them.

We flew over the island of Bau, the ancient home of the Fiji warrior kings. It was interesting to look down on the little speck in the ocean and recall that not so long ago an army of over two thousand native warriors were regularly retained on the tiny island. From the air, it looked as if there would have been standing room only. We returned to Viti Levu and, flying low, followed the reef past Suva down to Navua, where the coast is one of the most beautiful in the whole of Fiji. Joe accompanied me, making his first trip in an airplane. The newspaper story concluded, "Mr. Ekelund's idea after making the flight was 'Why not sell the yacht and buy a seaplane?'"

○ ○ ○

I suffered a real pang on leaving Suva. The Utleys had moved ashore to live, as I have said — and poor Temple Utley, to die there as well — which left the gallant little *Inyala* sitting in the blistering sun with only Haputu to watch her. Happy, as we called him, spent his days on her whitened decks, sometimes moving about and doing some job but mostly sitting alone under the red mainsail awning, staring into the distance. He told me he had gone ashore at first looking for companionship, but the great black Fijians and haughty Indians were completely alien to him in their ways as in their races, and they could not converse with him in French, the only foreign language he knew. He had long since given up the beach and was spending his time on board alone.

I suggested to Utley that Happy might be more content to sail with us in the *Pilgrim*, although it would still be the long way back to the Marquesas. I dropped the idea upon learning that he was suffering from tuberculosis and might have to be sent to a hospital in heaven-knew-what forsaken land, or shipped half way around the world as an invalid.

I never mentioned to Happy himself the possibility of his joining us, but it had apparently occurred to him. On the morning of our departure from Suva, he appeared togged out in his finest outfit — a straw boater, white trousers, and a pair of balloon-toed yellow shoes that were many sizes too large even for his great untrammeled feet. They had curled up into a permanent rocker shape, like the front ends of a pair of skis.

Having handed aboard the last case of Morris Hedstrom's rum, Happy clumped briskly all over the schooner, helping to take in the mooring lines and springing to anticipate whatever he thought someone's hand might do next. Now and again, in between these bursts of helpfulness, he would catch my eye and smile wistfully, as if to say: "*Amn't* I doin' fine? Wouldn't I make a good boy on your boat now?" I felt like what is commonly called a "heel" to leave him behind, but it was the only thing to do. I could not explain to the poor fellow why.

We left Charlie Lipscomb behind at Suva, too, because he was laid up with jaundice. Dr. Utley didn't want him to sail for some time, and we needed to get on to the west. Although Charlie was of an unhealthy hue at the time, he was a robust man and well able to look after himself. He told me he would meet the *Pilgrim* further along if he decided his conscience would let him stay away from home any longer. He did not rejoin us, as it turned out, but steamed home to Maryland and shortly afterward joined an expedition to Central Africa, which was to make a moving picture of something or other, including himself.

The ship's company was now pared down to six, which meant a working crew of five: that is, Pete, the Trader, the Chief, Joe, and myself; John was still doing the cooking. It was 12 August 1933, or one year and less than two months since we left Boston. We had traveled some 10,000 miles, and our approximate position was lat. 178°30′E, long. 18°30′S. The Pilot Chart showed fresh (Force 4 and 5) southeasterly winds prevailing for the season, with less than one day in twenty of light or variable winds or calm, and no westerlies to speak of. We were some 1,100 miles south of the Equator. Tahiti lay about 1,800 miles astern to the east, the northernmost point of New Zealand was about 1,000 miles to the south, 600 miles along on our course west-northwest were the New Hebrides, and 400 miles further the eastern end of New Guinea.

Except for the New Hebrides and New Caledonia and the Loyalty Islands group to the southwest, there were almost no obstructions in the sea, whereas the chart to the north up to the Equator and beyond is sprinkled with atolls as from a charge of bird shot. These include the Ellice and Gilbert Islands, the Solomons, and the Phoenix group.

To someone with most of his life ahead of him and no financial or other reasons for hastening home, much of this area invites investigation. The Skipper, in particular, was eager to meet, and possibly to compare skin markings, with the cannibals of the New Hebrides. Other spots, such as Phoenix Island with its two miles of abandoned guano tramway, one hut, thousands of rabbits, and no trees, inhabitants, water, or anchorage, were out of the running in any event. However, there were only a few months left before the northwest monsoon would set in against a comfortable passage through the East Indies. After so long among the relatively bland and primitive cultures of the Pacific, I was impatient for the more intensive evidences of the human condition found west of Australia.

Eschewing, then, the cannibals as well as the miasmas and fevers of the New Hebrides, we set a course to clear its capital and southernmost point, Port Vila. On this leg of the voyage, as on others, the expectations raised by the wind roses were dismally deflated. Instead of flying along the crests of the southerly swell with a near gale on our quarter, we wallowed and slatted in flat calms and gentle easterlies. Ordinarily, with airs dead astern, the square canvas was the sail to carry, but the long rollers up from some distant Australian blow rolled the *Pilgrim* like a powerboat. With the fore and aft sails set to check this movement somewhat, we could not head the course. With the wind light, the crashing of slatting gear was added to frequent icy downpours from a sunless sky to try our souls further. The engine came into play at times, and the light following breeze provided a variation in our discomfort by raking the ship from stem to stern with the smoke of burned fuel oil.

August 14. 8–12 A.M. Regular New Hebrides weather. Over-cast & rough with rain & irregular variable winds between SE and ENE. After breakfast took in fore and aft sails & set square-sail & raffee. This evolution accompanied by much swearing, everything being cold and wet.

Unpleasantness such as this is relatively trivial, and the extent to which we were concerned with it indicated, I think, the isolation each of us sometimes felt being at sea.

Our cat took to one of the boats the first day out & would only stick her head out from under the canvas cover every few hours. However, she appeared last night and ate as many flying fish as she could hold. They were coming aboard from all directions.... I tied one up by the tail for her to play with & she played with it for two hours with no let up.

On the evening of 18 August, Venus and Jupiter appeared close together, a phenomenon which Joe declared had always been understood by those on the inside to mean wind. Sure enough, about twenty-four hours later, a light breeze filled the limp lowers and main topsail. I can think of no example of the contrast between matter performing its proper function and its dejection in aimless desuetude as a sailing ship just now becalmed with drooping sails, once more met by a working wind.

August 16. 12–2 A.M. Lovely. After brief bobble of tide rip at midnight, nothing but very easy swell almost astern & enough wind to keep sails filled... Joe set lantern in lee rigging as lure for breakfast of fried flying fish, but fish apparently on to that one.

August 17. 12–2 A.M. Commenced boiling along in grand style. Mainsail, foresail, gaff topsail, fisherman staysail & balloon job all pulling strong. Fine trade wind abaft port beam & smooth sea.

As we overhauled the meridians of the New Hebrides, we

came into the lee of the Loyalty Islands and New Caledonia many miles to the southwest. These cut off the heavy swell coming up from New Zealand, and we slipped along in smooth water on a broad reach. The schooner would sail herself on this point for long periods at a time, leaving the helmsman free to go forward and watch the phosphorescent show set up by the cutwater at night, or now and then to race for a flying fish just hurtled into the bulwarks and still fluttering in the scuppers before Vahine Tahiti, not yet having had her evening fill of them, pounced with feral growl and robbed us of a fresh breakfast. It was also in this part of the ocean that we passed dangerously close one morning to the trunk of a tree about 80' long and 3' in diameter, and just awash.

> *August 17. 4–6 P.M. With the wind hauling aft & lightening a bit...set the square rig for the night. Looks clear up to windward & sunset auspiciously rosy. Have seen last of New Hebrides & are now in Coral Sea.*

> *August 18. All day same pleasant moderate breeze dead aft & sea quite smooth: at least it's plumb aft so we don't roll much. A bit of sun now & then but the clouds that seem to hang over the Western Pacific still persist to a considerable extent. Excellent meat & vegetable pie for lunch.*

The effect of the propinquity of Venus and Jupiter soon wore off and most of the rest of the passage was a tantalizing series of promising puffs of wind, paid for with long dull watches under power.

> *August 19. 2–4 A.M. Running under squaresail & raffee, easy going. No bunnies or frogs even attempted to come aboard, as far as can be ascertained by the helmsman, although an odor like kelp was noticed about 3 A.M.*

It is held by some that the Trader's slaying of a sea-bird

brought on this spell of calm weather.

Only as we drew up on the eastern end of New Guinea did the breeze really pipe up.

It was great out on the end of the bowsprit. Sometimes the turnbuckles on the outer end of the bobstay would be under water and then a big sea would lift her up & you'd be high up above the water and then you'd go rushing down as she'd go down into the trough of the seas...Before dark we rigged preventer braces on the yard braces as there is quite a strain on them in this breeze.

On the morning of 27 August, fifteen days and some 1,900 miles out of Suva, the *Pilgrim* was running into the haze under foresail alone before a 40-mile gale, trying to identify a range of mountains that looked down on our starboard bow. By noon, a welcome monument to someone's misfortune in the form of a rusty hulk, sitting up pretty well to her lines but with a deathly inertness, fixed our position near the remains of the steamer *Pruth* on Uateara Reef. The entrance to Basilisk Passage was easy to find, through which we floated "wing-and-wing" in a moderating breeze and dropped anchor in seven fathoms off the long wooden pier at Port Moresby, New Guinea.

August 27. 12–2 P.M. A fine smooth anchorage with the trade wind right off the beach. Bare hills with a few scrub trees & the town a homely lot of red painted shacks & cottages. As the Skipper remarked succinctly, "A hell of a desolate looking place."

chapter 13

Port Moresby
Through Torres Strait

THE AREA IMMEDIATELY SURROUNDING Port Moresby is a bald spot in the proliferating thatch that covers most of the huge island of New Guinea. The sloping foreshore of the harbor supports only the thinnest of a dusty green scrub vegetation, and even this is discouraged by the sandy soil beneath. Great patches of the soil were being whisked into dusty clouds which swirled about the stark red warehouses, the only evidence of energetic life as we approached the shore in our dory. I saw a rusty steamer, the *Papuan Chief*, baking beside the pier; dirtily dressed seamen were sleeping or moving lazily about her hot, shimmering decks. In spite of the most inauspicious appearance of the place, it proved to harbor a number of hospitable and agreeable hosts and to be the gateway to much more interesting country in the immediate vicinity.

> *From the ship's log: August 28. Anchored at Port Moresby. Blowing hard all day: SE right off the beach.... Met several people including the Lieutenant Governor, Sir Hubert Murray, the head of the government at Papua; Mr. Dupain, head of Burns, Philip, and Mr. Williams, an American prospector....*

Had a very good dinner at the Papuan Hotel. Mr. Dupain has been 30 years in the islands with B.P. Co. & has some very interesting stories. He was supercargo on schooners in the Solomons before the advent of power. Mr. Williams has equal stories & has been all over the world in the most remote places. They say the interior of this island is about the wildest spot left & you can go in by airplane to the gold region, but it is very expensive.

Only two miles down the shore was a typical Papuan village. It was composed entirely of shacks made of unfinished saplings and built up on stilts, most of which stood in the shallow water off the shore. The walls and roofs of such huts are of thatched grass. The design may have been for protection from enemies, enabling quick flight in canoes or possibly as a sanitary measure. The natives appeared poor and primitive. In spite of the nearness of the white colony, they wore almost no clothing: the men only G-strings with flaps in front, the women a fringe of dried grass.

From Hod Fuller's journal: While the men lie in the sun or work on their sailing canoes, the women do all the hard work. All the women are covered with geometric tattooing all over their bodies & faces. The canoes are made from huge logs about 75 feet long. They burn the insides out and shape the hulls with crude adzes. The outrigger is attached by means of a wooden framework on which they carry cargo. They paint the hulls with colored geometric patterns. These canoes sail well to windward & kept up with us in the motor dory doing 5 knots.

One eager fellow who knew a few words of English led me to his house, which I entered by climbing about 10' up a broad ladder of loosely fastened poles, worn to a hard slippery surface and awkwardly far apart. The only source of light was the

A typical Papuan village.

doorway and at the far end of the dark interior, I saw an old woman sitting by a fire which apparently rested on the wooden floor. She was cooking nothing, and it was a blistering hot day. The fire must have been some kind of bright comfort, or perhaps it was being preserved for later meals, possibly for want of matches to start a new one.

A few yams stood in a corner, and a shelf hung from the under side of the roof on wires, but for these items and a disintegrating shotgun, the room was quite bare. My host made it known that he had no shells for the gun and would like to beg a few, yet, as I left the village and rejoined others in the ship's company, he contrived to cross the path ahead of us and lope along, holding his weapon as if in readiness. Now and then he stole a glance out of the corner of his eye, as if to make sure that the picture of the mighty hunter going forth with the only fowling piece in town was not lost on us.

The grim bareness of the village dwellings was in sharp contrast to the structures called *dubas*, which stood in what might be called the road — it was almost indistinguishable from the

Papuan *Duba*.

surrounding barren landscape. These *dubas* were made simply: four posts about 8' or 10' tall supported a flat roof and were covered with bright-hued decoration. Each post bore a finial in the shape of a crab claw, which is also the shape of the sail of their canoes and catamarans. The whole was ornamented with carving and painting similar to that found on the totem poles of certain American Indians along the northwest coast of North America. We were told these structures had a religious significance, which led me to think that the bunches of bananas and coconuts hung from the roof were possibly offerings to the local deities.

Having established friendly relations in the little village, we were in turn visited the next day by those who had canoes. They paddled alongside the schooner and watched us for the whole morning. One made a present of a bow and unfeathered arrows, the tips of which were made of pointed bamboo colored with red clay. They may or may not have contained poison.

The chief use of this weapon was explained as, "Kill 'em wallaby." This phrase is an example of the pidgin English which is the *lingua franca* of these parts, the classic example of which is the remark of a native who, on first seeing an airplane that was probably one of those used to communicate with the gold fields of the interior, exclaimed, "My word! Wagon belong Jesus!" The language is also employed in the Dutch portion of Papua. Its most amusing form is said to have been the version rendered by some German emissaries to that part of the island before it became Dutch. They had studied the language from a book but were not familiar with English itself.

The craft which clustered about the topsides of the *Pilgrim* were as ramshackle in appearance as the houses in the village. Each was made of two dugout canoes, across which were laid sticks and poles of various sizes. The natives sat on these platforms and cooked food over the fires which burned continually in the bottom of one of the two canoes. I saw whole families crowded on these boats, together with numbers of the most nondescript dogs. These, to judge by their general dispiritedness, seemed to know their fate was the stew-pot and the sole reason for being kept alive was to preserve their carcasses from premature decomposition. Perhaps the most interesting thing about these watercraft, known as *latakoi,* was their rig: a burlap sail stretched between two curved poles which, because of a deep dip at the head, resembles a crab's claw.

August 30. A tattooed lady alongside in a canoe parted with a grass skirt for 2 bob (Australian).... A call from a few Papuans we met in the village & we traded off some cigarettes & an old coat for spears etc.

The next day, we went several miles into the bush behind Port Moresby to a village called Pari. Whether or not its inhabitants are commonly as dingy as those of the village on stilts, I do not know. Our only visit was on the occasion of a community dance. In a long open space between the thatch huts, what must have been nearly all the men and women of the village were spread out in a great column of fours, marking time with their feet to the steady *tomp* of drums. All looked straight ahead with impassive faces, except when one or another gave a loud shout, and their only motion was the swing of their haunches which was coordinated with their deliberate foot stamping.

The women wore only the *rami,* or grass skirt, together with such tattooing as they might bear, but the men were made up fit to frighten a Dutchman, as no doubt they often had. Their faces were streaked with scarlet, white, and gold paint, while wooden skewers about 6" long bristled from their noses and ears. Long pigtails made of feathers

Papuan villagers.

bobbed from hair luxuriant as that of the Fijians. The ferocious demeanor lent by these details was considerably softened, however, by anklets and bangles of fresh white and yellow flowers that might have adorned a maiden going to meet her lover in the shade.

The drums, which were scattered among the company, were each made of a piece of a hollow tree about 18" tall and 7" in diameter. Now and then, the drummer tightened the head, made of python skin, to a higher pitch by passing over it quickly — with bare fingers — a live coal kept in a brazier hung from his belt. These drums were sounded by slapping with four fingers held flat. The effect produced by a hundred or more men and women ceaselessly marking time together to the beat of drums is that of a community achieving some kind of spiritual unity having to do, in its original purpose, with either war or worship. I suspect, however, that on this occasion they were merely rehearsing for the next boat-load of tourists to arrive at Port Moresby from Australia.

Not that tribal wars no longer take place in New Guinea, or that war dances are the mere vestige of former warlike practices as they are in Tahiti. Although the Australians and British maintain order as best they can, beyond their control there are still wars and private murders. A year after our visit, a whole tribe with all its ancient customs intact was discovered in the interior for the first time. I was told by many that between the freedom with which the natives indulge their traditional head-hunting practices and the comparative police discipline near the white posts is every degree of outlawry.

A man who had done much to keep the natives in order was the Lieutenant Governor of Australian Papua, Sir Hubert Murray. A long, lean, and fit gentleman of over seventy years who once had been amateur light-heavyweight boxing champion of Australia, he received visiting yachtsmen in his undershirt. On my meeting him, he told how he had hit on a method of taming the spirits of some of the most troublesome murderers which, I thought, had the simplicity of genius. The first part of his program necessitated catching the criminals, which he did himself by going out into the bush and following their trails until he caught them, even if it took months. After making a perfect record for getting his man in this manner, his fame spread and earned him a sound respect.

The second element of his plan involved less perseverance but more originality. After catching a murderer, the Administrator would, instead of punishing him, make him a policeman. Apparently, the kind of murdering that is popular among the Papuan natives takes a combination of qualities which indicate a man superior to his fellows in courage and physical prowess (which is recognized in the kudos that goes with a fine collection of enemies' heads), and he reasoned that these were qualities which would serve a more civilized occupation. Murray also imagined that the glory of being in the king's constabulary, with a brass bound belt and badge to show the girls, would weigh more with a village bad boy than a now hazardous continuance of the old game. The fame of Murray himself undoubtedly had much to do with these men's eagerness to serve under him. There had been many protests from those who regarded murder as something "wrong" which ought to be punished, and who possibly felt uneasy under the aegis of their new policemen, but the new system was already established upon a firm bed of favorable statistics.

There was plenty of good water at Port Moresby, owing to a heavy rainy season, and we filled the *Pilgrim's* tanks free of charge. The customs regulations required forms to be filled out in quadruplicate, with a list of all stores on board upon arrival and another set for those at departure, but Mr. Byrne, the Collector, allowed the law to be satisfied with convenient generalities and estimates. He even filled out the forms himself, which saved a good deal of troublesome details and created international amity which some other Collectors and Port officers seem to try their utmost to destroy.

⊙ ⊙ ⊙

With the assistance of Mr. Dupain, the Manager of Burns, Philip Co., we engaged a crafty looking old native named Iagi Sulu as a pilot, and moved the *Pilgrim* out of Port Moresby and along the coast inside the fringing reef to the northwest. The captains of the Dutch Steamer *Van Rees* and the rusty local boat had plotted a course for us through the Bligh Entrance to the Torres Strait. They suggested we go along the Papuan coast, then to Yule or Ravao Island, more or less opposite the entrance, and proceed west from there. This first stretch of sixty miles or so, spotted with uncharted coral and shoals, could be covered safely only with local knowledge. Old Iagi was so conscientious about his trust that he would not relinquish the wheel even to eat, but sat all day on the wheel-box spitting red betel nut juice all about him on the deck, while we admired the 12,000', snow-covered peaks of the Owen Stanley range which followed the shore thirty miles inland.

> **Passed several native villages along the coast. As customary here, the houses are all built of grass and are set on piles up over the water with the natives' canoes dragged under them & stored up from the water's surface on scaffolds.... The coast is becoming prettier & much greener with palms along the beaches — not like dried up Port Moresby.**

In the afternoon, the trade wind blew up hard enough for us to proceed under the square sails alone and make Yule Island by dark. Iagi admired how easy it was to handle these sails compared with those of his native *latakoi* rig, but demurred at our setting the mainsail in light airs because "boom, he fly about too much." Passing into Hall Sound, we dropped anchor in soft mud close under the mainland side of the island.

With a letter from Mr. Dupain to the Resident Magistrate at Kairuku, the Skipper and I landed in the dory and followed a path through long grass and brush to the settlement. Later, after what we learned of venomous snakes on the island, we walked more warily. In our ignorance, we passed in safety by rice fields and groves of palms and mangoes to a small settlement where an English lady and gentleman were playing tennis. We soon joined them in doubles, with Mrs. Thompson, the wife of the Resident Magistrate, explaining that her game was not what it had been before she injured her arm driving a "lorry" in France. There were no side fences to the court. Instead, there were nearly naked little black boys who scrambled after the balls that went out and threw them inexpertly back to the wrong side, regardless of whether play had begun on the next point. This same misdirected eagerness had even greater scope when it came to bringing chairs and tea things from the house. Poor Mrs. Thompson plainly felt that things did not go at all as smoothly as they did in English gardens at home.

The following day, Mr. Thompson showed us around the settlement, and as the Skipper had expressed an interest in seeing a real cannibal, he showed us the jail in particular. A bare compound, enclosed by a fence only 4' high, contained a few simple board shacks in which the prisoners lived. Bare as it was, the place had more attractive surroundings than the Port Moresby village. The Resident Magistrate explained that the real penance done by an inmate was not in the confinement, but in being forced to do without a fire. I remembered the old woman bent over her fire in the house on a hot day.

Mr. Thompson called two chinless youths over to the fence for our inspection. They were wearing dirty, once-white breech flaps, on which were printed the arrowhead shaped mark with which the English tag their convicts. These were the cannibals he had promised to the Skipper. Their story was that a man had annoyed their sister, and they had, naturally enough, killed him. Although they had never eaten human flesh, it seemed like a splendid opportunity to try some and they each had taken a bit of a leg. After all, they had said to each other, their fathers and grandfathers had eaten human flesh, so there couldn't be anything really bad in it.

Sir Hubert Murray, before whom they were tried, had asked one of them whether he had enjoyed the experience, and received the reply that the flesh had not tasted very good, either because the defendant hoped to mitigate his offense or because he was as decadent as they both appeared to be and actually had not savored the dish. In any case, the boys obviously were not police material, and Sir Hubert had sentenced each to one year of imprisonment, without a fire, under the statute against indecent treatment of corpses.

The Skipper and I walked out beyond the settlement along a broad slope of rice fields, topped with a dazzling white limestone church complete with rose window and spire. A dozen black children ran out and shouted a greeting. They were followed instantly by a woman in a broad, roll-brimmed straw hat and voluminous dark blue gown of a cut believed by some to be helpful in disseminating the doctrines of the New Testament. She scurried after them like a mother hen, herding them out of sight under her skirts and into their houses. We marched in silence through the settlement with no other human figures in sight.

Beyond the mission, the path led down to the sea through an avenue of towering flamboyants, to another village called Chiria. Here, the houses were also built on stilts, but these were all on land. In contrast to the first village, they were neatly put together and kept, and the ground beneath them was of clean white pebbles, unblemished by even a stray twig or fallen leaf. Here and there, a small portion had been set off as a garden in which young coconut shoots and plants like tomatoes were set in even rows.

A young man, sitting on a veranda, was twisting vines into a flexible rope of about 1" in diameter with an ingenious apparatus made of sticks. Young pigs, dogs, and humans wearing no clothes were moving about. The adults wore necklaces of red and yellow beads and, for a further touch of decoration, chewed the usual betel nut cud mixed with lime juice, which stains it a bright vermilion. Not only are the chewer's lips colored, as the lips of women of our own country, but also the tongue and gums.

When the Skipper trained his camera on an old woman sitting

on the ground, a young girl who might have been her grand-daughter sprang to her protection with an expression of apparent puzzlement and fear which our explanation in English with gestures seemed unable to dispel. Further on, a feathered brave came down from a platform where he had been sitting examining himself from all angles in a hand mirror. "Shilling," he said, pointing at the camera. I guessed then it may well have been that the young girl's feelings had by no means sprung from ignorance of a camera's function but of outrage at what she regarded as a kind of petty larceny.

On the way back to the boat landing, the Skipper's eye fell on a red and white striped shirt and canary yellow *rami,* intended for gala use by natives. The shirts were for sale inside the store of the "Steamship Trading Co.," and he bought them to wear himself.

All that day on Yule Island, we had walked through long grass and brush in sneakers and bare ankles, with no more thought of snakes than we had in Polynesia where there are none. At dinner that evening, Mrs. Thompson told of hearing a hubbub in their fowl house one night and then finding a great python that had eaten or killed all of their poultry and wrecked the house, either in the chase or in its attempts to escape. A previous owner of their house, she went on, had built a small white gazebo on a knoll overlooking the sea, and shortly after their arrival she had gone there to read and enjoy the view. But soon she was startled by a rustling which proved to be that of poisonous snakes under its floor. On her hurried dash back to the house, she had to jump out of the way to avoid a death adder which dropped from a tree directly in her path. After that, she gave up going to the gazebo.

At the end of the evening, we groped our way down a long path to the little landing place. Mr. Thompson pointed out a stout stockade in the water designed to provide safety from sharks and alligators while swimming. Our boat for some reason had been moored to a buoy some yards out and there was no apparent way of reaching it. At the word of the Resident Magistrate, however, one of the native boys made a running leap into the water, swam frantically for the boat and tumbled aboard. No hungry jaws snapped at him, but it was evident that despite the stockade, he still regarded the possibility as not at all remote and still as not involving too great a risk to run for his boss's guests.

The next morning we sailed in the *Pilgrim* for Bramble Cay.

September 3....Proceeded to get underway: a process lengthened by the excellent holding ground which resisted the cleansing efforts of the hose to an unusual extent. Underway 7:45, under power. Practically no wind & a fine day. Mainsail & foresail up. Saluted the R. M. & his coterie by three blasts which so startled the Trader that he dropped the draw-bucket overboard: recovering it later with the boat-hook and an air of great dignity. Steamed out the pass south of Yule Island consuming an excellent breakfast of fresh oranges, bacon & eggs on toast, coffee.

Bramble Cay is a small island at the entrance to the Great Northeast Channel leading down the Torres Strait. Captain Anderson of the *Papuan Chief* had advised us to anchor there for the night so we would have the necessary advantage of daylight for spotting the coral reefs in the passage further along.

Had a good breeze later on & during my 6–8 watch did 18 miles which is a record for two hours.

After a fine run across the wind all day, we hove to after midnight, as the currents in that narrow region between Australia's northernmost point and New Guinea's southernmost are strong and unpredictable. In this situation, we were practically helpless against a flock of large white sea birds that swooped down out of the dark at the binnacle light, smashing into us clumsily and even threatening injury to our eyes. Finally, the

Skipper knocked one of them into the water with a stick, and this discouraged them gradually from further dive-bombing. Not long after daylight, Joe sighted the pyramid beacon on Bramble Cay, and as the wind had dropped under a heavy cold rain, we took in the slatting foresail. The weight of the wet sail broke the lee lazy jack. This was the first piece of standing rigging to part on the voyage, now over 12,000 miles long.

While we were still some distance off Bramble Cay, I saw another cloud of sea birds. As we approached closer, the sound of their confused cries filled the air. The beacon was the only part of the landscape that rose above the level of the flat island, the rest of which was so covered with birds it seemed impossible that even a small group of those swooping above us could find a resting place. It was not hard to believe that all the gulls, terns, boobies, albatrosses, and cormorants of that part of the world were convened there, as at a convention. As we approached from leeward, the air was far from fragrant.

Walking on shore was impeded by thousands of nests which lay all about in the low growth. These were loosely constructed of lumps of coral and bits of broken shells, and some contained a single egg, slightly smaller than a hen's egg. A large number of young in the pin-feather stage stumbled about on the ground. The adults were white, brown, and black with various markings which I had too little knowledge to identify.

Craters in the sand about 5' wide and tracks leading from them to the water attested to the presence of sea turtles. I tried digging both around the outside of these indentations where their eggs are said to be, and in their bottoms where the eggs are said never to be, but failed to uncover any eggs at all. In the shallows off the shore were many black and gray mottled *bêches-de-mer,* a kind of sea cucumber about 7" long. Also known as trepang, their eviscerated, dried, or smoked bodies are used for food. I had seen sacks of them in a warehouse at Port Moresby, destined for China

Shipmates.

and soup. In trying to get close to a bright green carp, I nearly put my foot into the jaws of a tridacna, or giant clam. Although it was not large enough to have held me, it could have given my foot a bad tweak. When I prodded it with a stick, its green and black scalloped jaws closed almost instantaneously and with the force of a captive mollusk whose sole means of making a living from the world is to do just that as efficiently as possible.

By getting the *Pilgrim* underway before dawn the next morning, we ran down the Great Northeast Channel in daylight and holed up at Coconut Island, from which we hoped to pass through Torres Strait the following day. Perhaps because we were now only fifty miles from mainland Australia, the signs of European civilization ashore were thick. The only white man on the island, the school teacher told us after we'd gone ashore, was a Frenchman who lived with a native wife and was "hiding from his sons." Although we passed by the Frenchman's house at the junction of the main road and "Eurydice Avenue Street," he did not emerge, and the schoolmaster was not on such terms as to intrude on his privacy.

In the teacher's schoolroom, we ran over the course of the *Pilgrim* on a Mercator's projection on the wall, to the apparently genuine interest of the man. On learning the schooner's name, he remarked: "It means going from place to place, does it not?" and that it "was a very good home." Despite the order of the island, right down to borders of white stones along the grassy streets and other evidences of the inevitable spread of Australian ways of doing things, the place was almost entirely devoid of charm. I mention it only for the sake of completeness.

As the ship's cat, Vahine Tahiti, seemed a bit restless today, we secured the services of a fine, strapping Coconut Island Tom. When he was introduced to Vahine, she put up a hell of a scrap. Later in the evening, the Trader and I went ashore & bought the tom cat for a carton of cigarettes. At present both cats are in the vegetable locker on deck, where we hope they will become better acquainted.

By turning out before daylight the next morning, we had the anchor chain "up and down," as the Skipper often said, and the mainsail set by the time it was light. We soon set off under full sail on the last leg of the Great Northeast Channel for Torres Strait, the gateway out of the Coral Sea and the Pacific Ocean. We were sailing now well inside the Great Barrier Reef and smooth water, ruffled slightly by a steady southeast wind. It was necessary to have a lookout aloft because of both imperfect charting and a strong westerly set. In my turn, I saw, in addition to the shoal spots, a half dozen well-wooded islands scattered about, a string of ketches hove-to and apparently fishing or pearling off a spot marked as "Grassy Sand Bank" and three brown porpoises playing under the bow. A flock of birds zoomed about the masthead, making in chorus a sound almost like that of sleigh-bells.

Now and then, one flew close enough to the spreaders, where I was perched, that I could make out its details. The bird had a grass green back that faded to a light blue rump, a canary yellow throat, orange underwings tipped with black, and a black head and tail. The tail was square and from the middle of it a single slender spike projected backward. On its end was what looked like a black pea. The waters beneath held creatures far less cheery. The Trader caught a forty-pound barracuda on the spinner that day. Even more sinister, the Chief hauled aboard a 3' yellow and black sea snake of the same general appearance as the one brought on board in Suva.

> ...Headed through the many islands & reefs on our way through Torres Strait. We passed one small island after another, all having the same appearance: very low, covered with low foliage & palm trees, & having white coral sand beaches. The sea through here has changed to an olive green color instead of a deep blue as it has been. The Skipper was busy rushing around getting many bearings on the different islands and did a slick job bringing us through the passage which is rather ticklish work with strong tides and many rocks and reefs.

We boiled through Prince of Wales Channel on a fair tide, showing Old Glory at the peak to the Australian lighthouse on Hammond Rock. We barely had time to notice on Goode Island some slender conical ant hills which must have been 10' high. Soon the *Pilgrim* was out on the other side and marching, wing and wing, into the Arafura Sea, which is part of the Indian Ocean.

chapter 14

Timor Laut, the Banda Islands, and Komodo

WE WERE NOW ON THE MAIN shipping route, heading for a lightship as a point of departure across the Arafura Sea. We were so exactly on our course, in fact, that a 5,000-ton steamer would have run us over from astern had the Skipper not played a powerful flashlight on the squaresail. Luckily, this caused the great vessel to change her course and pass us on our port quarter.

> **From Hod Fuller's journal: During the afternoon, the breeze died away & we are lazing along about 3 knots under the square rig with very little sea in here. We are having beautiful moonlit nights now & last night the moon came up directly aft over Australia & made a fine sight.**

The southeast wind held on for a few days but with diminishing strength. As we further reduced its relative force by traveling with it, we were soon reminded of our entrance into an enclosed tropical sea by a shimmering heat almost as lethal as an August heat wave in Boston. The tepid surface brine was apparently an ideal soup for the banded sea snakes. They appeared in greater and greater numbers and were an easy mark for a twelve-gauge shotgun, as their brilliant skins squirmed and reared against the dark water.

If you feel that our killing of these snakes, as they pursued their courses in their home waters, was a wanton offense against God's creatures, I would point out that not only are all marine serpents very poisonous, but this particular variety is also extremely aggressive. They are all members of the cobra clan and their poison sacs carry a powerful neurotoxin, for which there was at that time no available antivenom. Of the hundreds we were passing through, many reared their heads a foot and a half above the surface and swam menacingly toward the schooner. Years before, Joe had encountered one snake that had come aboard through the hawse hole of his ship anchored in the Hooghly River in India, at the head of the Bay of Bengal. A high percentage of the bites received by fishermen in Asiatic and Malayan waters are fatal.

> *From the ship's log: September 8. 12–2 A.M. Commenced drifting along before a faint easterly under the usual rig: squaresail & raffee. Fine night. Trade clouds flying over moon indicate a spot of wind aloft, which gradually came down & filled, to an appreciable extent, the sails of the American schooner yacht Pilgrim of Boston.*

We passed through the long yellowish streaks noted by previous mariners, including Captain Cook in his *Voyages,* which sometimes have been mistaken for shoals. When I examined them in a draw bucket, the discoloration seemed to be caused by countless bits of yellow matter, each of which was straight, thick as a hair, about ⅛" long, and with a vegetable odor.

> *September 10. 8–10 A.M. A flying fish morning. Loveliest kind of weather all day. Sea very smooth due presumably to the continent of Australia to windward. Very light trade wind about SE. Vessel easing along in the light air with no slatting. Very*

enjoyable even if the linear progress is rather slow. A particu-
larly good pudding produced by the Cook for lunch proved to be
composed principally of Cream of Wheat.

If you look at a chart of the Indonesian Archipelago, you see that, from a point just to the west of the tongue dangling down from Asia which is the Malay Peninsula and separated from it by the narrow Malacca Strait, there extends a long crescent of islands to the southeast and east, clear over to the western end of New Guinea. This string of islands represents an ancient mountain range, most massive in Sumatra and Java at the western end and diminishing in height toward the eastern end, which we were now approaching.

Enclosed by the crescent along its northern edge are Borneo, Celebes, the Spice Islands, and hundreds of others which break up the waters into the Java, Celebes, Flores, and Banda Seas. Farther to the north lie the China Sea and the Philippine Islands. To the south is the Indian Ocean, which pours and rushes through every gap in the chain and back again with each tide, setting up violent currents and tidal bores.

The Arafura Sea is the vestibule to the eastern end of Indonesia, and it was to one of the small islands in it, Timor Laut (Kepulauan Tanimbar), that we set our course. It was our first acquaintance with this part of the world, of which we had only the impressions from reading Joseph Conrad or seeing a movie of Clark Gable wearing a pith helmet and running a rubber plantation, reached by going up a river at night on a raft to the sound of innumerable cicadas.

Warwick Tompkins had cruised about these parts in the years before his acquisition of the *Wander Bird* in 1928 and warned me against Malay pirates. They probably would give you no trouble, he had said back in Boston, if they knew we were armed and on the alert — both of these conditions were necessary to safety. Pictures of Malay jungles and natives running amuck were mingled with what we had heard of the wonders of Bali. The liveliness of our expectations was exceeded only by their vagueness and confusion.

Most of the East Indies had been for centuries under Dutch control. This moved the Cook — for whom, as a Belgian, Dutch was a mother (or at least an aunt) tongue — to clean and brighten everything below decks with the especial thoroughness for which that nation is famous. At the same time, the gun locker was overhauled and the shotguns, rifles, and revolvers were cleaned and made ready; even the Very pistol and flares were brought out as a possibly humane but still effective protection.

To Captain Tompkins' general warning was added this somewhat sinister advice found in the *Sailing Directions (1889)*. Findlay says of Oliliet, a village not far from where we planned to land in Timor Laut: "Water may be got on the beach, but vessels should be very cautious in sending boats for it to guard against treachery, as several crews have been massacred here." The *East Indies Pilot* (here, as often, both the matter and the form indicate that Findlay has been freely drawn upon) said of the same place (page 273, lines 6-18): "Water could be procured on the beach, but a merchant vessel should be cautious in sending her boats for it, as the natives have a reputation for treachery." In this state of affairs we might have made a picture of very gallant fellows, indeed, sailing boldly into the range of such dangers, but the *Supplement to the Pilot,* which brought the information up to date from 1923, contained the following: "Page 273. Delete lines 6-18."

September 12. 12:10 P.M. Sighted Timor Laut or Yamdena Island in the Tenimber Group ahead. Apparently we have been set a little to the south. Stowed light mainsail & raffee & straightened things up. The Commander gave a prodigious burnishing job to the binnacle. Continued along & gradually identified Egeron Strait & Anger Masa Island. Hauled up northerly past Matkusa Island. The bearings on the chart don't check, but the general arrangement seems clear. We have a chart on a fairly big scale & are headed up the bay for where we suppose the settlement to lie.

The town of Saumlakki on Timor Laut is not a port which one would visit twice except to escape from adverse weather. We went ashore briefly. A row of neat little Dutch houses gave an air of substance on a small scale, which was relieved by more exotic touches such as orchids hanging in their yards and the presence of blue and red parrots. A man who was in charge of a pearl fishing enterprise and had not had anyone who understood English to speak with for a long time showed us the diving helmets and other gear used in bringing the shell and pearls up from the bottom. A few Malay women in dirty sarongs and tunics walked down the street with pumpkins on their heads. A little Malayan named Hussein sat on his porch making handles for ladies' handbags out of tortoise shell.

The people are Malays & speak Malaysian. They all wear European clothes & chew the beetle nut…. Their praus or sailing canoes are not dugouts but have hulls made of planks. They use double outriggers & strange kinds of sails — wide, but short, single squaresails — which they have to brace around whenever they come about. They seem to sail well to windward with this rig, although it's a job every time they tack.

September 13….Walked over to Oliliet where two big anchors & chains occupy a large plot in the middle of the village. The natives got them off a ship that was wrecked there a very long time ago. The anchors are about ten feet long, fitted for wooden stocks & with the sharp, straight arms of our best modern "fishing" anchors. The houses were all thatched & made of what looked like bamboo, & the people a sort of mixture. This place is on the edge of things & both the country & the people seem to

have a bit of the South Seas, the East & Australia. A consider-
able number of men met on the path were returning from
hunting with bows & arrows. The only bag seen was two small
birds about the size of blue jays.

But farewell to Timor Laut, and off to the Banda Islands. These
lay some 250 miles to the north of the island chain we planned to
follow to Java, but we were eager to visit the "home of the nutmeg
tree." None of us had ever seen a nutmeg except in its finished
commercial form. The ship's calendar said it was now the middle
of September. We were still riding along on the southeast
monsoon, although it was soon to breathe its last, and the rainy
season was over. The flying fish — a new species with canary
yellow wings bordered with black — flashed in the sunlight like
clouds of butterflies and disappeared as suddenly with a sound
like a sudden shower of rain while porpoises swam rings around
us, mocking our eight knots. Through a commotion like a tide-rip,
set up by a school of excited bonito, a great green whale rose half
out of the water almost perpendicularly, its thick head cleft by an
enormous but cruel smile.

After dinner a school of flying fish came aboard &
seven landed on deck. The cats grabbed three & we
rescued four for breakfast & put them in a bucket well
covered over. But by morning the cats had stolen one so
we were left only three which, when cooked, were
about the size of sardines!

September 15. Commences finest kind of a night. A broad reach
across the Banda Sea, smooth & a good little breeze about ESE,
a bit more aft than hitherto. The vessel is sporting eight sails &
they are all working. The cats are taking a kink in the coil of the
mainsheet, the slacking of which they appear to resent.

Entering through the Eastern Channel of the Banda Islands

between two of the most northeastern of the group, one anchors off the island of Neira in the shadow of Gunong Api. This volcano has many times devastated the Bandas but now merely emits the sulphurous fumes of a subterranean bellyache, shaking the earth some five hundred times each year.

A large part of the nutmegs of the world, and the best in the world, have been produced commercially in the Banda Islands since the early sixteenth century. I discovered that the natural beauty of the plantations which are carefully cultivated forests, the solid dignity of four centuries of building and planting by nutmegnates with the means to create surroundings both comfortable and elegant, and the leisure with which all activity, from picking the ripe seed to drinking Bols at the club, is carried on, all combine to produce an atmosphere of a peculiar and concentrated charm. Since the sixteenth century, the Portuguese, followed by the Dutch and for a time the English, have farmed the rich volcanic soil for the one indigenous product it produces better than any other spot in the world.

Galleons wallowed and clippers sped across 15,000 miles of ocean with countless tons of the precious nuts, completing the process of transmuting the belchings of the primeval crater of which Gunung Api is but a tiny grandchild into substantial fortunes. Most of the buildings on the island are made of stone, and this largely marble brought from Europe on return trips of the nutmeg ships. With this marble, they laid the floor of the church, from time to time raising a slab and interring one or another deceased citizen beneath, as many centuries-old epitaphs testify. One proprietor even imported from the Paris Exposition of 1900 an entire house of pink granite, complete with wrought iron balconies. Still another, homesick for the night sounds of his native lowlands, sent for a company of frogs, whose descendants still entertain the Bandanese with their song.

The little nuts were once more precious than they are now;

control of the islands, once won, had to be maintained by force of arms. To control the market, the Dutch for years prohibited the transplantation of the nutmeg tree, even going to the length of dipping the nut sold whole in lime to prevent it from sprouting roots. Two ancient forts, one in ruins and one still housing a doughty Dutch Garrison, stand as monuments of the struggle. The once twenty large proprietorships have dwindled to a few and the pink house from Paris was empty, but the alley of giant Canary trees along the waterfront remained, along with the gravestones, the crumbling forts, and the lichened gateposts of the residency, embossed with the arms of one of the conquering houses.

Joe & I went ashore yesterday afternoon & walked all through the town. The people are Chinese, Arab, & Javanese & they all have their separate churches & graveyards. The houses are made of split bamboo, & many of the others of whitewashed stone & plaster using parts of the old walls in the town.

A friendly invitation called from the veranda of the club led to a round of "splits" with the Dutch Administrator, a Chinese banker, and Mynheer Brumsen, manager of one of the nutmeg plantations. The Administrator was enjoying a kind of semi-retirement from the anxieties of a previous post in Dutch New Guinea (Irian Jaya), where the natives had eaten three of his policemen. Mynheer Brumsen had also visited those parts with his wife, for whom a native chief had offered a number of pigs in exchange. Madame Brumsen maintained proudly that the number had been a round hundred, but her husband ungallantly insisted that she had added a cipher and that the chief's purpose had not been matrimony but the cook-pot.

The woods which cover most of Neira hold no such terrors. Because nutmeg trees insist on shade, the plantations are forests of great Canary trees. Not more than 60' high, these form a protective roof over the little nut trees which live gratefully under them like lambs under their mothers. There is no underbrush, and scarcely a leaf is allowed to lie on the gravel paths that wind through the woods. Here and there on the plantation managed by Brumsen is a granite structure shaped like a large round-backed armchair without legs, bearing an engraved Chinese epitaph. This, reflecting the early Chinese trading throughout Indonesia, marks an ancient tomb.

A loincloth-clad Malayan walks slowly about, his practiced eye cocked upward for a fruit of just the right shade of yellow for plucking. He fingers the foliage with a little wicker trap on the end of a bamboo pole (he followed an expert picker for six months to learn how to judge and pick the fruit), gives a little twist, lowers the trap, throws away the split outer flesh, and pops the glistening mahogany nut, covered with a tracery of brilliant scarlet mace, into a basket hung from his waist. Because the nutmeg ripens at all times of the year, this unhurried harvesting never ends, bringing in a steady flow of guilders from the consumers of apple pies and eggnogs.

September 18....Mr. Brumsen showed us over the old nutmeg buildings, some of them 300 years old & still used in the various stages of curing mace & nutmeg.

The Brumsens introduced us to our first *rystafel,* or rice table, which is an experience no traveler to the East Indies can easily escape. It is as much a "sight" as the Boroboedoer in central Java. You first heap an enormous plate with rice for a foundation and accept a few shrimps which you place on the plate's rim. Next, watching your hostess, you mix the shrimp with some of the rice and swallow with a zest of appetite deferred and stimulated by several doses of Dutch gin, taken conversationally and neat. An ordinary appetite would never carry you through a *rystafel.* Some anchovies arrive at your left elbow, which taste even better, and then some red peppers, cut into strips.

Your beer glass has been filled in the meantime, and you take time out for a swallow to quench the fire of the peppers. Then you return to your plate only to find a platter of fish balls under your nose. You must take a little of everything, and that means you must keep on eating diligently enough to keep room on your overflowing plate for it. As the mixture gets hotter, particularly after a dab of chutney is added, you find yourself in a fine state of activity, what with the increasing necessity of more beer, attempting secretively to mop your brow, and telling your hostess what you think of Banda.

When at length your spirit is at the point of breaking, the serving boys call a truce. You sit back and heave a sigh which begins in relief but ends in an inner groan: you realize you have only just been breaking even up to now, and your plate is still covered. But your palate is nearly anesthetic by now and you feel as though you have been eating for as long as you can remember. You continue doggedly to go through the motions — swallow, mop, and gulp, "Yes, indeed, it is!" mop, swallow — until as with the tiger in the limerick, everything is inside. Unlike him, the only expression on your face is not a smile but a silly torpid leer. I went back to the *Pilgrim* alone that afternoon, probably on my hands and knees, and letting myself down gently by the binnacle, went sound asleep on the deck.

When I at length fought my way back to semi-consciousness, I became aware gradually of a periodic *whooshing*, fairly close aboard, which I could connect with no normal harbor activity. Over the bulwarks, the natives were paddling about by families in the narrow roadstead between Neira and Lontor, where we lay, the late afternoon sunshine lighting up their gaily-painted gondola-like *praus*. There was an excited, but not frightened, tenseness in the way they were guiding their craft in various directions, with alternate slow and frenzied strokes.

Suddenly, an enormous black whaleback emerged in the midst of the *praus*. The natives scattered in all directions, shouting and churning the water. With a sound like a tired locomotive, the "elephant fish" sank below the surface, only to reappear amid similar excitement further down the harbor. Just before he passed from sight, he won the game: one of the *prau* men had guessed wrong or ventured too close, and with his whole family was tumbled into the water. None of this appeared to engage even the attention, much less the interest, of the whale.

We put our Coconut Island tomcat ashore here, as he was getting to be a hell of a nuisance, & in place of him the Commander bought a fine white cockatoo parrot, which is yellow & white. He is reposing at present in a wooden cage on deck aft of the doghouse & is busy tearing the wooden slats of his cage to bits.

❂ ❂ ❂

The southeast wind filled the *Pilgrim's* sails just beyond the western channel of the Banda Islands, providing a gentle reach to the southwest across the Banda Sea to Portuguese Timor. It was at Koepang (Kupang), the chief port of the southern half of this island then under Dutch control that Captain Bligh and eighteen men landed their 23' open launch after their famous voyage from the scene of the mutiny. The chief port of the northern half of Timor is Dilli (D'li), and it was here that the southeast trade wind left us, apparently for the season. We were a disappointed crew who scanned a torrid and dusty settlement for some sign of the promise borne by the sandalwood-scented night wind that had come off the northern shore as we approached Timor.

The days are becoming hotter all the time, but it's great on board. At sea the clothing problem is very simple. I guess I've spent about twenty bucks on clothes in the

last fourteen months. At present I'm wearing out an old pair of white pants with the legs sheared off & the seat made of storm trysail canvas.

September 21. Commences running SW by W before a light breeze. Drifted along before it, having breakfast & locating the harbor east entrance from masthead. Nearly calm. Took in all sails just outside the reef & at same time were boarded by a dark man & the Portuguese pilot who had been sent out by the Captain of the Port. The dark bird took the wheel & the Pilot conned. The Chief started the engine. The Portuguese flag was hoisted at the fore, the US flag aft, the yellow flag at the main rigging & we triumphantly entered the harbor of Dilli.

While we saw nothing of southern Timor, the northern portion surely would have fulfilled no promises except to a weary crew of shipwrecked men. They would find, as we did on anchoring and going ashore, very dry land. There is little else of Nature's bounty here, short of snow-capped mountains many miles in the interior and the coffee grown on their foothills by Portuguese entrepreneurs. Each morning and evening, we saw a motley squad of jailbirds who were released from the barracks and drilled in a little square behind the waterfront. "Political prisoners" said to be in exile from Portugal were allowed the freedom of the town, at least during the day — mere existence in Dilli apparently being considered sufficient punishment for their offenses. Joe's capacity for finding the strange, wonderful, or enjoyable in any port was almost infinite, but here he returned from a trip ashore with a single prize: a dried salt cod from the Grand Banks, bought from a Chinese shopkeeper!

The skipper of the Dutch steamer *Reijeniersz,* Captain Grootenhuis, warned us of the strong tides and currents throughout the East Indies group and provided us with an elaborate table of the tides in Sapeh (Sape) Strait between Sumbawa and Komodo

Islands. The table covered the waters at every phase of the moon and was the product of much experience with the seven-knot current. However, we avoided the Strait altogether by passing south of the archipelago. We left Timor without a pang and continued our progress along the garland of islands to the westward — Alor, Solar, and Flores.

Joe made a fine roost for the parrot, & hitched him to it with a lanyard on a swivel on his leg. We can now carry him around & hang him anywhere.

"You must stop at Ende bay on Flores and see the colored lakes — red, green, and blue, all together," the Captain had encouraged.

We thought about it briefly as we neared the spot that was also the assistant resident's station on Flores. "Oh, the hell with the colored lakes," the Trader grumbled. "We know what they look like. Why not go on to Komodo and see what we've never seen: the dragon lizards?"

"Besides," the Skipper said, looking up from the *East Indies Pilot* and out toward land, "Ende Bay looks like a terrible place to lay."

Not for a yellow lake and a violet one thrown in would the Skipper willingly put in at "a terrible place to lay."

A light easterly wind expired completely, and the schooner became a power boat.

This is the third day we've been under power & I hope to hell the engine won't let us down from now on as we are getting into the waters where we will need it the most.

A whiff of burned diesel fuel will always conjure up for me a picture of a broken mountain range stretching endlessly along on the starboard hand, a slowly heaving oily sea, and a sulphur-crested cockatoo huddled in the shade of a dory, his crest drooping and his eyes looking out with listless resentment into the glare of sunlight that sends the thermometer below decks up to ninety-four degrees. Because the cockatoo ate wood and left about him a mess, I named him "Chips." Three days of this, with the fumes, smoke, and the heat becoming steadily more overpowering, found us heading up into the strait between Rinja and Komodo Islands, where we were in tide rips and bores, racing along with the current. Finally, we reached a quiet and protected anchorage behind an islet in the bay called Soro Go.

Here we saw no sign of human beings, only the dried brown mountainsides rising beyond a thick green thatch of mangroves which covered the shoreline. The only sounds were the occasional splash of a manta in the harbor and the cries of a flock of cockatoos, each identical with our own. Apparently they were calling Chips to join them, but he answered with spirit, presumably, to the effect that he was much safer and in general better off where he was, being regularly fed, made much of, and with plenty of fine ship's carpentry work to deface.

Just before rounding the point we hooked a fine "silver jack" on our troll & he went very well baked for dinner in the evening. This island has much the same appearance as the Galapagos.... This anchorage is completely shut off from the sea & we are enclosed by mountains rising right out of the water & going up 1,000 – 1,500 feet all about us. It's great scenery & very wild, rugged & desolate looking & "great lizard country," according to the Skipper.... It's 14,420 miles from Boston to here by the way we've come, so we're more than half way around the world at present.

Shortly before reaching Komodo, we discovered that the exhaust pipe had cracked at a not easily accessible joint well aft in the lazarette. Spare foresail, hawsers, ropes, fishing gear, and all the miscellaneous boatswain's stores, as well as every square inch of exposed timber and planking, were thickly covered with carbon black. A lovely day at anchor passed in removing and scrubbing clean every bit of the sooty gear and the lazarette, while Joe fitted a brass collar over the leak and fastened it with a stout serving, well-plastered with red lead.

The next day, we set out to find a dragon lizard, a prehistoric species endemic to the island. I had trouble conveying our purpose with my limited and recently acquired knowledge of the Malay language to two natives who had come alongside the *Pilgrim* in a canoe. *Tjitjak besar* seemed to describe the monster *Varanus* comprehensibly, but I also handed them a crude sketch of something like a dinosaur drawn by a four-year-old child. One of our native guides ashore wore only a sarong and walked with bare feet, while the more cosmopolitan of the two wore a pajama coat, dungarees, and flashy blue and white "sport" shoes. As we filed as silently as possible up the dried and stony stream bed, we startled a great variety of wild life, from parrots, yellow birds, and blue wood pigeons, to some wild boar and a kind of antelope.

First we proceeded through very flat, sun-baked country dotted with palms & thickets. We got into the bush as we got further up the valley. The old stream bed was overgrown with large trees & vines & in some places it was just like going through a tunnel.

After several hours in the merciless heat, which was considerably aggravated by the barrels of the shotgun I was carrying, we returned to a flat, hard-baked piece of ground behind the beach. It was there that we saw one of the famous dragon lizards, standing on all fours in the tufted grass. From our distance of about 60', he appeared to be a cross between a small lizard and a crocodile, and some 10' from the tip of the nose to the tip of the tail. His brownish olive color blended well with the dusty ground and parched vegetation, but as he immediately raised his belly from the ground and ran fast for cover, we were not able to get a very satisfactory view of him. I later learned that five of the creatures were brought to New York City's Bronx Zoo where, had we not been so far afield, we might have examined them more closely at our leisure — if, that is, we had gotten there before they all died, which was shortly after their arrival.

That afternoon, a giant albino manta appeared near the schooner. The Chief and the Trader immediately went after it in the motor dory, guided by directions which I waved from the masthead from where I followed his lazy dives and turns. They were unable to plant a harpoon in the creature. It was probably just as well, since the giant ray is said to be formidable when stirred up, and this one measured 15' from one wing tip to the other.

> *September 28. Anchored at Soro Go. Turned out 6 A.M. to find another fine day. Stowed awning & got our anchor up at same time the Cook purchased some fowls & eggs from some Malays in a canoe alongside. Underway at 7:15 & steamed out of the snug anchorage. Very little wind & that dead ahead, blowing up Linta Strait.*

For the passage from Komodo to the west along the south coasts of Sumbawa and Lombok, we called again on the engine. There was a light easterly breeze during some of the daylight hours, to be sure, and an all-sail enthusiast, by diligent use of the anchor, might have been able to keep from being sucked into one of the straits by the tide, and to hold steerageway for enough of the time even to make some westing, but the all-sail game has never seemed to me worth carrying to such a point. Even so, we were nearly reduced to the same situation by necessity, when the diesel rebelled by spurting fuel oil all over the engine room through worn pump packing. The Chief lost a good deal of sleep, though none of his good nature, before we had the engine turning over smoothly again.

September 29. When asked if he wanted to stop the engine, the Chief said, "Bali or Bust!"

chapter 15

Bali

THE BEST ANCHORAGE on the southern coast of Bali is at
Benoa, in a little bay which makes in from the east at the neck of
the southern peninsula called Tafel Hoek. For the benefit of those
who might breeze confidently up to the winding channel and be
suddenly confronted with what looks like a forest of spindles
bearing assorted wicker-work on their tops, together with
seventeen well-bunched sailing canoes all racing together for the
channel to catch the slack tide, it may avoid some of the confusion
and anxiety we experienced to know that the spherical cages are
to be passed on the starboard hand. Meanwhile, the dark brown
inverted scrap-baskets corresponding to our black or green buoys
should be kept to port.

Our neighbors at the anchorage were for the most part a fleet
of fishing sampans. Each was about 40' long and painted and
striped in bright yellows, reds, and blues, and almost entirely
decked over with steeply sloped thatched roofs. Figureheads and
boom crutches were carved into the likenesses of gamecocks and
griffins. Each carried a kind of lateen sail and appeared to be the
permanent dwelling for a whole family. A large Chinese junk
joined us and, after crashing into our port rail, discharged onto
the dock a cargo of heaven knows what, tied up in burlap sacks.

She then deliberately went aground for a bottom cleaning. The Oriental and rather primitive aspect of these craft contrasted with what I saw on the foreshore, which bore a modern Dutch cement wharf surrounded by a strictly geometrical fence of galvanized piping and wire mesh. The sight of this structure was a little disappointing to the ship's company, who murmured, "So *this* is Bali?" and wondered if we were too late to see the exotic beauty of the island before its transformation by Western enterprise.

Seven miles up the road from the waterfront is the principal town of southern Bali, Den Pasar, a town of tinkling pony cart bells and music. The road is lined with family compounds, or *kampongs,* enclosed by lichened brick walls and entered by humans through a main gateway normally ornamented with gray or red sandstone deeply sculptured with the forms of demons, gods, and sometimes Dutchmen in hard hats or even on bicycles. I have said that the *kampongs* are thus entered *by humans* because I discovered they are designed as well to prevent entry by unfriendly spirits. To this end, gargoyles are fashioned in the stone work, threatening and glaring at inimical intruders. Just inside the gate is a section of wall standing alone and placed so that to get inside, you must turn an abrupt corner — something which an evil spirit hell-bent for mischief is supposed to be unable to do.

Inside each compound is a collection of small isolated buildings made of wood and thatch, used for sleeping, cooking, and eating. In every case is one or more carved stone shrine or spirit shelters that resemble something like Chinese bird-houses. In these shrines are regularly placed offerings of rice, corn, flowers, and money. The offerings are renewed as often as they are used up by the god of the particular compound or other spirit for whom they were intended, either by the process of natural decomposition or through the depredations of hungry birds or passers-by. The family dead, at least until cremation, reside intimately within the compound in a tall, pagoda-like pile.

> From Hod Fuller's journal: The people are very child-like in many ways. The men fly huge kites about 18–20 feet high with bamboo cords. They also tie little wooden whistles to the birds' necks & then let them go & the whistles blow as the birds fly about.

> Inland the country is very green & luxurious with many bamboo groves and deep gorges full of water. The people are very industrious & spend much of their time building up old ruins, carving wooden & stone images, or working in the fields. They have a sort of water buffalo for cattle & also use them in carts.

> The women and girls sure are easy to look at & some of them are very beautiful. They have fine figures and wear nothing above the waist. They have long black hair, delicate features & very white teeth when they don't chew betel nut.

It is already evident to me that the Balinese are an intensely religious people, in the primary sense of believing in the existence of personified, non-human forces which have powers for both good and evil, and believing moreover that they can control, or at least influence, these spirits by cajolery with various forms of respect, paper money, and brick walls. I learned that an industrious Balinese gives a good half of his yearly produce or income to the gods. It seemed to me that not a day passed on the island without seeing at least one procession of young women bearing on their heads large and elaborately arranged offertory heaps of ripe fruits, vegetables, and flowers to some temple service. Each separate rice paddy, or *sawah*, has its own little shrine — raised on a pole and roofed for protection — to the god of that field and often others as well — for example, to the god of rice in general,

Shiva, the representative of the creative force.

The religion of the Balinese people is a hybrid form of Brahman Hinduism which involves conceptions of Brahma, Vishnu, Shiva, Krishna, and other deities. Aspects of these deities are interrelated in such a complicated way that surely only the most learned of priests could keep the theology straight. Brought up under the comparatively simple Western theological set-up, I found the Brahman theology as confusing and inarticulate as a Hindu design. Brahma is the beginning and end of everything, and yet Shiva represents the creative force — not only that but, unexpectedly, the destructive force as well and yet not unexpectedly, because Shiva is only an aspect of Brahma anyway. Other Balinese hold that Shiva is the highest god and ignore Brahma; still others that Vishnu alone is worthy of respect.

The variety of emphasis found among the followers of Hinduism, together with the unanimity with which the teachers declare Brahma to be the father of them all, might cause some surprise among Western visitors at the apparent flexibility of Brahman doctrine, were it not that an even greater elasticity, extending to head-on conflict of fundamental concepts, is found among the followers of the comparatively young Christian religion.

So far as I could determine, the various brands of Hinduism flourish peacefully side by side: at a monster religious festival at Besakih on Gunung Agung (God Mountain), the colors of Brahma, Shiva, Vishnu, and Krishna — red, white, black, and yellow respectively — flew together from the pavilions. For all that, the truth may be that the liveliest part of the Balinese people's religion is their animistic sense of being surrounded by the immediate spirits of everyday life. The truth may also be that the fear, wonder, and thankfulness engendered by this animism finds a ready means of personal and artistic expression in the forms and rituals of Brahmanistic observance, of which the priests alone know the official significance. I have ventured on these ill-informed remarks in an attempt to explain the pervasiveness of religion on Bali. There is scarcely any activity which is not colored by it, not the least of all their cockfights.

There is some feeling against cockfighting among the Dutch, who apparently disapprove of betting, at least by the natives. When I asked the manager of the Bali Hotel where I could see a cockfight, he replied that cockfighting was illegal. This was egregiously misleading. On special occasions, a license could be obtained to stage a cockfight legally. However that might be, all you had to do was inquire in fumbling Malay, using the word *djalan,* and you could find your way to a cockpit on any day of the week. It wasn't a hole-in-the-corner affair, either.

One day, I found a full acre of open ground near principal streets swarming with people, just as you would find at a fair. I already had seen hundreds of gamecocks kept in small wicker cages outside nearly every house, and watched as here and there two owners, each sitting on his haunches and holding a cage containing his favorite bird, discussed their bird's relative ferocity and courage. From time to time each idly advanced the cages to exhibit his gladiator's spirit. The hotel manager to the contrary, the gamecocks were not always so cooped up, cheated of the game for which they were bred — and for which they would die.

Coming upon a "main" in full swing, I saw a number of birds ranged around a square pit at the center of the crowd. A new fight was about to begin between a splendid black bird with a long restless neck and a rather quieter yellow one, whose neck feathers had a mangy appearance from being plucked by enemy beaks in previous encounters. The crowd looked them over while a 3", double-edged, and almost razor-sharp spur was bound to the right leg of each, and bets were made.

There was some laughing and kidding, but no disorder. A bet spoken across the twenty-four foot pit was easily heard: it was at first derided but finally accepted. I noticed a little cross-legged man, like all the other men wearing a turban and sarong, make an entry in a notebook. Then the birds were brought to the center of the pit by their handlers, approached a few times to whip up their mettle and released. They each made a short circle to their right and leapt into the air at each other. It looked like a harmless and bungling collision but in the next moment a black head was in the sand.

The next fight was not over so quickly. A red rooster had no heart for the battle and ran for the sideline. He was retrieved by his handler who put a bottomless cage, too small to allow for movement inside, over him and his adversary. The cage was raised a trifle and after a short interval the red bird emerged in a panic and again scurried for protection. This time, the little cross-legged man declared the bird remaining under the cage as the winner. The Chief, who had come with me, remarked with some pride that such a coward as the red bird would have his neck wrung in short order at any respectable cockfight in Massachusetts, where gamecocks have been raised with so much fear of ignominy that running out rarely occurs.

Everywhere you find fighting roosters in neat little round wicker cages & boys pass by with them under their arms. They also fight crickets in little bamboo tubes with slits cut in them so you can watch.

I...came on a big rooster fight. They use a slasher type of spur here & only tie one on the birds, but they seem to be able to do a hell of a lot of damage with them. There were several hundred natives at the fight & they all were doing a lot of betting before each fight & they had rules far different from the ones used at home.

At this point, an *entr'acte* took place. The sand of the pit was swept and a bamboo altar, standing on stilts about 5' high, was brought into the center by a priest. A vase of flowers, a bowl of water, and some *lontar* fruit were arranged on the raised platform while the priest uttered an invocation to the god of the cockpit. I was told that certain of the gods require blood sacrifices, which used to be satisfied with the blood of humans, but since that practice is outlawed, the blood of the fighting cocks effects the same expiation.

Those who were taking a rest from the fighting or perhaps had only come for socializing were strolling about in groups behind the ringside audience, now and then refreshing themselves with a snack handed up on a *lontar* leaf by a *vendeuse* who sat half-naked on the ground at her portable table. A mixture of black, white, and red rice, coconut, *pisang* (banana), and pig sausage, together with a grated scarlet substance as a condiment, sold for the price of two cash, or about a third of a cent.

I attended a special cock fighting "main" at which a hundred birds fought from dawn till dark at the estate of Mrs. P., the widow of an Australian bishop. After the battles were over and darkness had descended, the cockpit, illuminated by lightning, became the scene of an elaborate pantomime. This was executed by young girl dancers wearing heavily ornamented, gold paper headdresses, or *papier maché* demon's heads, according to the parts they played in stories from Hindu mythology. Although the entire dancer's body is swathed in an encircling sarong, or kind of winding sheet, their little feet are left free and skip over the sand with such amazing lightness that they seem continuously just above the ground. A ceaselessly fluttering fan, and sometimes two, one in each hand, enhanced the impression of a creature lighter than air. The fan's fluttering so heightened the impression of motion that at times the entire figure seemed fluid, to a point where I found it impossible to separate the movement of one part of the dancer's body from another.

At other times the rapid motion stopped, and the dancer

executed a series of postures, an important part of which were conventional grimaces which occurred again and again. They had, to my Western eye, no counterpart in any natural facial expression. It was with something of a shock then, that I saw this unreal little creature put out a hand in passing to adjust the wick of an oil lamp set on a box in the middle of the ring. At another point, it seemed to me an outrage on the dancer's remoteness when another little girl, perhaps her sister, stepped forward and, without interrupting the dance, rearranged her girdle. These incidents suggested the intimacy between the Balinese and their religious and artistic observances, and reminded me of the remark of a character in a book I had read: "The only truly religious countries are those in which the peasants light their cigarettes at the altar candles."

The dancing was accompanied by a full *gamelan*, or orchestra. The sounds of the *gamelan* were almost entirely percussion, the tune (or at least the predominating sounds — you could hardly say there was a separate melody) being carried by xylophones, accompanied by brass gongs ranging from little ones supported horizontally on cords to deep pendant boomers over 2' in diameter. There were a few flutes and an instrument which resembled a one-stringed violin. The notes played appeared to be all those in the Western scale, with the invariable, and, it seemed to me, rather perverse exception of the second and sixth, and with no chromatics.

A striking characteristic of the compositions worked out of these few notes was the persistent repetition of a simple motif by the smaller instruments playing more or less in unison, while the deep gongs boomed away on their own like fire bells in the distance. To anyone who has heard Balinese music, it will be evident that the foregoing are the remarks of a passing sailor rather than of a musician. This was brought home after listening one evening to a recital in Den Pasar. I thought it was charming and exciting enough, but it sounded pretty much like all the rest I had heard. "That," Mrs. P. remarked, leaning my way, "was caviar."

Worked with Joe cleaning the topsides during the morning. Then headed ashore for Den Pasar with the Skipper & walked around & saw several native festivals and the best dancing I've seen anywhere. At the dance I ran into a fellow named Hogan who was a year behind me in college. He is going around the world & just got out of business school last June. Had dinner at the Bali Hotel & then listened to a performance of the *gamelan* in front of the hotel. This *gamelan* playing is said to be the best in Bali. There was also some fine dancing here by some little Balinese girls. Returned to the vessel about midnight.

From the ship's log: October 7. Anchored at Benoa. Showers early. Reael, the Dutch steamer from Batavia, left at low water, 6:30 A.M., with 1,000 pigs in individual wicker crates for Singapore.

Once every five years, a religious festival takes place at Besakih, the great temple on the lower slopes of 10,000' high Gunung Agung in the interior, which thousands of Balinese attend. In a chartered automobile, the Skipper, the Trader, the Chief, and I climbed and circled the rolling hills and valleys of the country region, nearly every foot of which was intensely culti-vated for rice and, to some extent, coffee, sugar, and *kapok* — the silky fiber obtained from the fruit of the silk cotton tree. I learned that the rice terraces are connected by an irrigation system perfected over centuries by a close guild of experts, to maintain perfect balance and use all of the limited supply of water to the utmost. There are sometimes forty or fifty levels of these glassy terraces to a hill, and in places they are all one can see for miles, except for an occasional figure under a broad conical hat laboring at a dike, and hundreds of little shrines.

The villages along the way were decorated for the festival with long drooping leaves, the fronds of which stood 20' in the air, and with other leaves and grasses in geometrical designs, and streamers and pennons of the colors of the gods. As we approached Besakih, we fell in with an increasing number of devotees along the road, bearing squealing pigs and ornamental mounds of fruit to the feast.

There must have been five thousand Balinese collected at Besakih, a cluster of temples, for religious rites and feasts, with no more than fifty of us whites among them. I thought that as representatives of another culture we would excite at least mild curiosity, but the Balinese paid no attention to us whatever.

It is seldom that a Balinese man or woman even shifts the eyes to look at a car full of Americans or, for that matter, of Dutchmen either. This, I learned, is a real and not an affected indifference. The rural Balinese is secure in his way of living, his relations with his family, his fellows and his ancestors, and his religion. He has adopted none of the European customs or ways of thinking that have so changed the face of Polynesia. He continues to dress in a sarong and turban kerchief, and to eschew dungaree trousers and shirts. He has no movies nor does he ape the western *kau poi* as does the Tuamotuan, and the Christian religion has made no headway with him. There may well be a certain amount of contempt in his attitude. Early in the century, before World War I, the Dutch mistakenly sent a punitive expedition against South Bali, attacking natives from the water with shells and bullets. The reigning prince gathered his retinue and family about him and headed in a solemn procession to the shore, where, as a gesture of supreme contempt, all who had not been shot fell under the krisses of their own priests, the prince included.

The affair at Besakih was again like a Hindu design in that it seemed to the Western eye to be entirely without plan or form. People walked about the terraces of what looked like an abandoned temple up on the mountain side. Here and there a feast was in progress, the food spread all over the ground. Altars were scattered about, heaped high with ripe bananas and other fruits, and ghastly looking corpses of pigs. An outdoor theater held a continuous performance to a standing audience, most of the actors wearing grotesque masks of comic and fierce mien, and speaking in falsetto voices. A number of Brahman priests had set up shop at scattered points and were sitting cross-legged on covered bamboo platforms which were raised above the ground on stilts. One seamy-faced old fellow wearing a gold miter at least a foot high was kept very busy by supplicants who came before him with the names of relatives who had died since the last performance. For each of these, the old priest took a lotus flower from his collection, removed a petal, and with ritualistic movements of his long-nailed hands that were a dance in themselves, touched each to a little fire that burned in an urn before him, gave it the name of a departed soul, uttered an invocation over it in a precise monotone, and finally blew it off into space.

My understanding of all these rituals was the dimmer, of course, for my ignorance of the languages. While I had picked up a few words and expressions in the Malay tongue, these were merely of the *lingua franca* used by natives in dealing with foreigners. They gave no clue to what the Balinese were saying among themselves. There are three principal languages in Bali, we are given to understand, each of which is the language proper to one of the three main caste levels. A Balinese uses the language of the caste level of the person he is speaking to. Thus, it is at least theoretically, if not socially, likely for a conversation to be carried on in three different languages. A Balinese who is conversant only with his own language is presumably precluded from all conversation with his own fellow citizens, even his neighbors who are differently placed in the social scale.

However, we knew none of these languages. They are so far removed from the Malay we acquired as the usual tourist's equipment of handy phrases and elementary vocabulary that their words appear to have no common root whatsoever. Moreover, this sort of discussion, aside from being probably quite vulnerable to those who know about such things, gets the ship nowhere.

During the week the schooner lay at Benoa, time had been found to work on her. The Chief mended the leak in the fuel oil pumps, the port bumpkin was straightened and the topsides touched up to remove the traces of the collision with the junk, and the deck trim and teak were sandpapered and varnished. Bright and gleaming with these evidences of the sustained morale of her crew, the *Pilgrim* finally weighed anchor — although minus poor Vahine Tahiti, who had disappeared overboard into the strong tide, without a trace.

The *Pilgrim* put out into the turbulent, tide-driven waters of Benoa Channel and fought her way toward Bali Strait and the Java Sea. A flood tide should have been favorable on our northerly course, but there was instead a strong set to the south which, meeting a fresh breeze from east-southeast, set up a tide rip which rocked us like a dazed prize fighter assailed by a quick succession of right and left hooks to the chin. With all lowers pulling and the engine running, we forced our way in four hours through only fourteen miles of the devilish bobble. By nightfall, we were clear of Lombok Strait and taking a last look at Gunung Agung, its Olympian summit high above the clouds.

The question which I have been asked more than any other about Bali is, "But isn't Bali overrun with tourists now?" I know nothing of North Bali, where the cruise ships anchor in Buleleng Road, except that it is there that the largest city and the greatest commercial interests are. Because the women of those parts are now compelled to clothe themselves above the waist, and for other reasons as well, nearly every tourist motors over the mountains for a look at South Bali and its people. Even so, the proportion of whites seen on the streets in Den Pasar, where there are also several hundred Dutch officials, is so small as to be scarcely noticeable, and it is certainly far from what could be called "overrun."

chapter 16

To Singapore Via Java

From the ship's log: October 11. 2–4 P.M. Fine going. Swell dead astern & sails swung out to a freshening breeze. Continuing past Madura, which appears quite unlike Bali, the heights being about on an equal low level & giving a corrugated appearance to the skyline. 7:30 P.M. Off Surabaya. Can see the glare of the city.

In the Java Sea, once past the north coast of Madura, the island of bulls, the *Pilgrim* had a fair amount of company: a steamer, a tug, and a great many small fishing *praus* which carried a flimsy and unwieldy-looking lateen rig. The natives appeared to handle these craft with an ease born of long practice and familiarity. The winds were light those days, and I imagined a sudden or strong blow would call for phenomenal activity among the crews.

The *Pilgrim* carried her running lights at night as she always did without fail, no matter what the likelihood of meeting another ship. Some of the small craft, on seeing her approach, lighted flares to avoid being run down. One of them apparently failed to notice our lights, and we could have shaken hands over the quarter rail with her crew as we passed had they recovered sufficiently from their excitement before being left in the darkness astern. The next day we passed several gaff-rigged ketches, each carrying three jibs on a long jib boom, and two topsails. Each also had a high stern gallery projecting over the quarters and beyond the stern, and was clearly reminiscent in profile of the raised-pooped Western traders of centuries past.

October 12. 9 A.M.

We passed three ketches on the lee,
Exactly like the craft you'd see
In Fourteen Hundred Ninety-three.
They almost struck us dumb — O.
The Commander stared across the side,
At the jib booms raking far and wide.
"Today's Columbus Day!" he cried,
"And here comes CHRIS COLOMBO!"

October 13. 6–8 A.M. After breakfast wind died away. Hot but fine. Continued drifting along. A few native craft in sight. One, much resembling a pirate in appearance, came quite close before wearing around.

The variable easterly winds continued very light as we slid past the chain of mountains, with half-a-dozen peaks 10,000' to 12,000' high, which runs through Java. The temperature in the shade of the chart house reached ninety-five degrees in the middle of the day. It was deadly sea snake weather again, and we brought out the shot guns and picked off a few for fun. Despite the snowy peaks above the clouds in the distance, we were at sea level only a few hundred miles south of the Equator.

From Hod Fuller's journal: Hot as hell during the morning so we rigged a bosun's chair hung from the end of the bowsprit & sat in it dragging along in the water. It's a lot of fun & a fine way to keep cool.

By means of six-star fix at twilight and some dead reckoning, I estimated that at approximately 2:18 A.M. on 14 October 1933, the *Pilgrim* crossed the meridian 180 degrees from her starting point, one year, three months, and twenty-four days out of Boston. There was no celebration, nor even excitement at this statistical news, as everyone was asleep except me and the Skipper, and the Skipper was never given to expressions of his emotion.

> **Passed close to two great looking sailing *praus* which were becalmed. They had a crew of eight or ten, and were rowing along in the calm sea with their fishnets hung above them to act as awnings. The Trader threw several packages of cigarettes at the boats as we went by & completely disorganized the crews who started a mad scramble & even jumped overboard after some packages floating in the water.**

The shipping increased as we neared Tanjung Priok and Batavia (Jakarta), the principal port of the Dutch East Indies (Indonesia). On our last night offshore, an overtaking steamer showed no sign of heeding a bright searchlight the Skipper beamed against the mainsail and, had I not luffed-up to slow the schooner down at the last moment, would have run us over. Six days after leaving Benoa, we ran in past Tanjung Priok and recognized the white dome of the Royal Yacht Club which Captain Grootenhuis had roughly sketched for us at Timor Dilli on a hand-made chart of the anchorage.

Following his directions as closely as possible, we found ourselves in two and a half fathoms of water among a forest of fish weirs. Finally, we were guided out of the danger and our confusion by a friendly local yachtsman in a 6-meter boat who led us in through the obvious channel between two long breakwaters to a protected basin near the yacht club. The members at once opened the club house and welcomed us with unrestrained, though not undignified, cordiality.

The Trader lingered ashore that night after the dory had

returned to the schooner. Being lightly dressed and somewhat warm to boot, or so he claimed, he swam out to the schooner, hung his soaking clothes in the rigging and went happily to sleep. You can imagine his disgust on discovering the next morning that the canal which runs through populous Batavia, carrying all of its sewage, empties into the very basin where we lay at anchor. He gave himself and his clothes a frenzied scrubbing. He may have been over-squeamish. The Javanese constantly use the same canal for bathing, washing their clothes, and even brushing their teeth.

The Cook did not come back aboard at all that night. In the morning a uniformed messenger delivered a card on which was typewritten the following:

To the Captain & Owner, S/Y PILGRIM

Dear Sir,
 The Chief Steward is not abel te com on bord becorse he has to go to the genral politie had Quaters for investigation
Yuor truly
(Signature)

It turned out that our chief and only steward had by no means been misbehaving. While riding innocuously back to the wharf in a taxi cab, he was struck by a car driven by a white resident who was under the influence of alcohol and knocked into a nearby field. It was necessary to hire an English speaking Malay named Oudin to take over the galley work for the next few days while the poor fellow recovered from a number of cuts and bruises.

After a visit from several reporters, a two-column account of the ship, her company, and the voyage was published in *De Java-Bode*, in which appeared the following remarks upon the Skipper's appearance:

Met een grof gevlochten Panama van eigenaardig model op het hoofd, pijp in den mond, uilenbril voor de pienter twinkelende oogen, had de captain, wiens bovenlichaam met de prachtigste adelaren en ander gevogelte getatoueerd was en wiens onderlichaam in een kain Djocja was gehult, meer het voorkomen van een Chineeschen jonk-kapitein dan van den gezagvoerder van een Amerikaansch jacht.

[Translation: With a coarsely-woven, singularly-styled Panama hat on his head, a pipe in his mouth, and owlish spectacles before his brightly twinkling eyes, the captain, whose upper body was tattooed with the finest eagles and other birds and whose lower body was wrapped in a Jakja sarong, had more the appearance of a Chinese junk-captain than of the master of an American yacht.]

This gentle crack (of which, without John's help, we could only get the drift) was entirely good-natured and sympathetic. The account ended with the single flattering sentence: *Ons respect* (Our respect).

Ten leisurely days anchored at Tanjung Priok gave us time to spruce up the vessel — with sandpaper, varnish, and paint — as well as to replace the badly corroded copper exhaust pipe which had caused such a mess east of Komodo. For pardonable luxury as well as added safety (thinking of the steamer which had nearly run us down), the kerosene running lights were replaced by bright electric lights connected with the 32-volt battery circuit.

Sunday afternoon I went ashore with Joe to look for a bit of fun in the native quarter. We ran into a fellow named "Baltimore Charlie" who ran the "Radio Cafe" and camped there for a while sampling beer. I later took in the local moving picture (a Wild West thriller) with a cute little Sudanese girl in tow. We went to a native play after the moving pictures where the natives were acting out a wild west play as cowboys and hard-case cow punchers. It was funny as hell to see their idea of the western frontier as they really believe things still are in America. Returned to the Radio Cafe with my little packet in tow and heard a hell of a commotion in

the back street and looked into it & there was the *Pilgrim's* mate dressed in a sarong, hat & pair of sandals playing *rajah* with a harem of about twenty girls surrounding him. We had a few more drinks and raised hell with all the girls & natives there. They're a lot of fun and damned merry. Got back to the vessel so late that I had to swim aboard.

The Trader and I traveled by narrow gauge railway into the upland interior some 300 miles to the city of Djokakarta, the seat of one of the greater *rajahs*, who was like all the others, except under Dutch control. I saw no hint of political dependence in the sight of this proud fellow driving about in his ornate open carriage. He was attended by dozens of walking retainers, one carrying high the ruler's gold *sirii* box (containing His Highness' betel nut chewing mixture), another his ceremonial sword, and another his gold spittoon. My recollection of many interesting details of the procession is sketchy at best because I was occupied during most of its passage in attempting to record it with a motion picture camera, with which I was quite unfamiliar. The film, which was badly under-exposed, shows dimly some white horses and the silhouette of a boy on a bicycle crossing in the foreground.

There are many skilled artisans in Djokja, as it is usually called, who make gold and silver jewelry, and elaborately designed batiks for use as loin cloths, head dresses, and the like. The true batiks, commonly available now, are made by painting with hot wax held in a brass cup on the end of a stylus and dyeing the rest. Although every design is traditional and has a meaning, I managed to purchase a piece which an old lady, working constantly for a year, had decorated with 160 squares, in each of which was a different and complex pattern. The simple overall patterns denote districts, while others denote the property of specific clans and families, much like Scotch tartans.

Segment of the temple.

At the end of a short motor trip through the paddy fields from Djokja, the Trader and I came on the monument of the Boroboedoer. Built in the eighth century but mysteriously unfinished, it is the most important Buddhist monument in Java. Although some 60' high, it was once almost completely buried, possibly to preserve it from Islamic invaders, and lay undiscovered by foreigners for centuries. It is a mound in the shape of a pyramid, dressed and terraced in gray and lichened stone and surrounded by four galleries. The walls of the galleries are covered with relief carvings of gods and men which illustrate Sanskrit texts. The monument is decorated at frequent intervals with bell-like stupas, or shrines, inside of which are images of Buddha.

Aside from a pleasant sensation of elevated remoteness and a good view of the surrounding countryside, however, it is difficult for an Occidental of virtually no acquaintance with the culture which produced Boroboedoer to experience any specific or appropriate emotion while climbing its ancient steps. We were told it was a place for priests to walk about and meditate, but as no part of it offers a square foot of shade, I thought it fit only to fry lizards on in the blazing white sun of a Javanese summer's day. The Trader and I left the monument early. After a drink of Coca-Cola at the hotel, we rolled on the train down to the seacoast to rejoin our shipmates.

❂ ❂ ❂

After a simultaneous visit from a fuel oil barge, a water barge, and a ship chandler's delivery launch (known to us also in the Skipper's lexicon as a "pickle boat"), the schooner's depleted stores were replenished for her next passage. It is something of a pity that a ship is never really at home in what is supposed to be her element. Every winged flight across the water is a race from one base of supplies to the next. If her means of propulsion blows out or gives out, or if any one of a hundred fatal conditions,

Another segment of the temple.

whether from rot, worms, fire, stress, or weather, defies the most careful preparations and cannot be remedied at sea, her crew must eventually perish from lack of water or food or from scurvy.

It is a race which is sometimes lost by the crew but won by the ship — witness the great bark which, it is said, was abandoned among the Tuamotus some years ago, only to sail herself without a soul on board over the hundreds of miles of ocean to Tahiti and *through the narrow pass into Papeete Harbor* where her ragged sails hung becalmed while a photograph was taken in proof of the event. I do not wish to magnify the dangers which can beset even a well-found and well-handled vessel at sea or her crew, but only to indulge in the reflection that every voyage is, in some degree, a *tour de force*. A ship does not make man again the fish he was. Hence the oil barge, which unloaded 562 gallons of diesel fuel, the water barges, which unloaded 1,140 gallons, and the ship chandler's launch, which brought the usual array of supplies that suit a schooner and others that suit any boat.

Since Tanjung Priok, unlike Maupiti, is not the sort of place where the natives say goodbye by hauling in the anchor for you, we bent our backs to the windlass, making frequent stops to flush the black mud out of every chain link. We were soon powering out between the jetties and heading just east of north for Gaspar Strait (Salat Kelasa) and Sarawak. It was only one instance of the elasticity of the *Pilgrim's* plans that we did clear for Sarawak, armed with a letter of introduction to "the only white *rajah* in the world," with the intention of going on afterward to Bangkok. A day later we changed our course and headed, after passing through Gaspar Strait, for Singapore.

The regions which we forswore seemed then, as now, among the most interesting of places reached by water. Yet, there comes a time in every cruise when home is no longer the port you left behind so much as the port you are returning to. With the halfway meridian passed, that time had come. For one thing, the *Pilgrim* had turned out to be a fairly big vessel for one in relatively modest circumstances to maintain. For another, although we had completed more than half the voyage, there was still a long way to go, and we were sixteen months out of Boston. At 6:00 a.m. on October 30, 1933, we were off a rocky promontory called Tanjung Sau. The Skipper puffed on his pipe and said, "Very pretty: like Maine." I saw what he meant, and took it as another sign that the horses were smelling the stable.

> *October 25. 10–12 P.M. The new electric side lights illuminate the immediate vicinity like a drug store window. They should be visible at a considerable distance.*

> *October 27. 9 A.M. We are now in the China Sea. 10-12 P.M. Running NNW wing & wing. Smooth sea, light breeze, SSE. Very hazy sky with numerous "trade clouds" moving with fair speed across the face of the half-moon. Most of the outfit sleeping on deck.*

Joe has been busy recutting the clews to the raffee all day. They were badly pulled out of shape after all the good hard service the sail has seen.

On the afternoon of our fifth day out of Batavia, we brought up the schooner with a round turn in the harbor of Singapore. Lying midway between India and China, it is the most important port on the trade route to the Far East. At the direction of the Port Captain, we dropped anchor in the mud near several dozen steamers which, rusted and rotten, lay side by side at their anchors. There had been a similar "boneyard" at Tanjung Priok, and I was told it denoted a sudden depression in Eastern shipping.

Nevertheless, all around the harbor were Dutch, Chinese, Siamese, British, and Australian inter-island tramp freighters, junks, feluccas, catamarans, and schooners. Some of them were spotless, and some were in a most disreputable state of deterioration. A number were nondescript and unidentifiable. Some were being coaled by the primitive method of baskets handled by sweating coolies, while others were receiving or discharging bales, boxes, and bags of various descriptions and content. Much of the tin and rubber of the world then came from Malaya and was shipped from here.

The harbor itself was a viscous pool in which hundreds of sampans, most of which seemed to be moving most of the time, pushed their way through decayed vegetables, broken boxes, and general filth. They ferried seamen to and from the shore, looking for odd errands to do, and added to the impression I had of general blistering confusion. Since the harbor was as crowded as a dance floor, there was a constant jumble of sounds — toots, cries, the rattle of winches, the ribald laughter of American yachtsmen, and the churning of propellers. A sound like a gigantic wicker chair being slowly twisted that came in the night turned out to be a Chinese junk passing by. The smells were amazing and indescribable since they came mostly from Oriental cooking and such things as hides which no American board of health would allow at large.

The backdrop for this maritime "crossroads of the East" was a conventional white man's creation of a row of tall stone buildings — the Hong Kong and Shanghai Bank, the Singapore Club (this with a brownstone façade that might have been on Fifth Avenue) — and similar solid erections extending along the waterfront in unbroken blocks as far as one could see, clear to the famous Raffles Hotel. The intrinsically undistinguished name of "Raffles" was that of the man who first saw the strategic importance to trade in the Far East of the island at the tip of the Malay Peninsula. In 1819, Raffles purchased it for the British Government on behalf of the East India Company from the Sultan of Johore, once and for all stopping the Dutch in the fight for trade dominance. For this access of imagination, the colonial administrator became Sir Stamford Raffles and the Father of Singapore, now one of the busiest ports in the world.

There was an active Flying Club in Singapore. Planes flying over the harbor were so numerous and so sportive that "Pop" Stevens, then an octogenarian ship chandler who rowed daily several miles in a single-seat wherry, wore a scarlet pith helmet to avoid being picked off by them. His craft was also fitted with a rear view mirror and a foot-operated horn to help him navigate among the dense traffic of sampans.

The European front which Singapore presents to the harbor is but a superficial one. Behind it is an Asiatic city. In not many minutes sitting behind a trotting rickshaw coolie, one could arrive in a section that was, I understand, as completely Chinese as Peking. I saw nothing but Chinese people, Chinese shops, Chinese signs, Chinese clothes, and heard nothing, as best I could discern, but the Chinese language. In a square lit by flares were a number of open sheds where coolies gathered for their simple meals. For a few cents, a dingy old woman left her bowl of rice while she filled one for me from her simmering iron kettles. I was then free to eat, assuming that I was handy with chopsticks and didn't mind borrowing a pair of used ones while I sat on a wooden stool.

In another section of the city, I saw the mosques and huts of the ubiquitous Indians, while out in the vicinity of Geylang Road was the Japanese colony. In this latter section, a Mr. Kaneta operated the Japanese equivalent of an apothecary shop, which he obligingly closed with shutters and left when told there were in the *Pilgrim* some virgin areas of backs and arms whose owners had been looking forward to embellishment with his tattooing needles ever since his fame had been brought to Boston by the crew of the schooner *Chance*. The chart house was turned into an operating room while the Chief underwent some three days of suffering for a full size, shoulder-to-shoulder canvas of a cockfight, and Joe submitted himself to a similar agony for a writhing dragon of similar scope. The Skipper, meanwhile, acquired a dragon "gut-piece" which was necessarily small because of a limited area of the only remaining blank epidermis above his waist.

I settled for watching the procedures and easing my shipmates' pain. Mr. Kaneta worked from paper sketches, which he copied freely in outline with crayon onto the skin. Then he made his indelible marks with an instrument like a small spade whose blade was a closely set row of sharp needles dipped in green, blue, red, or yellow ink. It was not hard to persuade his walking canvases to display these labors.

This tattooing by hand sure is an unpleasant operation. My piece only took eight hours, while Joe had twenty hours work in all put in on his…. Yesterday I had another slight bit of tattooing put on by Kaneta. He put a beautiful flight of three Japanese storks with Fujiyama & a setting sun in the background on my left shoulder.

The island on which Singapore is built was once a thick Malay jungle, pestiferous and creeping with ferocious and deadly animals. The pestiferousness has been conquered by modern drainage and sanitation, while the animals survive only in the small numbers, confined in a zoo several miles outside the city. Here I saw leopards, civet cats, the small Malayan bear, orangutans, many small monkeys, tigers, and crocodiles.

The most vicious animal of all is the king cobra, or hamadryad, whose black, 12' length was confined in a wire-fronted cage. He apparently had not yet learned that the wire was too tough for him, because he bashed his nose bloody with repeated, resentful, and murderous attempts to attack his audience. This cobra is far more dangerous than the ordinary hooded cobra and is twice its length. I was told it is one of the few animals, if not the only one, that will attack a human being entirely unprovoked and for no good reason since he does not eat his victim. He feeds chiefly on other snakes.

> *November 6. The first day of the NE monsoon reaching Singa-*
> *pore. Night fine. Day commences with showers, and same*
> *continues all through the day. No work today (King of Siam's*
> *birthday). Skål!.... The old world still going around, new ideas,*
> *births, deaths, and Anglo-U.S. war debts decision is due today.*
> *On shipboard usual routine. And so ends the first day of the NE*
> *monsoon, Sweet Singapore. (Signed) Joe.*

In spite of its evil reputation, Singapore after dark was nearly as quiet as a country town. The seeker after waterfront dives harboring a picturesque crew of Malay pirates and assorted rough characters from the pages of a Conrad novel or the silver screen would have been disappointed. The movies, an amusement park with a roller skating rink, some Chinese theaters, and approximately three nearly empty saloons comprised almost the entire public night life of the city, once infamous for being a "sink" of intemperance and evil associations.

> **We went to an amusement park called "The New**
> **World" & did a bit of roller skating.... This whole town**
> **closes up tight at midnight. There are no cabarets or**
> **dives here now, the town having been cleaned up and**
> **had the clamps put on it a couple of years ago by some**
> **damned committee.**

On 17 November, having arranged with a British engineer who was going home on leave to take my place in the *Pilgrim,* I took temporary leave of the schooner and embarked on a Dutch steamer for Genoa.

chapter 17

From Singapore to Suez

By Harold Peters

THE DEPARTURE OF THE COMMANDER cast a gloom over those of us left on the *Pilgrim:* a gloom which a constant and torrential rain that started the instant he left did little to dispel.

The schooner was anchored some distance from the wharf, just clear of the many small coastal steamers working cargo from lighters. The steamers had lovely names — *Hong Kwong, Hong Ho, Sin Aik Lee, Hang Yon,* and *Ban Siong Bee.* Our connection with the shore was maintained by a small sampan hired by the Commander to attend the *Pilgrim* during her stay. The proprietor's name, unlikely as it may seem, was Ng. You can pronounce this if you know the language. We couldn't manage it and so called him O'Brien, a name which Mr. Ng, as a special favor to us, was obliging enough to answer. That this was fortunate is readily seen when you consider the prospect of getting results by shouting, "Hey, Ng! Are you there, Ng?" off the end of the dock on a dark, rainy night.

The *Pilgrim* left Singapore 27 November with a company of five. With the Commander gone, I considered my shipmates again and found no lack of beef. The Chief was a husky six-footer. Joe was as effective aboard a vessel as two ordinary men. The Trader could drive a harpoon completely through a 6' shark. And the

Cook, who weighed two hundred pounds, helped heave on lines any time it was necessary.

At 2 P.M. that day, we rounded Point Bulus, the southerly tip of Southeast Asia. Everyone looked at it and said, "There's the southerly tip of Southeast Asia." That is all that can be said of a place which is flat and low like the rest of the coast. Mangrove swamps lined it, mud flats extended out from it — in one case twelve miles — and the low hills back of the coast, seen through the usual drizzle of rain, all looked alike. The tidal currents there were also quite strong. In summary, the Malay shore of the Strait of Malacca was unattractive to a sailor.

We had calms, light variable airs, and rain squalls for weather. Great tufted masses of cloud often towered into the heavens, and with lightning and rain they looked as if they were about to blow the whole region up into China. In the season of the southwest monsoon I heard they do just this, when the notorious "Sumatra" squalls menace shipping. Named for the island over which they originate, we heard in Malacca that one of them recently had capsized and sunk a small steamer. However, when the *Pilgrim* was making her way northwest through the Strait, the desperate looking clouds produced very little wind. Occasionally, the clouds would disperse and a little breeze would suddenly stir. At first we tried to sail in these zephyrs, but as soon as we got the heavy sails hoisted and trimmed, the breeze fell flat or shifted to the opposite quarter. The second afternoon out, we did get a northeast breeze, and on this we sailed to the roadstead off the old town of Malacca where we anchored.

We stayed a day at Malacca to see a weird and gorgeous Chinese procession which Mr. Hayden, the United States Consul at Singapore, had urged us not to miss. It seems that every fourteen years, the Chinese, who make up a large part of Malacca's population, have a week's festival to quiet the evil spirits and reduce their numbers. This creditable ambition produced on this day a procession approximately one mile long. Having gone ashore and secured an advantageous position on a grassy hillside, we watched for two hours the gorgeous costumes, floats, banners, and whirling dancers against whom it appeared unlikely that even the most mighty evil spirits could prevail.

There was a paper dragon 50' long carried by ten skipping Chinese, while another human team dragged a chariot on wheels. This contained a piano-like instrument, the keys of which were pounded with sticks by an elaborately dressed individual of great age and, presumably, piety. The English agent for the little coastal steamers, Mr. Pierce, told us that on the last day of the festival, effigies of the evil spirits are put adrift in a boat, which is set on fire. All the spirits that escape burning fall overboard and drown.

Having to some extent digested a powerful dinner of roast beef, baked potatoes, Malay turnip, and apple pie on the night of this procession, we got underway at 8 P.M. and made sail in a good northeast breeze off the land. By morning, it was again calm, a desperate looking mass of cloud having produced nothing but rain. The following morning, when the fuel pump went bad, we were left at the mercy of the tides. The Chief decided nothing less than major repair would do, and he and the Trader labored at this mean job all day in a humid, ninety degree air. On deck, it was more comfortable as a little westerly breeze arose, against which Joe and I beat the vessel up the Strait.

There are few shoals in this part of the Strait. We planned to anchor for the night in Klang Strait, a swampy creek that forms the south entrance to Port Swettenham. But when, at dark, we were off the tributary strait, the wind was still holding and we decided, foolishly, to keep on. This meant Thanksgiving at sea, and it was one of the Cook's best, highlighted by our last canned roast chicken.

Good as that meal may sound and good as it was, Thanksgiving night was one of those occasions when the weather did everything possible to annoy us. After breezing up fresh from dead ahead and raising a choppy sea, the wind fell very light, and we banged around in drizzle until the tide turned. At 5 A.M., we anchored off a mangrove swamp in Klang Strait, the same place we had sailed past so hopefully the previous evening. Thirty-three hours at sea had netted eight miles. We turned in for a three-hour nap, tired and disgusted. We were close in under the trees of the jungle, but except for the crocodiles sloshing around among the mangroves, there was no sign of life — not even a mosquito.

When the tide turned fair at 9 A.M., the Chief started his contraption. We proceeded through the narrow and winding, but deep and easily followed, channel of Klang Strait, departing it that afternoon through the north entrance into the main Strait of Malacca again. On the way, we saw the tin and corrugated iron sheds of Port Swettenham. This is an important tin port and very aptly named. Tucked away in the jungle, it seemed to be actually stewing in the moist heat, steam rising up from its buildings as it does at the last stage of cooking chowder. The weather, for a change, held fine. We passed the usual number of junks, sampans, junk-sampans, and sampan-junks that somehow contrive to navigate this windless region under sail.

After another typical Straits night full of squalls and a continuous and drenching rain, we passed through the Sembian Islands, a few small, fairly high, and bold islets, and anchored off the Malay village of Pangkor in the Dinding islands. The harbor contained several big junks, some fully the size of the *Pilgrim*. A large number of the interesting Malay dugout canoes with carved ends were drawn up on the beach. There were no white men in the place. The honor of escorting us about it fell on a young Malay who had acquired an astonishing knowledge of English while making a voyage to New York in the crew of a tramp. He said some of the big canoes with sixteen men and a sail sometimes go to Singapore, taking about a month for the trip. They camp on shore at night.

We followed the outer edge of an extensive mud flat, using the lead away from Pangkor and toward the island of Penang, eighty miles further along. This island is 2,700' high, and the unusually clear weather allowed us to keep it in sight as we slowly worked our way against a light head wind and current. We brought up among a prodigious number of junks and other native craft, each very busy carrying mysterious cargoes to unknown destinations. The British require a license for all craft trading at Penang; Commander Owen, the Harbor Master, told me he has about five thousand on his list. The *Pilgrim* was anchored close in to the wharves of Georgetown, the name of the town, although it is usually referred to simply as Penang. It was here that Bill Cutting, our sixth crew member for the passage ahead, joined us. He proved just the right man for the trip to the south of France and fit right in. We all felt that under the circumstances a better shipmate could not have been found.

Theoretically, we were pretty well through the area of calms and rain. It was December and the northeast monsoon, the fine fresh winter breeze of the North Indian Ocean, could be expected at any time. On the morning of 8 December, under a gray sky and in a flat calm, we steamed out of Penang bound for the Nicobar Islands, 400 miles to the west. We picked up what we thought must be the monsoon late that afternoon and shut down the engine, but the wind never blew decently fresh and the weather continued squally the entire run.

> **From Hod Fuller's journal: The sea is very blue once more & it is a relief to be out of the dirty mud colored water around the Malay Peninsula.**

When, three days later, the murky hills of Great Nicobar Island appeared some thirty miles ahead, we were becalmed and wallowing in a heavy swell rolling up from the south. We decided to try for a harbor recommended by the pilot book between little Nicobar Island and a small neighbor called Pulo Milo. Our only chart was a tracing done for us by Commander Owen, and it showed an approach infested with rocks and shoals. I regarded it with great dislike, but if we were to visit the Nicobars, it seemed the only place sheltered from all threatening directions, particularly the south, where there was clearly some disturbance, and from the northeast, out of which the monsoon might strike at any moment.

We closed in with the land with the engine running and me on the foremast-head looking for shoals. This method of eyeball navigation is effective in the South Pacific where the sun usually shines, the water is transparent, and the brown coral heads can be seen in time to avoid them. Here, beneath the gray sky, the water was dark brown all the way to the rocky shore where considerable surf was breaking. There were several small nubbins just awash near which we had to pass that suggested the probability of other nubbins lurking invisibly under the surface. The chart tracing was on too small a scale to identify any of these hazards. However, when I thought of Magellan, Cook, and the many other early navigators sailing around the world with no charts, no engine, and in clumsy square-riggers, it did seem as though we ought to be able to poke a few miles around the Nicobars without getting wrecked.

Little Nicobar Harbor was a wild looking place. Dense jungle covered everything from the water's edge to the summits of a few hills appearing dimly through misty showers from low-hanging clouds. There was no sign of human habitation. The north end of Little Nicobar and the worst looking of the shoals having been cleared, the *Pilgrim* entered a sort of green tunnel between the main island and Pulo Milo. Beaches now appeared on both sides, backed by a few native huts under the palms where some naked

Nicobar canoe.

people were running about inspired, we hoped, by friendly enthusiasm at our arrival. The water was very deep, and we had to anchor in ten fathoms with just room to swing clear of a beautiful little beach on the south side of Pulo Milo.

Immediately, outrigger canoes appeared from behind a point and surrounded the schooner. These contained three or four men, each attired in a grass belt with a tassel falling down behind. They seemed a bit fearful but very curious. One canoe venturing close alongside revealed occupants medium sized, well-built, and wiry with what we thought a resemblance to the Polynesians of the eastern Pacific. Although the *Pilgrim* was pretty full of curios, we exchanged old clothes for paddles, spears, and so on. We saw no firearms.

They have very fine sailing canoes made from burned out logs with the topsides lashed to them and highly decorated bows and sterns.

Crew outing on Nicobar.

The most popular bargain aboard was struck by the Cook a day or two later when he swapped an old shirt for four fat ducks. The beach afforded excellent swimming, our last for some months to come, and with its background of palm trees and thick jungle resembled what one might expect of a movie set. There were not many natives and their thatch huts, or at least the ones I visited, contained very little. We never saw any women or children — invariably, they were rushed back into the bush whenever we went ashore. The Nicobars seemed as remote as any inhabited island we'd seen.

Ran the engine 11 hours. The fuel pressure has started jumping around again & it looks as though the check valves will have to be reseated & their seats rereamed when we get to Colombo. It's almost a year since they were touched and we've run nearly 500 hours since then. Took some quinine tonight before turning in.

Hooked one nice barracuda weighing about 30 pounds & had several other strikes but no luck. Had a fine swim during the afternoon and later went to a village about three miles up to the westward. Saw a few thatched huts built on scaffoldings along the beach under the palms & a few naked natives came to the beach for a "look see." Too much surf to land the dory so we had to head back again for the *Pilgrim*. Had another swim before dinner and then came aboard & had a powerful meal of roast duck, spaghetti, & hot biscuits.

The superstition that it is unlucky to sail on a Friday has no scientific basis, but it proved true once again when we left the Nicobars and were immediately beset by bad weather on our passage across the Bay of Bengal to Ceylon (Sri Lanka). We had hoped that the light easterly breeze would develop into the regular monsoon, but at dark it fell flat after running us slowly offshore. We spent the evening in a perfect deluge of rain, accompanied by a smart wind from the west. "Nicobar," a white hen just acquired by Joe, had been stowed on deck in a bucket for safety. She got into such a state that he allowed her to roost in the forecastle for the rest of the night.

Joe expects freshly laid eggs every morning for break- fast, but we all think the hen would do much better as a foundation for a stew.... We have offered a bottle of the best liquor a pound will buy in Ceylon to the fellow who picks up the northeast monsoon on his watch.

For several days, we rolled around, gradually drifting to the west under the propulsion of light airs that shifted constantly from the north to the southeast and back again. The engine was supposed to be only an auxiliary for getting in and out of small harbors or on an occasional short run between islands. Since leaving Batavia, however, the lack of wind had necessitated its constant use. This had put entirely too much work on the Chief, who certainly had not shipped to spend most of his time in the engine room covered with grease. We determined to sail to Ceylon no matter how long it took.

It took a long time. In five days out, we covered 309 miles, sixty-one of which were due to current. Although we got a trifle more wind after this, it constantly shifted and never amounted to much, and the *Pilgrim* floundered along to the westward with her canvas changed every few hours. In longitude eighty-nine degrees east, a giant ray who had been inspecting us with some interest suddenly rushed at the log rotator towing astern and bit it completely off. It was the only event of a tedious passage. The evening of 23 December, we picked up Little Basses light — Ceylon. The next noon, we found ourselves becalmed near the town of Galle. Finally, we had to call on the engine to take us the seventy miles up the west coast to Colombo, where we tied up at ten o'clock Christmas morning. Nine hundred two miles had taken ten days!

✪ ✪ ✪

The Vice-Consul, Mr. Livingston, came aboard with our mail and gave us an invitation to Christmas dinner with the Consul, Mr. Buell. Got our awning up and then changed and went ashore to the Galle Face Hotel for a fine Christmas dinner.

Walker's Yard at Colombo offered to haul the *Pilgrim* out and clean her bottom for such a reasonable price that I accepted, thinking the Commander, whose money I was spending, would be likely to see his vessel sooner if this was done. Although she had been in tropical waters over a year, including ten weeks at Tahiti where she was motionless, the copper plates that were clean and shiny when put on in Panama had only a few microscopic barnacles on them. Those smeared with sticky dirt had collected a splendid harvest of sea growth, as had the rudder.

There were numerous dhows in the harbor. We inspected one of the largest. With her gigantic lateen yard, blocks with no sheaves, and native grass ropes reeved through them, she seemed to me to be entirely unmanageable, and doubtless would be except for an unbelievably large crew and the blessing of Allah.

> **The dhows are about 100 feet long with big high carved poops like a Spanish galleon. The masts are raked forward at a terrible angle, and they have a big yard about 60 feet long slung on each mast. The natives make all the halyards and blocks themselves. Some of the blocks are about four feet long! The dhows carry rice to the Maldive Islands. They carry very light canvas & slide along easily in practically no air at all.**

Another day, some Hindu snake-charmers brought three cobras, each coiled in a basket, and a mongoose aboard the *Pilgrim.* The idea, they explained mostly through excited gesticulations, was that the mongoose, noted for its fearlessness in attacking poisonous reptiles, would take on each of the cobras in turn. The mongoose seemed dissatisfied with the conditions, however, and refused to tackle a single snake.

> **They had about half a dozen cobras in baskets and played little whistles which attracted the snakes out and they stood up & swayed back & forth to the music. All but one of the snakes had his fangs removed.**

> **The Trader & I installed the check valve unit after it had been renovated and the valves ground. The engine is running 100% better & smoother. I also had to install new gaskets on the head of the air compressor.**

On New Year's Day, 1934, the *Pilgrim* sailed from Colombo for

Aden (South Yemen). A fresh north-northeast wind steadily increased, accompanied by a threatening sky. By evening, the wind was blowing Force 8 and there was a rough sea chasing us. Sometime the next morning, the spare log rotator was bitten off by a fish. After towing the first one safely all the way from Boston, we had now lost two in less than three weeks in the Indian Ocean. One last spare remained, and we decided to depend on the "guess" method of dead reckoning and save it.

From 10–12 o'clock last night (1 January), we did 19 miles in two hours which is a record for us, as well as 217 miles, noon yesterday to noon today, being our record run so far for the trip.

Four days out, we passed about six miles north of Minicoi Island. It was here that we finally picked up the regular winter monsoon. For eight days, it blew more or less steadily, and for eight days, with this fine breeze abeam, we swung across the Arabian Sea at an average rate of 171 miles per day. To avoid the chance of being run down during thick weather or at night, we sailed about 25 miles north of the usual steamer track, and at dawn of 11 January, sighted the island of Socotra (Suqutra) topping the horizon on the port beam. On reaching the Gulf of Aden, the monsoon fell very light. Daylight four days later disclosed the Rock of Aden, high, bare, and jagged, with the peninsula of Little Aden, equally picturesque, to port. After two weeks at sea, sailing an average 152 miles per day, we were boarded in the harbor entrance by a pilot who berthed us to a buoy close off the town of Aden.

Aden harbor is well protected at this season, when the wind is off the land, and it wasn't as hot as I had expected. Ashore in the middle of the day, the sun baked down, but aboard the schooner it was always cool with usually a fresh breeze. If you like plenty of hot bare rock and sand, you will like Aden. I saw also plenty of camels and goats and dust and dreadful beggars.

> The town is built along the water and up on the hill-sides. Not a blade of grass anywhere... The streets of the native quarter are filled with goats and dromedaries, which are much better when viewed from windward.

> Loaded 234 gallons of fuel oil & 16 lube oil aboard from a dhow which came alongside. Took on also three tons of water.

Four days later, we sailed with a fair wind for Suez, some 1,300 miles up the Red Sea. With an increasing fair wind the next day, we rounded the island of Perim, which lies in the middle of the Straits of Bab-el-Mandeb ("Gates of Death"), the southern entrance to the Red Sea. I was glad when we had passed the Lebayir group, where the high islands spoil the wind and the low ones are hard to see at night, and reached Jebel Teir. This is a characteristic bare, volcanic rock about 800' high that suggests an enormous clinker of coal, picked out of a furnace and stuck in the Red Sea. There is a light on it, and I hope the keeper makes a large salary.

> Had quite a set-to with the cockroaches last night — they were walking all over me. I was dreaming that a bunch of sort of tassels were tickling my face & woke up to find roaches promenading over it. They are getting bad lately & often get inside your pajamas where they race around like hell.

At this season, the wind usually blows strongly from each end of the Red Sea towards the center, where exists an area of calms and variables. This whole system moves up and down the Sea to some extent, with the northerly winds extending ordinarily much further than the southerly. You might hold the southerly halfway up the Sea or, if particularly unlucky, you might meet the

northwester before you have really started. The *Pilgrim* secured
a position well up in the latter classification. We had scarcely
passed Jebel Teir on 22 January, when our southerly breeze,
which had been gradually dropping, disappeared entirely and
was succeeded by a moderate wind from the north-northwest,
dead ahead. It was accompanied by a peculiar short steep sea, out
of all proportion to the wind, into which the *Pilgrim* plunged to
her buffalo rail.

We could scarcely make headway under sail or power or both,
and the moon looked nearer to me than Suez, 1,000 miles dead to
windward. Furling the squaresail carefully along its jackstay just
forward of the foremast, we began the tedious and unpleasant
operation of bucking the head sea. For three days, we worked
slowly to the northwest until stopped by an increase of the wind
to a moderate gale. After we had been jogging for eighteen hours
under foresail and jumbo, the northwester suddenly moderated.
We had no sooner hoisted the mainsail and jibs and got the gear
coiled down and the vessel underway, than it fell to a faint air.
The schooner thrashed and wallowed so badly we had to take in
everything and start the engine.

I had never seen anything like these Red Sea waves. Although
of course not nearly so high as in the open ocean, they are higher
than seems possible in such a restricted area. They were spaced so
close together that the *Pilgrim*, 85' overall, could not ride over
them. High or low, they are invariably perpendicular. Managing
to gather a little headway, the vessel, standing nearly on her
stern, would stagger up one of these seas, pitch over the crest, and
land *kerplunk* on the face of the next one, taking water over the
buffalo rail forward and losing all headway completely. The wind,
nearly always north-northwest, was either very strong or merely
a faint air.

Had there not been interludes in this, I don't know that we
could have covered the distance up the Red Sea. On two succes-

sive nights, by keeping close under the desert mountains of Arabia, we caught a fresh easterly breeze off the land. While it looked as though the masts might go over the bow driving into the head sea, we managed on one of these runs with the wind abeam to cover 133 miles in twenty-four hours. This was 29 January, the day we crossed the Tropic of Cancer, and was followed by a day of 23 miles, most of which we spent hove-to in another gale off Yenbo. Keeping close to the Arabian coast in the hope of getting another night easterly (we did not), we had a fine view of this mountainous and arid region. It looked hot ashore, for the sun was shining most of the time, but aboard the schooner it often felt cold. As we approached the northern end, the thermometer fell at night into the forties.

> **Cold, bright, clear day with a northerly breeze about Force 7 blowing all day, and still in this damned head sea. Vessel rolling around quite a bit during the night & a nice leak in the deck has started over my bunk.... Can now receive about 20 w.p.m. on the radio according to the stop watch after practicing nearly every day since Pago Pago last July!**

When the *Pilgrim's* engine wasn't running — and without it we would be there still — the Chief didn't stand a wheel watch. Even so, he was on duty longer hours than the rest of us. He was on the wheel when, on 3 February, we saw the high barren mountains of the Sinai Peninsula in the north. Here the long narrow arm of the Gulf of Suez runs into the Red Sea. When we got there, the cold northwest wind was roaring out of it full blast. Beating up some particularly parched and unattractive islands on the Egyptian side of the strait, we anchored for twenty-four hours under one of them, Towila.

> **Found all the brass straps which held up the main exhaust pipe had carried away & were dangling by one**

screw holding each up. The exhaust pipe was being supported only by where it is joined to the engine & at a coupling in the line. Bill & I worked all morning putting in big spikes to hold it. The boys in Boothbay had little screws about one quarter of an inch long holding it up & which had broken off under the strain.

In lighter airs the following day, we started out under power for a try at the 170 miles separating us from the Suez Canal. North of the Straits of Jubal, the Gulf of Suez is very straight in about a northwest by west direction, with a width of ten to fifteen miles. With mountains on both sides, the place looks narrower than it is and forms a fine tunnel for the prevailing northwesters. The highest mountains are on the Sinai side, where we picked out Mount Sinai itself, 7,450' high, about 26 miles inland.

The end of the peninsula of Sinai is a terrible, desolate looking spot. High sun-baked mountains with not a tree or any green anywhere, and desert running from the foot of the mountains down to the sea. We could see Mt. Sinai where Noah's ark ran aground. I guess he wasn't busy enough with the sounding lead going around there.

The northwest wind remained light and by noon, 5 February, the *Pilgrim* had managed to struggle 73 miles up the Gulf. That afternoon, however, the sky clouded over. A falling barometer was accompanied at dark by a small south wind, the first since Jebel Teir.

About thirty miles from Suez, one passes a lighthouse on the Egyptian shore called Ras Abu Deraj. Above it, the Gulf widens out somewhat and forms an inland lake twelve miles wide. We had passed the lighthouse when, suddenly, the south wind increased to a gale. By the time the red flash of Newport Rock, which lies off the Suez waterfront, was visible from the masthead, a heavy sea was running. Not caring to approach the dead lee shore under these conditions, we hove-to under foresail shortly after midnight as near to the center of the Gulf as possible, with bearings on Ras Abu Deraj.

It quickly became too thick and rainy to see Newport Rock, and a little later I lost sight of the lighthouse. It blew harder here than at any time on the voyage before, the south wind coming right square up the Gulf at Force 6, 7, 8, 9, and 10. You could lean against the wind, it was blowing so hard. Although the wind had some ninety uninterrupted miles of Gulf to blow up, the place is so narrow it was hard to believe such seas could come with it. They washed the wedges right out from under the bowsprit.

We lay hove-to through it under the foresail very nicely, but she was diving & rolling like hell in the big seas. Everything broke loose in the cabin and was rolling & crashing about & making a hell of a mess & rumpus.

The schooner was all right, of course, provided we could keep her off the beach. We had perhaps a 12-mile offing when we hove-to, with only five or six miles on either side. We kept clear of trouble by wearing ship occasionally, until the wind increased to the point where we did not dare risk the foresail and gear on another jibe. At the time of the Force 10 wind, in the early morning hours of the sixth, the *Pilgrim* happened fortunately to be on the starboard tack.

The wind gradually hauled to the south and then the southwest toward dawn, allowing her to come up and face the sea, heading more parallel to the long axis of the Gulf, and, if my reckoning was anywhere near right, increasing considerably the distance she must drift to reach shoal water. We kept the lead going, taking soundings, and waited for daylight. Visibility was perhaps a quarter of a mile, and what currents might be set up in so restricted an area by such desperate conditions was a matter of pure speculation. All this in a little lake at the very north end of the Gulf of Suez!

Then, just after full light, the wind hauled to the west, off the desert, and our prospects immediately improved. Soon, the drizzle and mist started to clear up, and the wind fell with characteristic suddenness. Without further adventure, the *Pilgrim* finally passed Newport Rock and arrived at 10 A.M. off the waterfront of Port Tewfik, the port town of the Suez Canal. At no point did the vessel leak abnormally.

The port consisted, so far as I could see, of a stone wall that was being bombarded by the southerly roll to which it was fully exposed. At one end, some official looking structures and a jetty indicated the entrance to the canal. Joe hoisted the "Q" flag to announce our arrival in quarantine from foreign ports and the Trader the "S" flag to call for a pilot. For a long time these signals produced nothing whatever, and with the *Pilgrim* rolling drearily, we watched the gray seas smashing against the gray wall. Eventually, an Egyptian pilot arrived and guided us into a small, but not particularly clean, little basin behind a breakwater where we were tied up with anchor ahead and stern fast to the shore.

Have our stern lines made fast to a couple of cannons ashore & there are a hell of a lot of big bales of camel feed just astern of us which blow all over the vessel.

Two days later, I was talking with Captain Edwin Huffman, owner and skipper of the 85' schooner *Astrild,* whom I'd met in Singapore. He had fared somewhat better than we by being a day behind us. We wondered how the *Joanna,* a 45' schooner also first met in Singapore, would manage. As we were speaking, her skipper appeared on the wharf. Exchanging greetings, I asked Culley where the *Joanna* was, supposing he had left her in Aden and come up by steamer. He pointed to the bay: there she was at anchor!

"The Red Sea?" said Culley. "Not a bad place. We left Aden five days after you, had a fair wind to twenty-one degrees north, then a couple of calm days, then more fair wind to here. Only ran the engine two days. And you?"

chapter 18

The Suez Canal and Eastern Mediterranean

by Harold Peters

THE PARTICULARLY GLUTINOUS AND evil-smelling mud of Port Tewfik having been hosed from the anchor chain, the *Pilgrim* started up the Suez Canal early on 9 February, with a fair tide counteracting a cold head wind. She was in the charge of a pilot, a genial Frenchman. It is about ninety miles up the canal to Port Said, with Lake Timsa and the desert town of Ismailia about half-way. Here we anchored in the afternoon and went ashore. We walked around the desert looking at the camels, the sand, and about one thousand small boats drawn up on the shore of the lake, which we understood to be "netters."

> **From Hod Fuller's journal: Saw some very interesting native sailing feluccas here with a tremendously high sprit from which the sail is hung. Some of them must have been about 125 feet high & slung from the mast-head from which they pivot. All hands turned in very early.**

The Suez Canal, which unlike the Panama Canal has no locks, is a narrow ditch through the desert that allows ocean going ships to traverse the isthmus between Asia and Africa. When a particularly large steamer passes through, she is given the right of way, and vessels bound in the opposite direction tie up against the bank until she passes. Accordingly, when we met the big German steamer *Resolute* the next morning, our pilot ran the *Pilgrim* alongside the sandy bank and ordered two lines ashore. When the *Resolute,* which was flying a Hitler flag on the jack staff forward, passed, she sucked the water down so that the *Pilgrim* was left rolling on her bilge in the sand.

This was an alarming and unexpected circumstance to us, if not the pilot. We were almost high and dry. I had a vision of the vessel stuck in the desert and being gradually buried in sand while we stood watches on the mastheads with rifles to keep off the packs of wolves or wild dogs which Joe, who had gone ashore with the lines, reported seeing from the top of the bank. Considerably shaken by this maneuver, we proceeded when the water returned, and that afternoon tied up stern to the wall in the Arsenal Basin at Port Said.

It was forty-six degrees on deck when we left Suez, and when we arrived at Port Said, in a penetrating rain driven by a strong west wind, it was forty-two degrees. After two days, the rain stopped but the westerly did not, so when our decks were clear of water they filled with sand off the desert. We had to keep everything shut tight to keep the sand out of the soup or the eggs, and even then plenty of it got below.

> **Received our mail from home and things still continue to go from Bad to Worse. I wish to hell this boat would stay out another year. It would be slick, all right. Heard from the Commander and we are to bring the vessel to the Riviera as soon as possible.**

> **The town here is rather dull but has a couple of pretty fair cabarets. The streets are filled with pimps who follow you around everywhere…. For the first two days**

we were tied up here no traffic could get in or out because of the heavy seas running & at present two steamers are aground in the canal because of poor visibility at night during these sand storms.

My one pleasant recollection of Port Said is Billy Thompson, the provision dealer and "agent." But before going further, here is some background. When a yacht arrives at any considerable seaport in the East, she is instantly stormed by all the local tradesmen. Jewelry and goats she can manage without, but not fresh provisions. The provision dealer selected always assumes an air of devotion to the ship's interests and brushes aside the matter of payment as one of no importance. "Why, *Capitaine*, your credit is good. We trust. Pay when sail."

The idea behind their devotion is to present an outrageous bill on the eve of your departure, with the expectation that you will pay it, or most of it, rather than delay sailing. In the *Pilgrim*, we insisted each load of provisions be paid for on delivery and a receipt given. The dealer doesn't like this but will do it rather than lose your business. He also, in competition with others, wants to become the ship's "agent," who enters and clears the ship and arranges for all supplies. Having escaped all "agents" to this point by entering and clearing the schooner myself, I assumed the same could be done at Port Said, but it could not. There is the French Canal Office and the Egyptian Port Office, and both require separate documentary formalities. I survived the canal office but not the port office, where no one spoke anything except Egyptian.

Billy Thompson is an Egyptian — he said I couldn't pronounce his real name — and a gentleman who had been supplying us with provisions under the *Pilgrim's* usual arrangement. Although his charges were reasonable, I had told him we needed no "agent" as I would clear the vessel myself. At the end of my futile session at the port office, when I was wondering how to proceed without knowing the language, Billy Thompson offered to do it, and to do it for nothing, which he did. Apparently, no Captain had ever tried to clear his own ship except through some hired "agent," and the idea of anyone attempting this without knowing the language seemed to appeal to Billy Thompson's sense of humor.

❂ ❂ ❂

The *Pilgrim* sailed from Port Said on 18 February, a fine morning with a light southwest wind, bound for any port she could reach on the French Riviera. If you can steer a straight course, it is about 1,400 miles in a west-northwesterly direction. "You can't make it in this vessel at this time of year," the Suez Canal pilot had said. "All you get is westerly gales." He paused and added, "I suppose you can steam a short way to the west in an occasional calm, but that's the only way you'll get there at this season. Maybe by April there will be east wind, here in the eastern Mediterranean. But not now."

I had spent two weeks once in another schooner in Cádiz and Tangier at this precise season, waiting for a strong east wind to *stop* blowing through the Straits of Gibraltar. They had called this easterly a "levanter," and I had supposed, I still think with some justification, that it came from the Levant. Having sailed about thirty miles out of Port Said, the wind hauled west-northwest and stayed there for five miserable days of heavy rain squalls, driving hail storms, and cold. One day I wrote in the log, "Blowing up fresh with increasing head sea and after several plunges of the bowsprit under water took in mainsail. Feels like snow."

As the Skipper says, "Hurrah for the sunny Mediterranean!"

Except that they were bigger, these Mediterranean waves were the same as those we fought in the Red Sea, too steep and closely spaced for the *Pilgrim* to ride. She plunged and wrenched and got nowhere. Our company of five and the cook was just right for running the Trades, and I don't suppose we could really have been called short-handed. However, the schooner's lower sails were made of heavy Number 3 canvas, and the operation of hoisting them, sopping wet and cold and stiff as a board, only to take them down again in a rattling fire of hailstones, began to lose its appeal. Our zest, if we had any, for palm and needle work was considerably blunted by having to renew, amidst all this weather, large sections of the stitches holding the mainsail to its boltrope.

Having been warned to avoid the African coast, where many vessels have been wrecked, we sagged gradually in these moderate gales across the Mediterranean in a northerly direction. On the morning of 22 February, the island of Cyprus was visible, in clear spells, some thirty miles to the northeast. At this point, the westerly weather culminated in an exceptionally heavy northwest gale, with seas so big their crests broke aboard, swirling around the skylights and cabin tops. There's no use claiming we were comfortable or dry because we weren't. But Joe had kept the gear and rigging in excellent condition, so we did not have to worry about anything carrying away. Hove-to under the foresail with the wheel lashed nearly, but not quite, hard over, the *Pilgrim* looked after herself, usually lying four points from the wind and drifting very little to leeward. There was nothing for us to do but tough it out and wonder how so much water could get below through tarpaulins, hatches, and skylights.

At one time we were heeled over enough to put the lee rail under by the force of the wind alone, which is something in this heavy ark. Very difficult to write in the cabin because of the motion.

The next morning, the wind came north and moderated, allowing us to make sail for the eastern end of Crete, about 230 miles distant. I saw that one of the heavy wooden strips spiked to the bowsprit to hold the jib stops had been torn off by the seas during the night. The weather side of the main topmast looked like that of a telegraph pole after a snowstorm where the spray had dried, leaving a coat of white salt stuck to the wax on the mast.

The north wind did not hold for long. There was hardly a breath of wind for four days. With frequent stops for engine repairs, which kept the Chief up for as many as twenty-three hours at a stretch, the *Pilgrim* crept to the west.

Slept most of the morning & then spent the rest of the day in the engine room repacking fuel pumps & cleaning strainers etc. Almost flat calm all day with quite a northwest roll. Very warm, 66° for a change. The boys bent on a new jib as our old one had nearly carried away from the bowsprit while we were hove-to. Its roping was pretty rotten.

At dawn of 26 February, we saw the snow-covered mountains of Crete off the port bow. Passing through Kasos Strait, we steamed along the island's much indented and precipitous north coast, where at times a light breeze off the land allowed the sails to help the engine. The next morning, we anchored in Suda Bay, about fifty miles from Crete's west end, alongside a solitary little Greek schooner. This was the first sailing vessel we had seen since leaving Port Said nine days earlier, half of them spent in a gale and half in calm.

The surroundings of Suda Bay, the only completely protected anchorage the island offers, are barren but picturesque. The little village lies in a rocky and sterile region whose bare slopes soon merge into a mountain that sweeps up 7,000' into the sky. At this time, it was covered with snow and ice to within a short distance of the village. The inhabitants, most of whom seem to earn a living in various small ways connected with the sea, did all in their power to help us, with no idea of being paid for it. Everything was Greek, including the labels on goods. Even the Cook, who previously had interpreted in Spanish, French, and Dutch, could make nothing of it. We were able to get supplies and fuel oil in the considerable town of Khania, three miles to the west.

Wonderful scenery here in Suda Bay, very green hillsides with terraces that slope back from the shore to very high snow-covered mountain peaks. The little towns are of whitewashed plaster with red roofs and set off well against the green hillsides. Many old forts & walls on the hilltops. Spent the morning at work patching up the diesel. It's getting quite a bit of exercise through here, having been run a total of 464 hours since Singapore alone!

The evening after our arrival, Bill Cutting came down with a chill and the next day was running a fever. The Trader concentrated on our medical book and decided Bill might have bronchitis. By the morning of 2 March, his fever had broken. Although it was a Friday we decided to make a start. Passing Agria Grabusa Light, the northwest tip of Crete, that evening, we headed for Sicily, about 400 miles across the Ionian Sea. Although the engine was out of commission at this point due to trouble with the fuel pressure, we picked up a little breeze from the northeast and next day were running our course at eight knots.

Under a gray and gloomy sky and with a steadily falling barometer, the wind gradually increased. In the early hours of 4 March, it backed into the northwest with gale force. We hove to in conditions which soon equaled those of the blow off Cyprus, with winds at Force 10 for most of the daylight hours. We had replaced the old foresail with the spare, and under this new sail with a reef in it, the *Pilgrim* battled the winds and waves through to the next day. At one point, I set a deck chair in the main gaff bridle to help hold her into the wind, and it made an excellent spanker.

> Very rough night hove-to in a northerly gale & practically impossible to sleep & stay in your bunk. Everything wet & leaking & the vessel rolling like hell & pitching in big short steep seas. Sky overcast & gray low clouds tearing downwind with occasional rain squalls.... Three of our kerosene boxes along the leeward rail carried away & went overboard as the rail went under, despite lashings. What a miserable tough passage we're having in this Mediterranean Sea, shorthanded with Bill in his bunk & the Trader with a temperature & it blowing a gale!

Bill Cutting had a tough time. He was laid up in the Commander's stateroom, which was cold and not entirely dry. Because we had to keep the tarpaulin over the skylight, the cabin was also dark. How he managed to recover under these circumstances, I cannot say, but he did. When he spoke of standing his watch again and began to growl about this "Yankee hell-ship," I knew he was out of danger. Our position on 7 March was thirteen miles northwest of the 4 March position, the line connecting them showing an interesting but not very profitable cruise of about 35 miles to the south-southwest and return.

> Sighted a couple of steamers last night but they did not come within hailing distance so none of us could get aboard them!

> By noon the wind & sea...had moderated quite a bit so the mighty diesel was started and we bore away NW by N for the Straits of Messina under jib, forestaysail, & foresail & engine with a head sea against us.... We are making about four knots under this rig & the diesel seems to still hold together for some unknown reason.

It is only a question of time until she stops entirely, having been run over one thousand hours and no overhaul! I seem to manage to keep it running by everlasting patching up & frigging when something goes.

After this blow, the weather continued unfavorable. Headwinds, squalls, and that particular Mediterranean short steep sea from the west held us back. It was not until the morning of 10 March that we entered the Straits of Messina, between Sicily and the toe of the boot of Italy. Here, with the snow-capped volcano of Mt. Aetna belching smoke in front of us, it fell calm. We had intended to make Malta, farther to the south, since the Straits at this time of the year are not an encouraging prospect for a sailor. The currents are strong, and conditions at their northern end, where the wind is against the tide, are reportedly desperate. But where you plan to go in the Mediterranean in winter, and where you do go are two separate things. The previous day the wind had gotten enough into the southwest to enable us to just fetch the Straits on the port tack, which we did. We were mighty glad to get there.

Except for a long list of historical associations, the Straits of Messina offer nothing unusual. The shores are bare and rocky, like plenty of other shores, and the towns as seen from the deck of a passing schooner are not inspiring. The diesel having been once again coaxed into operation by the Chief, we steamed up them in the company of several little barkentines and various unnameable varieties of brigantine and topsail schooners which the calm gave us a chance to admire. That afternoon, we tied up, once more under the direction of a local pilot, in the little artificial harbor of Messina, on Sicily. We moored with the *Pilgrim's* stern made fast to the shore, as we had done in Papeete. Instead of lovely tropical scenery for background, we now had a freight train which constantly moved back and forth under our stern with a penetrating rattle and clatter without appearing to get anywhere in either direction.

On Tuesday, 13 March — no more Friday starts for the *Pilgrim* — we rushed out of the Straits with a fair wind. I got a good look at Scylla, a rock on the Italian shore, and we passed through Charybdis, marked on the chart as a whirlpool, without noticing any disturbance, mythological or otherwise. Aeolus is the God of Winds, and one can easily see how, when he blows against the swift currents setting out of the north entrance to the Straits, he could make the passage "between Scylla and Charybdis" pretty desperate, whatever else the phrase has come to mean. I was told that even today steamers avoid this place in heavy onshore winds.

The course up the middle of the Tyrrhenian Sea, which is bounded by Italy, Sicily, Sardinia, and Corsica, is about northwest by north. I kept the schooner on it, in the middle of this region, to avoid lee shores. The weather was generally bad, illuminated at night by plenty of lightning, but the wind providentially allowed us to head the course most of the time. One day, we actually covered 143 miles, with enough time off to attack the cockroach headquarters in the sail locker. When we passed the little island of Monte Cristo, whose 2,000' height appeared barren and desolate, the northwester jumped us again with its accustomed violence. With the snow-covered mountains of Corsica in sight to the west, we fell off to the east and made a lee under Elba. We soon dragged the *Pilgrim* into Port Longone, on the island's east side, where we anchored in a rattling deluge of giant hailstones.

The *Pilgrim's* anchors weigh four hundred pounds each, and it took both of them, with fifty fathoms of chain apiece, to hold her against the tremendous williwaws that roared out of the harbor. While Port Longone lies a little further north than Boston, the desperate cold made us feel we were inside the Arctic Circle. Down below, with the galley stove going and plenty of hot buttered rum circulating around the table, we listened to the roaring of the wind and the hailstones rattling overhead on the deck. The old toast, "She's howling for somebody else tonight," was never given with more enthusiasm.

This blow lasted two days. We walked around the barren hills where people were loading little donkeys with sticks for firewood. We also looked over the town where there was a big prison said to contain some three thousand political prisoners. Our guide, an old man who claimed once to have lived in Boston out of which he sailed as second mate of a five-masted schooner, said the place where Napoleon was incarcerated could be seen in the interior, but we passed on the opportunity to pay our respects.

Very pretty little fishing village. A nice schooner & some small sailing craft tied up along the sea wall where many fish nets were hanging to dry. The town is made up of yellow plaster houses with red tile roofs built on sloping ground back from the water. The streets are all paved with big stones and are very steep & crooked. Heard some good guitar & mandolin playing in the street while ashore.

When the northwester let go, which it did with extreme suddenness, of course, we pulled out of Port Longone. Outside, we found a flat calm and a mixed cross sea — the Mediterranean alternative to a gale. The *Pilgrim* weathered bleak Cape Corse, the northern tip of Corsica, and finally, over a month out of Port Said, tied up in a little pool in the inner harbor of Nice.

The Commander was on the dock and boarded us immediately. The log does not say that we turned in early that night, and we didn't.

chapter 19

Through the Western
Mediterranean to Las Palmas

ON THE FIRST DAY OF SPRING in 1934, the *Pilgrim* ended her long battle with the winter gales of the Mediterranean by poking her salt-caked bowsprit wearily in through the narrow breakwater entrance to the harbor of Nice, on the southern coast of France a few miles from the Italian border, where she settled stern to the granite quay in a maze of sooty mooring lines. The tiny port was crowded with wintering yachts, both power and sail, of all sizes. Many of their owners were suffering out the season among the often exaggerated pleasures of shore life along the Riviera. A few, for whom the shelter of villa or hotel and the life of the casinos was either insupportable or too expensive, remained aboard their boats doing a bit of work on deck when the weather was fine, but for the most part lying low in their cabins while the mistral howled through the rigging.

Since arriving in Europe from Singapore, I, too, was spending some time along the Riviera, and before that I had been in Paris. There also had been two weeks in Genoa where I renewed and improved an acquaintance that suffered an interruption of more than a year by stepping into an Italian registry office and replying "*Si*" at the proper moment during a marriage ceremony. If it had not been that my recently acquired wife, who entertained a strong distaste for life afloat, had no intention of joining me for the voyage home, my pleasure at seeing the schooner again would have been unalloyed.

Soon after the arrival of the *Pilgrim* at Nice, we brought her the twenty-odd miles to the westward, past Cap d'Antibes and the Isle St. Honorat, where there is an old monks' castle dating back to the fourth century, into the cleaner and less congested harbor of Cannes, where both work and much-needed relaxation would be more pleasant for the crew. In plunging up the Red Sea against a stubborn northerly, the ship had stretched her fore and aft stays, and they all needed setting up. Many suns and much tropical rain had mottled the golden bloom of the wooden shells of the blocks with gray patches of decay. In between the spells of cold rain, these were scraped down, bleached with lemon juice, and varnished. The booms and gaffs were painted white and other spars were varnished. There was some visiting with the crews of other yachts tied up to the mole, but these were for the most part used as winter houseboats, and their well-dressed owners, with a few single exceptions, were not of the type to swap a yarn with a man wielding a paint-scraper with a horny and grimy hand.

> *From the ship's log: March 29. At Cannes.... Received a number of packages, some of which, from Kelvin White, have been to Batavia, Honolulu, Singapore, Colombo, Marseilles and Nice.*

My wife and I had made the acquaintance in Paris of another Yankee who had done a good deal of sailing in both commercial and pleasure vessels as a young man, and whose academic and social pursuits did not prevent his undertaking to join the *Pilgrim* for the voyage home across the Atlantic. Andy Hepburn joined us at Cannes. I am sad to record that a cable received in Cannes soon brought him news of the death of his brother which required his immediate departure for America by steamship. However, he did not leave before he applied several coats of varnish to the bowsprit and enthralled the local population by blowing Gaelic dirges across the water from his bagpipes in the stillness of the night.

Before my wife left for home in a steamer, she delivered aboard the schooner a large quantity of assorted merchandise as cargo. For each bureau, gilded mirror, and package of crockery, room had to be found in the crowded food and gear lockers. The most difficult item of all to accommodate was a cubical crate of about a yard in each dimension. It contained, well nested in its center among a mass of crumpled paper, excelsior, and cotton batting, a wax head of Christ, believed to have been fashioned in the fifteenth century. After tucking it well into the port provision locker, I gave it no further thought.

Before leaving Cannes, the Trader and I attended a dinner given by the local Chamber of Commerce for the yachtsmen then in port. Reporters were present, and since strangers always took for the owner of the *Pilgrim* either the Trader or the Cook (the Cook was not present on that occasion), and since newspaper reporters are very apt to be wrong about facts of minor public importance, the following extract from a newspaper of the following day is not surprising:

> Malheureusement, Mrs. Cammon n'aime pas la mer. C'est assez ennuyeux quand on a un mari qui fait le tour du monde dans un petit bateau. En raison de cette aversion marquée, on ne sait pas si le Pilgrim arrivera en rade de Boston, le 1er juillet prochain, avec son équipage augmenté d'une unité feminine ou privé d'une unité masculine.

> [Unfortunately, Mrs. Cammon doesn't love the sea. It is rather tiresome when one has a husband who is making a trip around the world on a small boat. Because of this marked aversion, one cannot tell whether the *Pilgrim* will arrive in Boston Harbor the first of next July, with the addition of a feminine unit or the

subtraction of a masculine unit.]

After the departure of the feminine unit by steamer from nearby Villefranche, the *Pilgrim* set off across the Gulf of Lyons for the Balearic Islands, with a chart of that region obtained from a local optician's shop. As we approached the notorious gulf, the glass tumbled and the sky darkened. Out of the north, then out of the northwest, came a succession of rain, thunder, lightning, and hail squalls. The wind finally reached gale force, and the seas making up quite steep, now and then slopping aboard. Fortunately, the course for Port Mahón, Minorca, was well south of west, so that with shortened sail these violent attacks of nature helped us on our way and made short work of the run of 270 miles.

> *April 22. Commences rain & lightning. Soon commenced to breeze up NNW. Glass 29.56 at 12:45 A.M. 2-4 A.M. Thunder. Much lightning, heavy rain & hail squalls. One calm spell with high sea. After 3 commenced to blow very hard from about N, gradually hauling NNW in heavy squall. Took in jib. After daylight, wind backing westerly. Barometer, having hit 29.40, starts up. Fine time made under foresail & jumbo until 8 A.M. Wind backed more westerly then. Sheeted in foresail & jogged heading SxWrly in general direction of Minorca.*

> *Weather clearing & glass rising, but rough sea — altho much less than last night. Wind WxS. 10:10 A.M. sighted Minorca ahead. Noon: less wind & sea but concluded too far to go to Port Mahón before dark so continued jogging SxW & SSW. Weather fine. P.M. closed with Minorca quicker than expected & at 4 off Cape Favorite Light, set jib & stood along the shore. Wind now blowing hard off the land. After supper decided to have a try at Port Mahón, the weather looking unfavorable for getting along as wind now strong SW. Worked up around La Mola Peninsula under engine, jumbo & foresail & then up the slick narrow*

entrance to Port Mahón where we anchored in 5 fathoms, mud,
at 9:45 P.M., just west of the little islet of Pinta, off the town.
First appearance of the Pilgrim in Spanish waters.

"Junio, Julio, Agosto, y Puerto Mahón
Los mejores puertos del Mediterraneo son."

Port Mahón, once the Carthaginian settlement of "Mago," is not only the best harbor in the Mediterranean (aside from the three months referred to by the poet), but surely one of the best in the world. From a narrow entrance, it extends northwest some three and a half miles inland. About one and a half miles wide, it is protected by high land from the severest winds in that region, which come from the north. Its advantages have caused it to be fought over many times in the course of the centuries. From the time that Mahón was a *municipium* under the Roman Empire, the harbor has been successively in the hands of the Moors, James of Aragon, the all-Mediterranean sea bandit Khair-ed-Din Barbarossa, the Corsairs, the British, the French, and the Spanish.

The Moorish and Spanish influences are architecturally the most evident in the twisted columns and the whitewashed simplicity of patio walls in the town, although the ancient stone battlements which crawl up the steep shores of the inner harbor speak of an earlier age when refinements of design were secondary to the main concern of safety from sea rovers. Mahón is probably also one of the neatest ports in the world: the stone quays which line the waterfront and the brick and limestone warehouses behind them were as free of dirt as a Dutch kitchen.

From Hod Fuller's journal: Across the harbor from where we are lying is the house where I'm told Lord Nelson & Emma Hamilton, his mistress, used to hang out in the years before Trafalgar. It is the biggest house here and is built on the top of a hill overlooking the sea on one side and the harbor on the other.

Although Minorca nourishes the usual small Mediterranean fruits, it is, in general aspect, rather bare of vegetation due to the fact that in the winter, northerlies' salt spray sometimes drenches the entire island, discouraging the more generous growth characteristic of its sister island of Majorca (Mallorca). The two islands, but twenty miles apart, are portions of the same subterranean mountain, the depths between them being only about forty fathoms, while on all sides the sea bottom slopes sharply away to over six hundred fathoms.

An overnight run through a sea of the bobbing lights of scores of fishing boats brought us to the Bay of Palma, on the south side of Majorca. The high, flat face of the town's cathedral dominates this port at its head. Majorca, even in those days of 1934, had been "discovered" by the knowing expatriates and "escapologists." While there were still a few of those left behind to make the lives of visiting yachtsmen as gay as even that abandoned species could wish, most of the modern discoverers had departed for some other pristine spot. They left behind them the tangible monuments of Christian and Muslim civilizations going back at least two thousand years, cropping out all over the island from the limestone and olive tree scenery.

April 27. Moored at Palma. Another fine morning. We seem to have suddenly left what looked like endless winter & run into summer at last.

At the mole where the *Pilgrim* was tied up lay a brigantine, several Spanish coasting schooners and smaller, lateen-rigged local vessels, some used for fishing and others heaped to the rail with oranges. They formed a scene into which the *Pilgrim* blended more harmoniously than I had supposed. It was here that an American tourist paused for a moment opposite the schooner's stern, passed his eye over her decks and rigging, and remarked to his companion: "There's an old-timer." His impression may have been due somewhat to our having spent time in the resorts of Majorca rather than scrubbing the topsides. Another tourist asked if it were true, as he had heard, that we were planning to cross the ocean in "that little boat." Upon being told that we were going to try, he went off shaking his head as if too tender-hearted to continue looking at men who were so soon to die.

From the mole, a cobbled avenue fans out into shaded streets and narrow wagon lanes, winding up the slopes past lichened stone watch towers, Moorish balconies, and arches through which you can rest your eyes on the cool, stone-floored patios of large and ancient houses. The people are called Catalans, although the blood of early Roman, Vandal, and Byzantine settlers must run in them too. At night, you can hear the high pitched wails of flamenco singing that mingles the voice of northern Africa with the thrum of the Spanish guitar.

After I had bought for my wife a Siamese cat on such scant inspection as I could make, since only the head, set with round China-blue eyes, appeared above the rim of a raffia carrying basket, we cast off from the mole and steamed out into a head sea for Gibraltar, a little over 500 miles to the southwest.

May 2. The mountains of Spain are topping the horizon to starboard. Passed the meridian of Greenwich this morning & are now in west longitude for the first time since August 1, 1933.

May 3. Breeze & sea increasing from the west all night & we continued to plug along under power until after breakfast when we could make nothing against the increasing seas, so shut the engine off & hove to under foresail & jumbo.... The ship's cat is still laid low & seasick. Joe says, "These fancy parlor cats are not good for going to sea" & that you want a good barroom cat or tough alley cat for a ship's cat. Evening, the same conditions prevail & we are getting nowhere fast.

We were one hand short, since the Trader was laid up with a high temperature and Bill Cutting, on arriving in Nice, had gone on overland to England. A moderate gale soon made up from dead ahead. There was nothing we could do but lie to and suffer it out, the only work required being that of wearing ship every now and then, once to avoid running up on the Algerian shore, and several times to put the schooner on the starboard tack so the Cook's stove would draw properly.

May 7. Passed a good many small steam trawlers this morning. High mountains all along the coast and many old towers and forts are built along the shore, most of which are in ruins.

After seven days, during one of which we made good only eleven miles on our course, we steamed into Gibraltar, the northern "Pillar of Hercules," to take on water, combustible kerosene to replace the recalcitrant fluid supplied at Cannes, and general stores for the voyage across the Atlantic.

Waiting for me at Gibraltar was a cable from my wife. We previously corresponded by means of a traveler's code, but the matter of this message was beyond the scope of that special and limited vocabulary in which travelers speak to their agents and family. Some of the message was in another code. The whole was translated, and then confusedly into telegraphic English, only after I had visited several commercial houses in search of different ciphers. The text at first appeared to be a request to return home immediately on the liner *Rex* which was shortly to head that way.

What awful turn of affairs this portended I did not dare to imagine, and cabled for enlightenment. All codes were cast aside in a flood of expense before it was made clear to me that my description of the gale in the Gulf of Lyons, perhaps a little exaggerated, had aroused fears of damage to the wax head of Christ, resting in perfect security in its nest of packing below, and

An enviable craft.

that it was the head which must return home, not I, under more reliable auspices. After a full day of activity, during which I had to employ powers of diplomacy and administrative efficiency long declined from disuse, the head was at last installed in a first class cabin in the deluxe liner, with promises of daily inspection by the Chief Mate and a steward. Both were awed by the responsibility of a sacred relic and grateful for a supply of fine cigars.

Everyone who goes to Gibraltar hears the story of the two square-rigger captains who went to a bullfight just over the town line in Spain while waiting for an easterly wind to take their ships through the Strait into the Atlantic. Just before the last bull was killed, a puff of easterly breeze stirred the air. One captain hot-footed it for his ship while the other waited to see the last inning, saying he would follow along presently. The conclusion of the story is that the first ship reached America, reloaded, and was back at Gibraltar before the second one had been able to get away at all.

When we heard this tale at the luncheon table of Mr. Horatio Sprague, the American consul (the last of the family to hold the office in an unbroken line for more than a century), a fine easterly had been making up for several days. Since the Trader was now well enough to stand watch again, all hands were eager to start the last lap of our voyage, and we shortly did. Williwaws swooped down invisibly from around the Rock as we got in the anchor and whipped the squaresail roughly about as Joe let its gaskets go. Soon the *Pilgrim* was scudding handsomely out through the Strait. We overhauled a large gaff-rigged ketch which was forced to tack down wind and re-entered the Atlantic Ocean, last left at Cristóbal twenty-two months before.

Home lay more than 3,000 miles over the horizon, on a great circle course to the north of west. As head winds and a head current also lay in that direction, we set our course for the southwest, nearly at right angles to the shortest way home, and went to look for the northeast Trades. The prevailing winds of the North Atlantic move in a clockwise direction to form a huge ellipse, while a great whirlpool, formed partly by the Gulf Stream, describes roughly the same pattern in the sea below. The southern section of the ellipse comprises the northeast tradewinds, which swing up into the southwesterlies of the American east coast, while the fitful northerlies at the easterly end, as they pass the coast of Spain, are called the "Portuguese Trade" — when they are found.

As soon as the levanter which had driven the *Pilgrim* out into the Atlantic commenced to dissipate itself beyond the funneling effect of the strait, we began to look for the "Portuguese Trade" and charged the Skipper personally with its absence. The *Lloyd W. Berry* had, from his account, found it blowing in great shape just here in 1920. The sudden appearance of a brisk westerly in place of it was treated by the crew of the *Pilgrim* as, at best, evidence of a gross misapprehension on the Skipper's part and, at worst, of his own personal dereliction. The absent fair wind was constantly referred to as "his," and not until we had tacked laboriously to within a day's sail of Gran Canaria, where we intended to put in, did it finally appear to justify and reinstate him.

> *May 17. 4–6 A.M. Overcast & cold but a fine NNW breeze. After breakfast set fisherman staysail & jib topsail. Lovely going. Wind about a point abaft starboard beam. 10-12. Noon sun coming out. Making nearly 8 knots. The Portuguese Trades at last!*

As we drew up on the entrance to Las Palmas, a black squall from the northwest gave the signal for taking in all the light canvas. I unwisely carried out my part in this operation with no clothes on, as though I were still in the tropics, and as a result spent most of the following week in the port recovering from an attack of grippe. The more prudent members of the ship's company, once we were anchored, gave the "old-timer's" topsides a coat of glossy white paint in preparation for her homecoming. Joe went over her running rigging, here changing a nip, there fitting a new pendant, until all was ready for the next stage. With these activities and visits to and from other boats in the busy harbor, we saw little of the island. Indeed, the immediate shore of Las Palmas seemed to me to offer little of attraction.

The city itself was like a part of the outskirts of a city outside the center of activity and interest, but not far enough out to include the houses, gardens, and parks which, released from the compression of commercial expediency, expand graciously into the open country — a suburb without a city, with trolley cars raising dust. Doubtless, it had charms to which we were blind. We had been out nearly two years now, and the attitude of expectancy which had invested every sensation on the outward passage with novelty and excitement now gave place to some impatience to complete the voyage and be at home again.

Near our anchorage was the hulk of a Spanish sail and steam auxiliary warship of the last century, the *Oceania*. From her raised poop, there stretched along the rail a row of gun ports, forward to the raised forecastle, which was finished off by an elaborate gold figurehead of the Spirit of the Absolute Supremacy of All the Oceans. Below, the bow projected forward under the waterline for ramming any possible contender.

The double-ended, 38' pilot cutter *Ho-Ho* was resting nearby after a long and difficult winter passage from the North Sea. Her Norwegian crew of four amateurs planned to round the Cape of Good Hope and go on to Australia. Another of the many yachts was formerly owned by the late German Kaiser, Wilhelm II. This one, a racing schooner once called the *Meteor* and now the *Alta Vela,* was undergoing a kind of reconditioning before a projected passage to Buenos Aires and delivery to a new owner. Her former elegance was sadly dimmed — the mahogany paneling of her main saloon had been many times painted over, blurring the forms of splendid carving. Her decks were white, and her racing spars, even though they were cut down, still seemed to be too great a burden for her thin, corroded steel hull. Back on board the *Pilgrim,* Joe remarked in a low voice: "I could have put my foot t'rough her side."

There was an old bark, still in commission, and many more modern vessels — cargo steamers from Africa and South America, two- and three-masted schooners, and commercial ketches. Bumboats plied the harbor carrying monkeys and canary birds for sale. The *Pilgrim* had had one monkey for a pet and, at various times white rats, a sloth, a coati mundi, a tortoise, a cockatoo, and we were on our fourth cat — a dirty and silly fellow who used to climb to the mainmast and then complain because he could not get down — but never a sprightly and musical canary. A man in a bumboat exhibited a little beauty to us — pure yellow and full of song. With a little haggling, a bargain was made. A piece of silver changed hands, and the man in the boat, after turning his back for an instant, as if in catching his balance, handed up the cage and rowed away — with his decoy. It was an old trick. The bird he delivered never sang a note and died several days later, perhaps of fright at Kiki, our Siamese cat.

chapter 20

Bermuda and Boston

WE LEFT LAS PALMAS on 25 May 1934 in light airs which teased and baffled us all the way down to the twenty-second parallel. The North Atlantic wind ellipse was suffering from a hiatus for the time being, and not until our track had described a long sweep well to the south of the charted northerly limit of the northeast Trades did we pick it up. Even then, and for the entire passage of 3,300 miles to Bermuda, no strong breeze was encountered, with the exception of a brief succession of squalls when we were back in twenty-six degrees north, within three days of the Bermuda islands.

> **From Hod Fuller's journal: Fixed up a leaking air valve in the engine in the afternoon & had to manufacture a new spring for it as the old one was rusted away. Joe has made a fine chip log to use instead of our patent log. We have only one spinner left for it (the others have been taken by fish), and we are saving it for coasting.**

> *From the ship's log: May 28. 6–8 P.M. Nice little air, more than we have had for two days. Full moon, which should change the weather, according to Joe.*

Joe at work, watched by the Chief.

Day after day, the sun appeared astern, swung up over the mastheads, and sank, sizzling, over the horizon beyond the bowsprit. At each morning and afternoon sight, we crept a little further along on the paper chart, but no change in the balmy waste of water and sky marked our progress along the meridians. The simple requirements of steering and, at long intervals, adjusting a sheet or brace, released our attentions from the relation of the ship to her surrounding elements and allowed us to attend to the schooner herself.

Although she had been scrubbed, painted, varnished, oiled, and tarred thoroughly when she left the Canaries, there was, as there always is, a good deal more to be done. If you can once attain that condition when every square inch of a boat glistens like a brand new model (but rarely will), you can barely take enough time out to step back, paint brush in hand, and gloat over the sight before you must immediately start running again in order to stay in the same place.

The Commander & the Trader have been giving the brass on deck hell today. Joe is turning out a new set of wire pennants for the jib sheets — a very neat eye splicing job all served with wire.

The Chief was an inveterate beautifier. He went over the engine room with rag and brush, shining to a dazzle every brass pipe, knuckle, and cap, and touching up the cylinder heads and other high spots with scarlet paint. The insides of the cabin trunks, while white, were still of a variety of white which spoke of two years of rising fumes from beef goulashes and the smoke of many a late yarn session. While no one ever looked at them except when seeking something to do, they came in for a coat of enamel for good measure.

The housekeeping fever seized the Skipper, who turned his mind to the problem with the condition of the port stateroom, a double cabin he had occupied alone ever since Hawthorn's departure at Panama. These capacious quarters, accommodating a dresser, a clothes locker, a fixed berth, and an extension transom, had presented no problem at all at first. The Skipper's seamanly qualities included the tidy habits of the seafaring man, and as he traveled light, he had fairly rattled around in the space. As port after port was visited, however, he gradually acquired a collection of new and curious objects of all sorts. Shell hatbands, model outrigger canoes, grass dancing skirts, stuffed birds, grotesque masks, multiple-barbed spears, a canoe paddle, a conical Malayan sun-hat — all these and more.

In the beginning, apparently feeling that an explanation was needed for such extensive acquisitiveness, he would mention the name of some relative or child of a friend for whom he got the latest souvenir. It became apparent, however, as the assortment grew and all possible beneficiaries were provided for, that the Skipper was truly a human magpie. The reverse of the medal of which the face was his unusual neatness was an overpowering passion for collecting objects. As the accumulation continued, finally overflowing onto the transom and dresser, the Skipper gradually evicted himself from his own stateroom, the victim of his uncontrollable propensity, and took up quarters in the charthouse. Now, with housecleaning in his eye, he was not daunted as he surveyed this bulging bin and pondered the problem of painting the nearly obscured bulkheads, his spirit wavered. After days of grim industry, all the objects had been removed tenderly to the main cabin, one by one, and, the painting done, just as tenderly replaced. No one could perceive any difference in the appearance of the scene.

> *June 5. 6–8. Continued painting, scraping, etc. Weather lovely. Kept along making about SW true until 3:30 P.M., wind a fine Force 4. Then decided we are far enough south (lat. 18°46′ N, long. 30°47′ W) to be pretty sure of holding the Trades reasonably strong. So shifted light mainsail to port side, wore round & struck out W by N ¾ N. A fine breeze about ENE on starboard quarter. Set fisherman staysail, light mainstaysail & balloon jib & then hove the log which gives us eight and a half knots! Squaresail & raffee, which have been up since May 28, still pulling strong with yard braced up a bit.*

It was during the days of these domestic occupations that Kiki, the Siamese cat, was missed. She had not appeared to be happy on board from the first moment she was released from her basket and looked about at her comfortless surroundings with disdain. She was not so repelled by her situation that, like the Taboga cats, she jumped overboard, but instead made the best of her lot. She had been actively sick several times but in spite of suffering from worms, she gained her sea-legs eventually and ate with great ferocity a number of flying fish as well as a squid which Joe brought up with a dip net. As these manifestations of normality appeared, the ship's company came to accept her as a proper ship's cat and so felt some regret at her disappearance. Some three days later, however, a howl of indignation — and outrage — blasted up through the open skylight of the Skipper's cabin.

"Look at my coat, look at it! And my best shoregoing hat! Get *out* of here!"

The first of these adjurations was addressed to all in general. The Skipper's best, and indeed only, white duck coat, reserved for calling on island governors and occasions of similar formality, was not hung on a hanger in the ordinary way, but had been carefully folded, wrapped in brown paper, and placed on the floor of his clothes locker. The missing cat had torn away enough of the wrapping to expose a well-laundered nest and then deposited in it three white kittens. It was a mess. In the agony of her *accouchement*, Kiki had also chewed large pieces out of the hat. The touching charm of the family scene was lost on the Skipper. Mother and young were promptly given a properly upholstered whiskey case in another cabin. However, Kiki repeatedly carried her two youngsters that survived by the scruffs of their necks back to the place of their birth until it was locked against her.

> *June 8. 8–10 A.M. Took in light mainsail which had chafed through against spreader. Also halyard had chafed through one and a half strands against the backstay. This did not, however, deter Joe from trusting his weight to it in going aloft in the bosun's chair to reeve a new one.*

The evenings, like the days, were uniformly fine and were the regular occasion of the mostly superfluous star and planet observations which are characteristic of all leisurely amateur ocean voyages. We were not attempting to sail a great circle course, but only to hold a fair wind to the west, so that carefully plotted fixes of Antares, Kochab, Pollux, Alioth, Arcturus, and others served only for the personal gratification every navigator feels when his lines of position form a definitely minute polygon on the plotting sheet. A serious impediment to this self-congratulation was encountered on 7 June in the shape of a brilliant celestial body gleaming in the southwest sky at an altitude of about fourteen degrees. No method of identification in the *Nautical Almanac* pointed to any star or planet. Only after a week of exasperated night work did a reference, come across by chance in a text, to the infrequent and brief appearances of the planet Mercury reveal it as the mysterious stranger.

> *We sure are making time & roaring along. Also have the fisherman staysail set. It's too wet for the cat on deck in this kind of weather & after getting washed down the scuppers by a sea while heeled over she took to below & stowed herself away with her kittens.... This sort of weather must be unusual for the horse latitudes as we have had a Force 3 or 4 breeze ever since leaving the Trades & it was in this same latitude that we were becalmed coming down from Boston two years ago.*

On the morning of our twenty-eighth day out of Las Palmas, the solitude of the ocean, hitherto shared only with an occasional whale or mammoth sea turtle, was broken by the appearance of a number of gulls, terns, and bosun birds whose presence spoke of the nearness of land. We had already overlapped the most easterly point of our track to the Canal Zone, made two years before, and so had already circumnavigated the globe. As we approached Bermuda, the nostalgic fragrance of freesia and horse manure off the land made me feel as though we were virtually at home again, off merely on a little cruise. Several hours later, after picking up the pilot off St. David's Head and steaming up through the long channel, we let the anchor down in Hamilton

Harbor, off a little island on the Paget side.

We had just time for a refreshing dip when an approaching boat, carrying a white-clad lady who was leaning expectantly forward from the bows, caused some of us to reach for the protection of pareus and the rest to duck below.

"Mr. Taylor?" she called as the launch slowed off our quarter.

"There's no one named Taylor on board," I said.

"Oh! Where is he?"

"I don't know a Mr. Taylor."

"But this is his boat, isn't it?" she said, sweeping her eyes along the sheer.

"No. She's not connected in any way with anyone named Taylor."

"Whose is she?"

"Belongs to a man named Starr," the Skipper said.

"How long has he owned her?"

"Ever since she was a set of blue prints," the Skipper said. "Would you like to come aboard?"

"No, thank you," she said, now looking very confused and yet still studying the schooner's lines. "Listen, are you sure?" They sped away.

The next morning, the Skipper brought back from a trip ashore the Bermuda newspaper. In it was a short item that referred to the *Pilgrim* and yet ascribed her ownership to a Mr. Taylor of New York.

A lady in Panama once tried to convince me that the *Pilgrim* was the *Chance*, renamed, and departed obviously unconvinced. It is appalling to think of the number of gross misconceptions of pure fact-finding lodgment in the human mind against which not even such tangible and verifiable means of refutation can be brought as the registered identity of a 73-ton schooner. These misconceptions persist, to the continued complacency of their hosts and the progressive perpetuation of unnecessary error.

We lay at anchor for a week in Hamilton, protected by the awnings from the late June heat of day. The only sounds were the occasional tinkle of a bicycle bell or the clopping of hooves from the winding road along the shore.

> *June 25. Anchored at Hamilton. SS Monarch of Bermuda arrived at 8:30 & tied to dock. A three-masted schooner from Nassau with a deck load of lumber, which was anchored just outside the harbor yesterday, also came in & tied up. Fine morning & light southerly breeze. Sandpapered & oiled deck. Tarred forerigging.*

The Skipper and I pedaled out to Flatts one day to Mr. Mowbray's aquarium. We had been told we might find some old friends we would recognize, brought there by Vincent Astor after a voyage in his 263' diesel-powered yacht *Nourmahal*, a name which means "light of the harem." We recognized them in the shape of a dozen odd tortoises, one black and yellow iguana, a frigate bird, a flightless cormorant, and a company of penguins, all from the Galapagos.

On 27 June, the ketch *Vamarie* crossed the finish line of the Newport to Bermuda Race, followed by the schooners *High Tide*, *Water Gypsy*, *Grenadier*, and several dozen more yachts. Afterwards, their combined crews gathered in the bar of the Royal Bermuda Yacht Club, a room designed to accommodate a much smaller number of guests, and talked it over. The *Edlu*, a sloop, won the race on corrected time. We of the *Pilgrim* listened and enjoyed the company but had little to contribute.

It was great to see the boys from home after being away for two years. We had a good many coming aboard & being very interested in the vessel & hearing about the trip. They all made very good time on the way down, the weather being fine & plenty of wind rather than lack of it. The corrected time of the *Edlu* was sixty-nine

and a half hours, which is some going.

When finally the discussion died away a day or so later, it was time for the *Pilgrim* to head for home. After the payment of a whacking big exaction to the port office, second only to the fee at American Samoa, she was free to do so. Just before the anchor was hove short, the Skipper discovered that the steering gear was stuck fast. It had resisted ordinary force after the stay at Cannes, but this time it could not be moved at all from the deck. Joe had to go over the side and reeve quarter lines through the hole in the after edge of the rudder, designed to meet just such a contingency. Alternate heaves on these lines, together with working the wheel, finally freed the rudder of what was probably marine growth around the stock. The mechanism seemed to be in good order and there was no further trouble. After taking on a ton and a half of water from a barge in the harbor, we ran down Dundonald and the Narrows Channels, past St. David's Head, and squared away for home.

> *July 1. Commenced with a nice breeze but a head sea persists, which slows us up some.... A fine day & good breeze W and W by S. Considerable head sea occasionally smoothing out, but on the whole a pretty good chance along.... The Siamese kittens are growing big & frisky... Towards dark wind backed to WSW & we started a bit the sheets. The head sea having gone down considerably, we are roaring along in fine style.*

The waters through which we were about to pass have given plenty of trouble to mariners, especially in the Gulf Stream, but our passage on this occasion before a moderate southwest breeze was entirely uneventful. On our third Fourth of July aboard the schooner (the second we dressed the ship in Pago Pago, and the first we spent becalmed on the way to Panama), we were off the Nantucket Shoals, listening through patches of fog for the hoots of invisible steamers. A brown butterfly alighted on the main boom for a short breather, then took off again in the direction of Martha's Vineyard. Signs of the nearness of our native land were accumulating, but the crew seemed far from elated at the prospect of a homecoming.

> **Very smooth nice going with a breeze a hair forward of the beam; chilly weather here and we all feel it after being in warm climates for so long.... Have got the engine room all cleaned up and the brass polished for port.**

July 3. 6 A.M. Fog ahead. 6:30. Thick — seems like home at last.

A complaint in the log about the evening temperature of fifty-one degrees spoke rather of irritability than of a joyful anticipation which would have disregarded minor discomfort.

As the schooner tore along the back side of Cape Cod, her boiling wake led astern through some 28,500 miles of days and nights of life afloat with good companions, threading the channels and ports of strange but friendly waters and lands with no disaster to mar the recollection. The grief at Panama was long since swallowed up in our overcoming of it, just as the memory of every hour of calm and every shadow of disillusionment was submerged under a composite picture of every anticipation fulfilled or exceeded. The fragrance of Hiva Oa as we came upon it after a three weeks' passage across the southeastern Pacific blended into the sunlit coral bottom of the lagoon at Papeete, the roaring reach from Vavau to Samoa, and the pony bells of Bali.

Remembered were many a plate of baked *varo* and many a friendly glass but not a pinch of bicarbonate of soda. I could look astern and remember these things past with sad pleasure, because the coming home meant they were to end. Ahead lay perhaps half a life again. If the scene of it were to be no longer the soft and enervating background of the tropics, I had experienced a good bit of that for a time, and the hard bite of a New England winter on the cheek would bring its own satisfaction. From now on, I would have to get up betimes of a morning. On the other hand, I should not have to turn out in the middle of the night to prop my eyelids open during a mid-watch — except, that is, when I might do a little middle-aged cruising along the coast. I could look at it either way, but I could no longer take my choice. We were racing past Highland Light for home, with everything drawing.

It would have been a glorious finish to stand in through the Narrows as we were going now, with the weather rigging taut and the afternoon sun gleaming from every sail and block, but the sun and the wind both had dropped by the time we came up to Harding Ledge. We putt-putted up Boston Harbor in a flat calm and dropped anchor just after midnight 5 July 1934 under a silent and darkened city. The Chief produced a bottle and proposed a toast, to which we all drank, but the fact and the circumstance of our homecoming made it a quiet and thoughtful ceremony.

Early the next morning, we received our first greeting from a fellow in a boat which had come alongside.

"Hey! You can't anchor here."

Joe was on deck, wiping the night's soot from the rail. "Why? I was in a ship like this once. She anchored right here."

"That don't make no difference. You godda ged ouda here. An' right away, too."

appendix A

Crew of the Schooner Pilgrim

by Richard M. Dey

The Commander, **Donald C. Starr**, owner of the schooner, in effect the First Mate, and author of this narrative. Starr, an attorney in Boston, was thirty-one at the start of the voyage. He was graduated from Phillips Andover Academy in 1918, Harvard College in 1922, and Harvard Law School in 1925. An Assistant Attorney General in Massachusetts before the voyage, Starr returned to the law in private practice afterwards.

The Skipper, **Harold Peters,** captain of the schooner. A native of Boston, he was forty-four at the start of the voyage. He was graduated from Harvard College in 1910. Peters sailed in commercial schooners out of Maine before World War I, and served in various naval ships during the war. Afterwards, he managed to do considerable sailing, making a trans-Atlantic round-trip in 1920 as master of the schooner *Lloyd W. Berry* and serving as navigator on yachts in the Bermuda, Transatlantic, and Fastnet Races. His brother, Andrew J. Peters, had been the Mayor of Boston.

The Chief, **Horace W. Fuller**, Chief Engineer of the schooner. Raised just outside of Boston, in Milton, "Hod," as he was also known, was twenty-four at the start of the voyage. He was

Part of the crew.

graduated from Milton Academy in 1926 and Harvard College in 1930. He had been director of the Harvard Flying Club and worked briefly as a transport pilot and in finance on State Street. After an exceptionally distinguished military career during World War II, in which he fought in France and Guadalcanal, retiring from the Marine Corps as a Brigadier General, he ran charter yachts in Greece.

The Trader, **Joseph McCammon**, in effect the Assistant Engineer and Second Mate. A native of Washington, D.C. and briefly in the business of selling airplanes, he was twenty-five at the start of the voyage. He later went into investment banking and became president of the Washington Stock Exchange.

The boatswain for the schooner, **Joseph Ekelund,** forty-one, was a hired hand. Born and raised in Sweden, Joe had worked aboard a number of yachts, including the *Highland Light* and the *Yankee* owned by Frank Paine. Joe and the Skipper previously sailed together in the *Highland Light*. He was described by John Parkinson in *Nowhere is Too Far* variously as "colorful," "a mighty physical specimen," and "the shipmate and friend of many [Cruising Club of America] members." Joe later served as captain aboard General George C. Patton's schooners *Arcturus* and *When And If*. He named one of his two children after Wilfrid O. "Kelvin" White.

The Cook, **John Vranken**. Born in Belgium and a resident of East Boston, he was forty at the start of the voyage.

The Doc, **Richard C. Durant**, twenty-six, began the voyage in Boston but left a year later in Samoa to return to Harvard Medical School, from which he was graduated in 1934. He previously was graduated from Yale, where he was a varsity oarsman. After working as a surgeon in New York and as Chief of Surgery at Annapolis, he retired in Honolulu. The Doc was a medical witness at the First Atomic Tests in the Pacific and died in Pago Pago, Samoa, where he had left the *Pilgrim* nearly forty years earlier.

Langley Hawthorn was a friend and contemporary of the Skipper's from their World War I convoy days. Hawthorn had done some yacht racing in Long Island Sound. He left the schooner in Panama.

Murph, **Charles B. G. Murphy**, joined the schooner in Panama and stayed aboard until family matters called him back to Detroit, Michigan, from Tahiti. He was a Yale graduate, where he was perhaps an acquaintance of The Doc's.

Kelvin, **Wilfrid O. White**, was the nautical instrument inventor and manufacturer who ran a ship's chandlery in Boston. It was White who outfitted the *Pilgrim* and served as a communications link between the schooner and the New England yachting community, which was then small enough that it passed through White's doors on State Street routinely. "Kelvin" joined the schooner in Tahiti and made a two-week passage to Raiatea.

Charlie, **Charles Lipscomb**, was from Easton, Maryland. He had been with a yacht brokerage in Annapolis and seems to have been about the same age as The Chief and The Trader. He sailed aboard the schooner from Tahiti to Suva and might have stayed longer had he not come down with jaundice.

Bill, **S. C. M. Cutting**, was a British engineer who signed aboard in Singapore and made the run to Nice.

appendix B

The Making of a Schooner
by Donald C. Starr

HAVING GROWN UP NEAR FRESH WATER in Winchester, Massachusetts, I operated in rafts, canoes, skiffs, and powerboats. I did no salt water sailing (except once for some catboating in Buzzard's Bay in 1916) or cruising until 1920, when I was nineteen. That summer before my sophomore year in college, I had the opportunity to range the waters between Nantucket and Block Island with Quincy Howe in his family's 22' catboat. She had little navigational equipment, and the bottom was often tested with the centerboard by the cat's whisker method; even when we grounded, the removal of human and, in the last resort, of lead ballast always floated her off. While this kind of sailing was the worst possible training in pilotage, other aspects of those cruises out of Cotuit, such as the absence of power and ice, did prepare me for extended cruising.

After chartering a small schooner out of Fairhaven, Massachusetts, in the late 1920s for a cruise down Long Island Sound, I bought a 41' Casey ketch in 1931. With the help of Mark Howe, who had sailed there before, I made my way from buoy to buoy in dense fog to St. Andrews, New Brunswick, an especially rewarding spot in those days. That summer, I decided to make a longer voyage and began a search for an appropriate vessel. One

80' schooner built by Arthur D. Story at Essex, Massachusetts, while just the right type was too expensive. Another about the same size, and quite able and fast, had relatively slack bilges and outside ballast which would not have made for comfort on an ocean voyage. These two just about constituted the whole market as I saw it.

Due to my inexperience of deep water then, I was looking for a somewhat larger vessel than I would want now for the same purpose. In 1931, the gaff-schooner rig had still not been displaced by the new type of offshore sailing vessel typified by the Sparkman & Stephens yawl *Dorade* as a dependable and easily handled rig for deep-sea cruising in foreign waters. The idea then was not, as now, to go off in a small boat that is part of a flotilla connected by radio, but to have a vessel that could go safely off on its own over the seas of the globe.

Warwick Tompkins and the *Wander Bird*, his famous 85' North Sea pilot schooner, were working out of Boston at about that time. They confirmed my ideas regarding the size, rig, and accommodations of a vessel, and suggested many of the elements that went into the *Pilgrim*. Tompkins himself attended the launching of my schooner in Boothbay and became a life-long friend. Another schoonerman in Boothbay Harbor then was Sterling Hayden. A boy of about fifteen at the time, he lived there and took great interest in the *Pilgrim's* construction. He wanted to go along with me, but I felt at the time that it was too much of a responsibility to take along a lad so young. I subsequently felt sure that he would have been a great addition to the crew.

I had the schooner designed by John Alden primarily because he had revolutionized yachting by adapting the fishing schooner of New England waters to the abilities and requirements of yachtsmen. He also admired Tompkins' schooner, having written: "I consider *Wander Bird* the best-designed and best-built vessel of her size in America." Alden's own highly regarded *Malabars* gave yachtsmen the ability to go offshore with the assurance that their boats were designed for that purpose while also affording the speed every yachtsman appreciates, provided it is not purchased at the price of his idea of minimum comfort and ability. Alden's *Malabars* were proving very successful in ocean racing then, but he could not have been more pleased than by my order for a strictly cruising design. No one could have done a better job at it.

❋ ❋ ❋

The *Pilgrim's* dimensions were 85', l.o.a., 70' l.w.l., 20' 8" beam, and 12' draft. She had a billet head that added 3' 10" to her length and her bow sprit added another 17'. The billet head is the timber, fastened to the stem, that results in the clipper bow. John G. Alden, her designer, gave her the clipper bow because it was more in keeping with her high freeboard and bulwarks. She had a long straight keel with considerable forefoot. Her counter stern was short. Planked with long leaf unbled yellow pine on white oak, she was bronze spike fastened to one foot above the waterline. The rest of the fastenings were galvanized nails. Her decks were white pine. Chinese teak was used for the wheel box, rail cap and various pieces of trim. Her fittings were of galvanized iron. All her ballast was inside, amounting finally to some forty tons.

There was a comfortable sunken deck, or "dog" house, aft, with two berths and a chart table. The diesel was below this. There were two staterooms aft, a double for the Owner and a single for the Skipper, with a head between them. A large main cabin 18' long had four fixed berths, two on each side. A large galley, a second head, ample storage space, large closets, a forward stateroom, and a fo'c'sle big enough for four paid hands completed the accommodations.

She was rigged as a gaff topsail schooner and carried a 40' yard permanently mounted on her foremast. Her two masts and topmasts, all booms, and gaffs were of Oregon pine. Her standing rigging was galvanized steel, connected to the chain plates by lanyards and deadeyes. The running rigging was manila rope. All the sails were of cotton duck, machine sewed. A raffee with a 6' club at the head was set above the yard and a squaresail below it. With the main mast stepped well aft and both masts of nearly the same size and height, the sail area was pretty well equally divided, making sail handling relatively easy. The normal head rig was fore staysail, inner and outer jibs, and flying jib. We carried and used a main gaff topsail but did not bother with a fore topsail. In light air, we used a ballooner, fisherman staysail, and a lower staysail of about the same shape. We also had a large jib-headed mainsail that was attached to hoops on the main low-ermast and set flying to the topmast. When the wind was broad on the quarter, this big sail was sheeted to a block on the end of the main boom which was guyed out. With that and both stay-sails, raffee, squaresail, and ballooner, we could set quite a spread of canvas to a moderate trade wind.

The *Pilgrim* was powered by a rebuilt 85-horsepower Winton diesel which burned slightly less than three gallons an hour and pushed her along at about five knots. Her fuel tanks held about 550 gallons and we carried extra fuel in 75-gallon drums. A small diesel generator provided electricity for lights and windlass; she had no refrigeration, however. She had a Kelvin & White compen-sating yacht binnacle fitted with a 7" spherical compass that sat in front of a 49" wide mahogany wheel. The only radio equipment was a small and primitive National Company receiving set which sometimes produced a time-tick but usually received transmis-sions in the International Morse Code. There were three chronom-eters. Cooking was done on a Shipmate equipped with pressure kerosene burners. Water capacity was about 1,100 gallons. Ground tackle included galvanized loose stock Fisherman type anchors, one 350 pounds, one 250 pounds, and one 125 pounds. Anchor chains were ¾" close link galvanized, two lengths of 40 fathoms each. We carried two dories, the 14' "peapod" dory nested inside the slightly larger Swampscott dory, lashed down on the forward starboard deck.

The *Pilgrim* was built by the Reed-Cook Construction Company of Boothbay Harbor, Maine, between the fall of 1931 and the spring of 1932. She was outfitted by Kelvin & Wilfrid O. White Company, of Boston. She cost about $35,000 by the time she reached Boston in July 1932, preparatory to final outfitting, provisioning, and departure.

❂ ❂ ❂

Brief Biography of a Schooner

by Richard M. Dey

The following is a compilation of information found in various press releases, books, journals, magazine articles, letters, and interviews.

"During the morning, we put the small boat overboard & the Doc & Trader rowed off from the *Pilgrim* and got some pictures of her under jib topsail, flying jib, jib, staysail, foresail, fisherman staysail, mains'l & main gaff topsail. We are all very keen to see how they turn out as these are the first pictures ever taken of the vessel underway."

Hod Fuller, 4 June 1933
Lat. 20°41' S, Long. 170°05' W.

The *Pilgrim* was, in 1934, the largest Alden yacht to complete a circumnavigation — the smallest being William A. Robinson's

32' ketch *Svaap,* which went around between 1928 and 1931.

Donald Starr, on going ashore in Boston, returned to his career in law. After leasing the *Pilgrim* to a treasure seeking expedition that went to the Canaries and Haiti in 1935, he sold the schooner to Phillips Lord, better known as "Seth Parker" to radio fans. Too busy to use her as much as he had hoped, Lord sold her, and in 1937, she went through the Panama Canal up to California. That year, she was featured in the August issue of *The National Geographic* in an article by Harold Peters, her skipper for the circumnavigation, "The *Pilgrim* Sails the Seven Seas."

A wealthy Fullerton, California, rancher bought the schooner to establish a training vessel for boys. Before he was able to put his plan into effect, however, he died, willing the *Pilgrim* to the Christian Science Church. The schooner was then sold at auction to movie actor Lewis Stone, who achieved fame as Judge Hardy in the *Andy Hardy* movies. An avid sailor, he used her weekends until World War II closed the coastal waters to yachtsmen. He turned the schooner over to the Coast Guard, and she became a floating schoolhouse for trainees. After the war, he sold the ship.

In those days, shark liver was a highly commercial commodity as a vitamin source, and her new owner sent the *Pilgrim* on a shark fishing venture off Costa Rica. The proud schooner then experienced her darkest days. Another new owner virtually dismantled her, installed bait tanks, and anchored her off Redondo Beach, California, as a sport fishing barge. This operation failed and the *Pilgrim* lay neglected in Los Angeles Harbor for a few years before being purchased by Harry S. McGill of Wilmington, California.

McGill, his wife, and their three young sons reconditioned her and lived aboard. They made frequent trips to the neighboring islands and began leasing her to 20th Century-Fox, the movie studio.

The schooner's life before Hollywood cameras began in the

movies *Sealed Cargo* (1951) and *Pearl of the South Pacific* (1955). She became known to millions between 1959 and 1962 as the *Tiki* in the ABC TV series *Adventures in Paradise*. The program was originated by James Michener and starred Gardner McKay. In those days, she sailed out of Newport Harbor. Filming took place off California's Channel Islands.

After the TV series, the *Tiki* became the *Pilgrim* again and was purchased by the popular folksinger Glenn Yarbrough in 1965. Two years later, James Ready and Bruce Martens, two young men looking to get into the charter business, formed a corporation with Yarbrough. They renamed her the *Tiki* and refitted her in San Juan, Puerto Rico. She was totally refurbished to accommodate twenty passengers on five-day cruises in the Virgin Islands.

From Port Royal, Jamaica, Bruce Martens wrote Starr in December of 1966: "I have been reconditioning the *Pilgrim*... She has been rebuilt forward — stem piece, cants, knight heads and bitts, with new decking under the winch heads and to aft of the scuttle hatch. She is tight, her planking being sound and well-pickled. Below I have opened her up by taking out some cabins and going pilot boat style for more light and air. The Master's cabin extends for the full width under the skylight forward of the engine room. For part of our trip we had seventeen people aboard and were not crowded.

"The *Pilgrim* was bald-headed when I got her, but I have now rigged her with topmasts, course (squaresail) and raffee.... I am continually surprised that she moves in just light airs, and takes two sixty-knot gales beautifully.

"I am inspecting the possibilities of charter either here or St. Thomas. She is a vessel that catches the eye and, as my wife says, 'She sails like a Cadillac rides.'"

She sailed in the charter trade out of St. Thomas throughout the 1970s. Representing the Seven Seas Sailing Club of New York, she participated in Operation Sail, 1976, which commemorated the Bicentennial of the Declaration of Independence.

She was sunk in Admiralty Bay, Bequia, in August 1980, when Hurricane Allen struck. She had opened up while on a passage from Antigua to St. Vincent with a cargo of refrigerators and was in Bequia for repairs. Her owner at that time, a jazz musician from the States, left her there some months earlier. Eventually, she was sold to a man from Union Island, who pulled the sticks out of her and stripped her to rig a vessel he was building. The hull was towed west of the island and sunk. She had sailed for forty-eight years.

In March of 1976, before she headed north from the Caribbean for New York, Starr wrote a letter in response to someone who had come upon Harold Peters' article in the 1937 *National Geographic.* Starr noted some of her film history, including *Adventures in Paradise,* "in which she always appeared with the main strapped down hard, as if she never had the good fortune to meet with a fair wind. I am happy to recollect that in sailing around the world, that is what you have by far the most of. She is still called the *Tiki.* With new bulwarks, which I have reason to believe were added at least partly to conceal some hogging of her sheer, she only slightly resembles the beauty that came off the ways at Boothbay Harbor in April of 1932."

The Pilgrim's *Leak*

Following is Report No. 729, submitted by William Ruxton, Surveyor to American Bureau of Shipping and made in Balboa, 3 August 1932.

This is to certify that the undersigned Surveyor to this Bureau did at the request of the Owners attend the Wood Auxiliary Yacht *Pilgrim* of Boston, 73 gross tons, Harold Peters, Master, as she lay in the dry dock at Mount Hope, C. Z., on August 2, 1932, in order to examine and report upon leaky condition of Hull.

1. Reported that hull developed slight leakage from the sea during the voyage.
2. Yacht placed in dry dock at Mount Hope, C. Z. for purpose of copper sheathing outside of hull below the water line.
3. Seams of hull planking gone over and dealt with as necessary. Copper sheathing installed as intended and vessel undocked.
4. After floating of Yacht it was discovered she was leaking and was redocked for examination.
5. Several strakes of copper sheathing entirely removed from keelson to well up vessel's sides, port and starboard, and from stem to stern. Hull part filled with water internally in effort to locate source of leakage. Examination by Surveyor at this time disclosed considerable number of bronze spike fastenings as

Preparing the *Pilgrim* for hoisting.

leaking where the hull planking is secured to frames. Approximately 25%, a number showed leaking heavy, indicating that fastenings apparently did not properly fill the hole, or possibly straining by stress of weather. No evidence of leaky seams noted.

6. The Yacht was not examined internally by Surveyor due to presence of water for hull testing purposes, also considerable amount of sash weights for ballast purposes stowed in bottom portion of hull.

In my opinion, Yacht in her present condition is considered unseaworthy for the long voyage of two years as proposed.

(signed) Surveyor to American Bureau of Shipping

❂ ❂ ❂

Following is the complete text of an undated, unsigned affidavit by Mr. Shreves. It probably was written at the time the Pilgrim *left the Mt. Hope dry dock, 18 August 1932.*

My name is Sheppard J. Shreves, foreman shipwright and dock master at Cristóbal, Canal Zone. I have been an apprentice, journeyman shipwright, foreman shipwright and dock master for thirty-two years, the last nineteen years having been spent in the employ of the United States Government at Cristóbal. Other places include Newport News, V.A., ten years, New York Shipbuilding Company, Camden, N.J., Cramps' and Bath Iron Works.

I first saw the schooner yacht *Pilgrim* on July 18, 1932. It was stated to me at that time that she was leaking, and she was put into dry dock in order to locate and stop the leak and copper her bottom. I found several places in forefoot keel and stern where stopwaters were needed. These were inserted. There were two old worm holes in the false keel. These were cut out and graving-pieces put in. I found also that the forefoot was of an inferior piece of timber, soft and split in several places, and was leaking heavily. Three stopwaters were put in this and it was caulked. Several places in this forefoot were tested with a caulking iron, which was driven in easily to a depth of an inch and a half, and yards of cotton were put in.

On examination of the planking, it was found that the putty had squeezed out of the seams, which would indicate that the planking had been working. It was further discovered, after removing the putty from several seams and butts that a caulking iron could be driven about one and one half inches into the seams, and further in the butts.

I reefed out one seam and small places in several different seams and there appeared to be very little oakum in them — I judge two thin threads. It was considered necessary to recaulk the entire hull up to the water line, which was done.

I also found one plank under the port fore rigging about halfway from the keel to the water line which was badly split through to the inside, which I ascertained by inserting a hacksaw blade from the outside through to the inside. The plank, fourteen feet long, was removed and replaced with a new plank. After this was completed about eighteen inches of water were pumped into the vessel to test her while lying in dry dock. It was discovered that she was leaking in four places through the plugs of the fastenings in both garboard strakes. These plugs were cut out and the spikes set up and the holes replugged. The vessel then showed no leak as she then lay, and she was painted and coppered and floated out of dry dock.

The following day it was discovered that the vessel was leaking about three-fourths as much as she had before. In order to find the leak, lead and iron ballast and several pieces of the ceiling were removed. Also some of the cement ballast, with iron punchings and window weights, round the fore and mainmasts, without revealing the cause of the leak.

I then discovered that a general leak was coming from round all the exposed frames. I could pass a hacksaw blade between the planks and the frames, striking the main fastenings, the blade showing water, which led me to the conclusion that the leak was in the main fastenings. At these points, the planks were not tight against the frames at the points where the spikes passed through.

It was also found that the seacock in the ship's side from the galley sink drain pump could not be closed on account of the handles coming into contact with the planking, and that one of the valves in the pump was adrift, which allowed water to back up into the sink. Also in the pipe from the sink to the pump there was a very bad leak in one of the elbows, which was continuous since the seacock could not be shut. This leak was stopped by refitting the pipe, and the pump and the handle of the seacock were repaired.

This vessel was again put into dry dock and about a third of the copper removed. She was then refloated in a cradle, the keel blocks removed, and filled with water up to the floor. About a third of the plugs then exposed showed considerable leaking, but no further leak in the keel.

I then removed all exposed plugs and set up all spikes from one-eighth to one-quarter of an inch as it appeared to me that most of them were not driven home. I turned up white pine end-grain plugs and inserted them with white lead in place of the original machine plugs.

Upon being refloated again it was found that about a third of the leak had been stopped, which convinced me that the trouble had been found. The vessel was accordingly redocked, the remainder of the copper removed, and all the spikes and plugs below the water line similarly treated. While doing this work I found three plugs over holes into which no spikes had been driven: one of these on strake nine, port side, abreast the fore-rigging, the second on strake twelve forward of main-rigging, the third on the starboard side about one foot aft of the main rigging in plank twelve. These three holes were plugged with dowels and then plugged like the others. All felt and copper was then replaced and the vessel floated.

(signed) Sheppard J. Shreves

❂ ❂ ❂

Following is the complete text of a signed affidavit by Lt. Cowdrey, dated 12 November 1932, Balboa, C.Z.

The undersigned, Roy T. Cowdrey, is Production Assistant to the Superintendent of the Mechanical Division of the Panama Canal, and holds a commission as a Naval Constructor, U.S.N.

I have held this position for one year and four months and my experience with wooden ship construction stands from a period of four years and was acquired at Boston and Philadelphia Navy Yards.

At the request of the owner, Donald C. Starr, of the Schooner Yacht *Pilgrim*, that she be replanked or that her leaky condition be otherwise remedied, I directed the operation of hoisting the said Schooner out of the water at Paraiso, Canal Zone, for this work to be done. Prior to the hoisting out, all portable ballast, most of fuel oil and water on board, anchors, chains, sails and other loose gear were put ashore in safe storage. All the copper was removed from her bottom, as well as felt and tar, and the hull scraped clean. The plugs over all spikes below the floor line (or below the level of the water then inside the vessel) showed water issuing therefrom in drops and trickles. I observed that some of the spikes were driven off the center of the counterbore, so that in some instances the head of the spike had bruised the wood around the counterbore, and in other cases the spikes were bent so that heads would clear edge of counterbore. Into some of the holes an awl or wire could be easily inserted past the head of the spike to a depth of several inches, and in some instances as far as the frame. The spike was found to be driven at a sharp angle to a line fair with the plank. The removal of one of the plugs uncovered a hole into which no spike had been driven.

One complete strake was removed from each side, consisting of staggered planks at or near the water line. Each of the four planks when split offered evidence that the round holes were larger than the spikes which were inserted in them. This condition plainly appears from the samples of wood to which I have affixed my initials for identification. I observed no portion of any of these planks where this condition did not exist. The wood around the spikes, as shown by some of these samples, has been blackened, in my opinion from water, and the plug holes from some of these samples, and in many other portions of the hull, showed a similar condition.

All of the plug holes below the water line are to be and are being tapped, and a gun inserted for the introduction of a mixture of equal parts of red lead, white lead and litharge softened with varnish into the spike holes under pressure. At the date of making this statement, approximately 1,750 of the holes have been so treated out of approximately 4,900 holes below the water line. The above described lead and litharge mixture has been used in an amount of 150# up to this date.

I examined the quality and workmanship of the planking and of the caulking, and find them to be good.

(signed) Roy T. Cowdrey

Glossary

by Richard M. Dey

Note: This glossary is not meant to substitute for a sea dictionary or any good, standard dictionary. It is provided to help the reader with the arcane words and terms unique to a schooner found in this narrative.

Backing: change in the wind direction contrary to its normal pattern. In northern latitudes, the wind is backing when it moves counter-clockwise. In southern latitudes, clockwise. In all latitudes, a backing wind is taken as a sign the wind will freshen.

Bale: a curved metal hoop or band to which blocks are shackled. In a schooner, bales are found at the ends of booms and gaffs, and sometimes aloft at the crosstrees.

Band: metal fitted around the end of a spar to which stays are attached, sometimes to a bale mounted on it.

Beaufort Scale: a numerical scale devised by British admiral Beaufort to indicate the force of the wind. Ranging from Force 0 to Force 12, the number indicates not only the strength of the wind in nautical miles per hour and in description (Calm, Moderate Breeze, Near Gale, Storm, and so on), but the height and state of the sea ("Large wavelets, crests begin to break" in the case of Force 3 or "Large waves, streaky foam" for Force 7).

Bend: to rig a sail.

Bight: a long, not necessarily deep coastal indentation or curve bigger than a bay or cove.

Bilge: the outside turn of the hull below the waterline, or the area about the keelson inside the hull where water collects and various items are sometimes stored.

Boatswain: in yachting circles, a hired hand responsible for rigging, anchors, sails, and routine maintenance on deck and aloft. Also spelled as commonly pronounced: bosun.

Bob Stay: the stay that runs between the end of the bowsprit and the stem of a ship to support the bowsprit from beneath.

Boltrope: rope sewn to the edge of a sail to add strength and prevent tearing.

Boom Crutch: support for the boom's end when the sail is not up. It is usually a Y-shaped piece of wood.

Boom Gallows: permanent support for the main boom in the shape of a frame spanning the after deck, aft of the wheel.

Bower: a heavy anchor used in ordinary circumstances.

Brace: a line or block and tackle rig used for trimming the yard.

Brailing: the system for setting, reefing and furling a squaresail.

Brake: another word for the handle of a pump.

Breaker: a small water cask in a ship's lifeboat.

Bridle: rope or chain whose ends are made fast to a spar or another rope, and whose mid-section becomes the purchase point.

Broach: A vessel is said to broach, or broach-to when, running before or off the wind, she is suddenly driven up into the wind and, in the process, shoved hard over by a sea onto her beam ends or side.

Buffalo Rail: a low rail mounted on top of the bulwarks and running from the bow aft to a point about even with the forecastle hatch.

Bulwarks: the sides of a vessel above the deck; more generally, the rail.

Bumpkin: V-shaped strut that extends beyond the afterdeck to hold the lower end of the main or mizzen backstay, making the stay free of the main or mizzen boom.

Bung: a round wooden plug placed over a screw or spike that is countersunk.

Burton: block and tackle used to pull a heavy anchor up from its hanging position at the waterline, over the rail, and onto the deck for storage. Also to pull it up to the cathead, with which the *Pilgrim* eventually was fitted.

Butt: the joint between the ends of two planks.

Cabin Sole: a cabin's floor.

Cable's Length: 200 yards or one-tenth of a nautical mile.

Cathead: a curved beam extending from a frame out over the bow of a ship, used to let down and haul up the anchor.

Caulking: material, usually cotton or oakum, hammered in between planks to insure watertightness and some elasticity. Oakum is made of tarred rope fibers.

Ceiling: planking fastened to the frames *inside* the vessel.

Chain Plate: a metal strip that is bolted to the hull and to which, at the top, a stay is attached.

Chance Along: a good start to a passage.

Charley Noble: the galley smoke pipe or any chimney fitted to the deck for a source of heat.

Checked: wood having splits, chinks, or cracks.

Chock: a fitting which serves as a lead for dock lines.

Cockbilled: said of a yard when it is not positioned in its usual manner perpendicular to the mast, but angled.

Counter: the stern.

Covering Boards: the outermost deck planks that run the length of the ship and cover the frame tops.

Crosstrees: spreaders.

Cutwater: where the stem of the bow cuts through the water.

❂ ❂ ❂

Dead Reckoning: the method of navigation using time, speed, and distance to find the ship's position.

Drift: Velocity of the current.

❂ ❂ ❂

Fashion Pieces: aftermost timbers below the waterline which shape the vessel's stern.

Fo'c'sle: short for forecastle, the forwardmost cabin or enclosed space in a vessel.

Forefoot: the place where the stem — at the bow — joins the keel.

Force: see Beaufort Scale.

Freeboard: the distance between the waterline and the top of the rail.

❂ ❂ ❂

Gangway: an opening or door in the bulwarks for getting on and off the vessel; more generally, the structure, composed of a ladder with platforms at its top and bottom, used for getting up onto or down off of a vessel.

Garboard Strakes: the hull planking immediately next to the keel.

Gaskets: ropes or bands of sail cloth used to secure sails to spars.

Graving Piece: a new, shaped piece of wood inserted in place of wood that has rotted. Also called a "dutchman."

Gripes: ropes used to secure a dory to chocks on deck or when a dory is slung from davits. In the latter case, they prevent the small boat from swinging.

Guy: any rope or wire that supports, steadies, or guides a horizontal or slightly inclined spar, such as a bowsprit or a boom.

Gybe: see jibe.

❂ ❂ ❂

Hank: a device used to connect the luff (leading edge) of a sail to the stay.

Hauling: used with regard to wind, it means moving in a clockwise direction. Also called "veering." It is a sign that the wind is moderating.

Hawse-Hole: the opening in the bows of a vessel through which the anchor chain passes.

Heading Up: pointing the vessel higher into the wind.

Heave-to: to lay the vessel on the wind in a storm with the helm to leeward and the reduced sail — in a schooner, usually the foresail — sheeted in tight.

Hermaphrodite Brig: a two-masted vessel rigged with squaresails on the foremast and fore-and-aft sails.

Hoop: a round, light device, usually made of laminated wood which attaches to a sail and travels over a spar as the sail is set or taken in.

Hove-to: see heave-to.

Hull Speed: the fastest the boat can go, according to mathematical calculation based on design factors.

✪ ✪ ✪

Jackstay: any stay that does an odd, usually secondary job, or is without a specific name.

Jaws: the concave piece of wood or metal that is attached to the forward end of a boom or gaff and fits around the mast, connecting the two spars.

Jibe: to run off before the wind and change tacks with the boom shifting over, sometimes violently.

Jog: to tack back and forth, or to run up and down a course.

Jumbo: the fore staysail.

✪ ✪ ✪

Keelson: the timber bolted to the top of the keel for reinforcement.

❂ ❂ ❂

Lace Lines or Lacing: rope that holds a sail to a spar.

Lateen: a triangular sail set from a long yard which is attached obliquely to a short mast.

Lazarette: space below the deck at the very stern, used for stowage.

Lazy-Jacks: lines rigged on either side of a sail to prevent the sail from spilling away from the boom.

Lead Line: a line usually fifty or one hundred fathoms long at the end of which is a chunk of lead used for taking soundings.

Line: a rope on a vessel.

Log Line: the line trailed astern a vessel at sea at the end of which is a rotator that turns according to how fast the vessel is going. These revolutions, transmitted by the line, are then calculated by the log, a mechanical device mounted on the taffrail, and converted into distance figures.

Log or Patent Log: The whole mechanism of case, line, and rotator used to measure distance traveled and determine speed.

❂ ❂ ❂

Manrope Knot: a knot at the end of a rope.

Mole: a wharf or pier.

❂ ❂ ❂

Nip: the part of a rope around a thimble, as in the nip of an eye splice.

❂ ❂ ❂

Parcel: to wrap around with a material such as canvas or leather.

Parrel: a half-ring of rope or wire, commonly fitted with wooden trucks or beads, that is attached to the ends of the gaff jaws once the jaws are in place around the mast, enabling them to slide up or down the mast, or to work from side to side without pulling clear of it.

Parrel Truck: a small wooden, often maple, bead strung on the parrel that enables the parrel to slide easily and without chafing.

Patent Log: device used to measure the distance the vessel sails and her speed.

Peak: the end of a gaff.

Pelorus: a fixed compass card on which bearings relative to the ship's position are taken.

Pendant: wire or rope with one end made fast to a yard, sail, or gaff.

Pig: cast iron or lead, weighing five to three hundred pounds, in the shape of a brick or ingot.

Point: any of the thirty-two equal divisions marked at the circumference of a compass card that indicate direction. One point is equivalent to 11° 25'.

Pratique: permission to enter port granted by a health officer. Until this is given, a ship entering a foreign port is considered in temporary quarantine and must fly the yellow "Q" flag.

❂ ❂ ❂

Quarter: the port or starboard side of a vessel to any point forty-five degrees forward of dead astern.

✪ ✪ ✪

Raffee: the small triangular sail set between the yard and foremast head.

Range: the straight line that extends from two or more objects lined up one in front of the other. It is frequently used in coastal navigation, especially for entering harbors, to indicate a course to steer or a danger to avoid.

Reef: to make a sail temporarily smaller.

Reef Out: to remove caulking from a seam.

Relieving Tackle: tackles used to hold the booms close to the leeward rail, preventing them from jibing or swinging at random.

Rhumb Line: the path of a ship on a fixed compass course, shown on a chart as crossing all meridians at the same angle.

Rotator: the device towed at the end of the patent log line whose sleek, finned design makes it rotate.

Round-to: to turn into the wind or current, bow first. Also round-up.

Rudder Post: the aftermost vertical timber which supports the rudder.

Rudder Stock: the forward edge of the rudder as well as that part which passes up through the rudder port into the ship where the steering mechanism is attached.

✪ ✪ ✪

Seam: the space between planks.

Set: the direction a current moves a vessel.

Set up: in the context of spikes, the meaning is to drive the spike home, all the way up into its countersunk bung hole.

Sheave: the roller in a block.

Sheet: the rope used to control a sail by hauling, or sheeting, it in or letting it out.

Shroud: the major side ropes or wires supporting a mast.

Slip: space alongside a wharf used for lodging a boat.

Spanker: the quadrilateral, fore-and-aft sail set from the aftermast of a squarerigged vessel to help drive it better to windward.

Spar: any pole in the rigging of any craft: mast, boom, gaff, yard, bowsprit, spreader, and so forth.

Spike: a long nail.

Spring Stay: the wire running between mastheads.

Sprit: a long spar run diagonally up from the lower mast to hold up the peak of the sail.

Stay: any rope or wire that supports a mast or bowsprit.

Stern Sheets: the place in the after part of the boat where the sheets are handled.

Stop: a length of rope or strip of sail cloth used to lash down a sail.

Stop-water: a nail driven through the keel and stem where they join at the forefoot. Also, a felt packing set in lead between planks to make a watertight joint.

Supercargo: an officer or person aboard a ship whose responsibility is for the cargo alone, having nothing to do with running the ship.

Swinging-ship: the process of finding the deviation, if any, of a compass on every compass point of the ship's head.

❂ ❂ ❂

Tack: a vessel is on the port tack when the wind is coming over her port bow, on the starboard tack when the wind is over her starboard bow. When a vessel is tacked, she's brought from one tack, through the eye of the wind, to the other.

Tackle: gear of rope and two or more blocks used to multiply the power exerted on the rope, and so make work easier.

Taffrail: the flat or rounded upper part of the rail that runs around the stern of a vessel above the counter.

Throat: the forward end of a gaff, close by the mast. A throat halyard is what hoists the gaff and the sail attached to it at that point. Compare peak.

Topsides: the sides of the hull above the waterline. Also, generally, the deck area in opposition to the below decks area.

Transom: Figuratively, the stern of the ship above the waterline. Specifically, transoms are the athwartship timbers of a vessel bolted to the stern post.

Traveler: a track or rail running across deck. The lower sheet block is attached around it so the block can slide from one side to the other as the vessel is tacked or jibed.

Triatic Stay: in a schooner, the stay leading from the fore-topmast head back and down to the main-crosstrees.

Truck: the top of the mast or the circular piece of wood topping the mast in which are sheaves used for reeving flag halyards.

Trysail: a small triangular sail used for heaving-to in a gale.

✪ ✪ ✪

Up and Down: the anchor is said to be this way when the rode, or chain, leads straight down directly beneath the bow.

✪ ✪ ✪

Vang: the line that controls the peak of a gaff or other spar.

Veer: the clockwise change in wind direction.

✪ ✪ ✪

Warp: a line used for hauling a vessel ahead by an anchor, a buoy, a piling, or a wharf. To warp a vessel is to move it ahead in this manner.

Washboard: coaming or thin plank fastened to the side of a hatchway to keep out the sea.

Wind Rose: a symbol on pilot charts distinguished by its many arrows showing the average wind directions and velocities over particular patches of the ocean for each month of the year.

Wing-and-Wing: having one sail broadly out to port and another out to starboard when the vessel is running dead before the wind.

Worm: to lay "small stuff" in between the strands of rope, before parceling and serving it. Also called worming.

✪ ✪ ✪

Yard: a spar rigged perpendicular to a mast.

Richard M. Dey

Brief Bibliography

Anon. "Noted Sailing Ship On Rocks of Devon." *New York Times,* 26 April 1936.

Brown, Alexander Crosby. *Horizon's Rim.* New York: Dodd, Mead & Company, 1935. The second half of the story of the Schooner *Chance's* circumnavigation.

Carrick, Robert W. and Henderson, Richard. *John G. Alden and His Yacht Designs.* Camden, Maine: International Marine Publishing Company, 1983.

Crocker, Templeton. *The Cruise of the* Zaca. New York and London: Harper, 1933. Circumnavigation in a 110' schooner.

Dodd, Edward H. Jr., *Great Dipper to Southern Cross.* New York: Dodd, Mead & Company, 1930. The first half the schooner *Chance's* circumnavigation.

Griswold, Roger. "The Cruise of the *Lloyd W. Berry.*" *Harvard Alumni Bulletin,* 11 January 1923 and 18 January 1923. Substantially the same account, under the title "Eleven Thousand Miles of North Atlantic in a Sixty-Footer," was run in the April, May, June, and July 1923 issues of *Yachting*. Harold Peters was Skipper.

Hansen, Art. *Photographic Memories of a T-Wharfer.* Boston;

Privately published, 1984.

Hayden, Sterling. *Wanderer*. New York: Alfred A. Knopf, 1963.

Henry, Teuira. "Ancient Tahiti" in *Bernice P. Bishop Museum Bulletin* 48. Honolulu: Bernice P. Bishop Museum, 1928.

Holm, Donald. *The Circumnavigators*. Englewood Cliffs, New Jersey: Prentice-Hall, Inc., 1974.

Johnson, Captain and Mrs. Irving. *Westward Bound in the Schooner Yankee*. New York: W. W. Norton & Company, 1936.

Moorehead, Alan. *The Fatal Impact: An Account of the Invasion of the South Pacific 1767–1840*. New York: Harper & Row, 1966.

Nordhoff, Charles B. "Saved By the Durian!" Cambridge, Mass: *The Harvard Graduates' Magazine*, September 1929. Light verse.

Parkinson, John, Jr. *Nowhere is Too Far*. New York: The Cruising Club of America, Inc., 1960. An informal history of the CCA and therefore, unavoidably, a history of yachting before the fiberglass revolution. There is a nice account of the *Pilgrim* voyage.

Peters, Harold. "The *Pilgrim* Sails the Seven Seas." *The National Geographic*, August 1937. Photographs greatly enhance this *Geographic* travelogue, written by the schooner's Skipper.

Pidgeon, Harry. *Around the World Single-Handed: The Cruise of the Islander*. New York and London: D. Appleton, 1932.

Robinson, William Albert. *10,000 Leagues Over the Sea*. New York: Brewer, Warren & Putnam, 1932. This narrative was published in The Mariners Library series as *Deep Water & Shoal*.

Robinson, William Albert. *Voyage to Galapagos*. New York: Harcourt, Brace and Company, 1936. The author attempts to solve the mystery of the disappearance of the Baroness and her lover, Philipson.

Shurcliff, Sidney N. *Jungle Islands: The* Illyria *in the South Seas.* The Record of the Crane Pacific Expedition, Field Museum of Natural History, Chicago, Illinois. With a Scientific Appendix by Karl Patterson Schmidt. New York: G. P. Putnam's Sons, 1930.

Tompkins, Warwick M. *Fifty South to Fifty South.* New York: W. W. Norton & Company, 1938. One of the best nautical books ever written, not least for its schooner jargon.

Utley, Temple. *A Modern Sea Beggar.* London: Peter Davies, 1938. Utley recounts getting help from Peters, Fuller, and "Mr. White" in taking the *Inyala,* a yawl, out of Papeete.

West, Isabel White. *Wilfrid O. White, 1878–1955, A Family Journal.* Vineyard Haven, MA: Privately Printed, 1990. The biography of "Kelvin" White and the story of his chandlery and instrument business.

Wittmer, Margaret. *Floreana Adventure.* Translated from the German by Oliver Coburn. New York: E. P. Dutton & Co., Inc., 1961.

Annotations by Richard M. Dey

Editorial Notes

Chapter 1

Art Hansen, in his *Photographic Memories of a T-Wharfer*, published in 1984, wrote: "From our window we could watch Donald Starr and his crew fitting out the beautiful schooner *Pilgrim* for his famous round-the-world cruise." A circumnavigation was news then, and the fact that the Skipper's brother, Andrew J. Peters, had been Mayor of Boston and that Starr had been an Assistant Attorney General contributed to the newsworthiness of the voyage from beginning to end.

The Rime of the Ancient Mariner, Colderidge writes: "The Sun…, etc."

A well-known superstition of sailors: Whistling in a calm brings a breeze, while whistling in a breeze brings a gale. It is considered bad luck to whistle aboard a boat in any conditions other than flat calm. Less well known is the double superstition of sticking a knife into a mast and whistling in order to raise a breeze.

"Bosun bird" is the sailor's name for the red-billed Tropicbird, distinguished by its shrill, piping cry.

To Euclid we owe basic geometry, to Napier the invention of logarithms, to Bowditch *The American Practical Navigator*, to Marcq St. Hilaire the altitude method of finding a ship's position using a chronometer and nautical almanac, and to Arthur A. Ageton the formulaic designs for H.O. *Pub. No. 211, Dead Reckoning Altitude and Azimuth Table.*

A schooner's four lowers, or working sails, are the mainsail, foresail, staysail, and working jib.

Chapter 2

One survey, dated 3 August 1932, was conducted by a surveyor for the American Bureau of Shipping. After noting that "several strakes of copper sheathing (were) entirely removed," and that the hull was filled with water internally, it states: "Examination by Surveyor at this time disclosed (a) considerable number of bronze spike fastenings as leaking where hull planking is secured to frames... indicating that fastenings apparently did not properly fill the hole or, possibly, straining by stress of weather." While this ascertains the true nature of the problem, it still allows for another, less drastic explanation — seams opening due to stress of heavy weather. This was discounted, however, since no real heavy weather had been encountered. It concludes, "In my opinion, Yacht in her present condition is considered unseaworthy for the long voyage of two years as proposed." The second survey was done by a surveyor to Lloyd's Register of Shipping, first on 4 August and subsequently at several points over the next six weeks. The schooner was insured by Lloyds. The document appears to be more a summary report than an official survey. While it is more detailed, it is less informative than the first and makes no pronouncements. For more detailed and technical accounts of the *Pilgrim*'s problem, see Appendix D.

Harry Pidgeon returned from his first circumnavigation, which lasted nearly four years, to Los Angeles in October 1925. His second voyage, which began within days of the *Pilgrim*'s return, also took four years (1934–1938) and made him the first single-hander to complete the circumnavigation twice. In 1947, at the age of seventy-three, he and his wife set off on a third circumnavigation in *Islander*. The yawl was wrecked in a hurricane in the New Hebrides. He built his last boat, a 25-footer, in California and lived aboard with his wife until shortly before his death in 1955.

Alexander George Findlay (1812–1875) was the British geographer and hydrographer whose six nautical directories, including *The South Pacific Ocean*, were accepted as standard authorities in every quarter of the globe.

Chapter 3

There is some confusion over the names of the Galapagos Islands, since each one has three — that of an English duke or king given it by the early buccaneers, that of fancy given by various Spaniards, and that given by the Ecuadorian government. The name commonly used by American sailors is used here.

Baroness Wagner de Bousquet had gone in October 1932 to Floreana Island, apparently to establish a hotel. She was accompanied by three men. One of them was a German named Rudolf Lorenz, and he proved to be one of the two men found dead. The other was a Norwegian who owned a fishing boat and was taking Lorenz from Floreana to Chatham, from which he planned to depart for Ecuador on his way back to Germany. The boat apparently developed engine trouble, and the pair decided their chances for survival were better on the island than on the boat, caught in the swift north current. The boat, along with an Ecuadorian who elected to stay aboard, was never seen again. The articles referred to appear in the October, November, and December, 1931 issues of *The Atlantic Monthly*.

Dr. Karl Frederick Ritter, a German dentist, left civilization behind in 1929 with Frau Dore Strauch in order to practice a back-to-nature philosophy of life. Ritter died on the island of food poisoning in November 1934.

Much publicity was given Ritter and his island experiment initially — he and Dore were known to the world as the Adam and Eve of the Galapagos, but it later went to the Austrian baroness whom the press called the "Empress of Floreana" and whose "Hacienda Paradiso" was in fact first a tent and then a one-room shack in the middle of a vegetable garden. Baroness Wagner, as mentioned earlier, arrived in Floreana with three men — Lorenz, Robert Philipson, and an Ecuadorian named Valdivieso whom she met in Paris. A difficult and imperious woman, she immediately antagonized Dr. Ritter. She sent Valdivieso away. She constantly humiliated and, with Philipson, physically abused Lorenz who was in poor health. Lorenz claimed to have helped finance the baroness and was likely her lover before Philipson. One day early in 1934, she and Philipson disappeared, apparently aboard a ship bound for Tahiti. Neither was ever seen or heard of again. It was thought, though never proved, that Lorenz, or Lorenz and Ritter, murdered the baroness and her boyfriend. For a full account of this bizarre story, see Margaret Wittmer's *Floreana Adventure*. William A. Robinson also offers an account of these events in *Voyage to Galapagos*.

Charles Hubbard, football star and Class of 1924 at Harvard College, wrote in his twenty-fifth reunion book: "I bought an ocean going schooner and lived on her for a couple of years. Having a deep water ship is a restless business, and so I made a voyage to the Pacific and sold the hooker in California."

Tanganyika was a former nation of east central Africa that joined with Zanzibar in 1964 to form Tanzania.

From the last line of John Keats' sonnet, "On First Looking into Chapman's Homer."

Chapter 5

Dégustation is the practice of giving customers free samplings of wine.

Paul Gauguin, the French artist famous for his South Seas work, lived and painted in a house in Atuona for twenty months before dying there in 1903. He had lived in Tahiti for many years previously, until getting into trouble with the authorities.

(Author's note.) In the usual spelling of Polynesian words, each vowel is pronounced separately. Thus, Ua Poa should be pronounced as though it were spelled Oo-a Po-aa.

Chapter 7

Quirós today is credited with having discovered part of the Tuamotu Archipelago, which his description suits.

The vexed question of who was responsible for introducing sexually transmitted diseases into Tahiti is dealt with by Alan Moorehead in *The Fatal Impact*. Both Wallis and Bougainville claimed their crews were free of disease.

Chapter 9

Directed by F. W. Murnau and produced by Murnau and Robert Flaherty, the silent movie was filmed in 1929 and released by Paramount in 1931. It won the Academy Award for cinematography. "Tabu" means death, the fate of anyone who tried to love a native girl designated by the high priest as a sacred virgin. In the film, the girl already had a lover when she was appointed and they attempt to flee the island and their fate.

Chapter 14

(Author's note.) A split is, by definition, a Scotch and soda which is supposed to contain only half the quantity of whiskey of a full Scotch and soda. Since the order is always for a "split" and the mixture actually contains as much whiskey as a full one anywhere else, the term appears to be nothing more than a euphemistic sop to the conscience. The phenomenon can be observed in Singapore, where the same drink goes by the name of "s'tengah" (Malay for "half"), and in America where various full sized drinks, and sometimes a number of them, follow an invitation to have a "little touch," a "splash," or a "spot."

Appendix C

Quincy Howe, well-known radio broadcaster, journalist and historian.

Mark DeWolfe Howe, Quincy's younger brother, was secretary to Justice Oliver Wendell Holmes and later edited some of his letters and wrote a biography of him. A law school professor at Harvard, Mark Howe was also active in the civil rights movement.

Dorade, one of Olin Stephens' first designs, was a 52' yawl launched in 1930. She won the 1931 Transatlantic Race, the first small yacht to do so, and went on to have an extremely successful ocean racing career.

Hayden became well known as a movie actor. Before that, he served in Gloucester fishing schooners, including Ben Pine's famous racer *Gertrude L. Thebaud.* He sailed as Irving Johnson's first mate on the second circumnavigation of the Schooner *Yankee,* whose many voyages with young, paying crews during the 1930's, 1940's, and 1950's Johnson chronicled in a series of books, articles in *The National Geographic,* and films. Hayden later sailed a big schooner of his own, the adventures of which are brilliantly recounted in his book, *Wanderer.*

Richard M. Dey

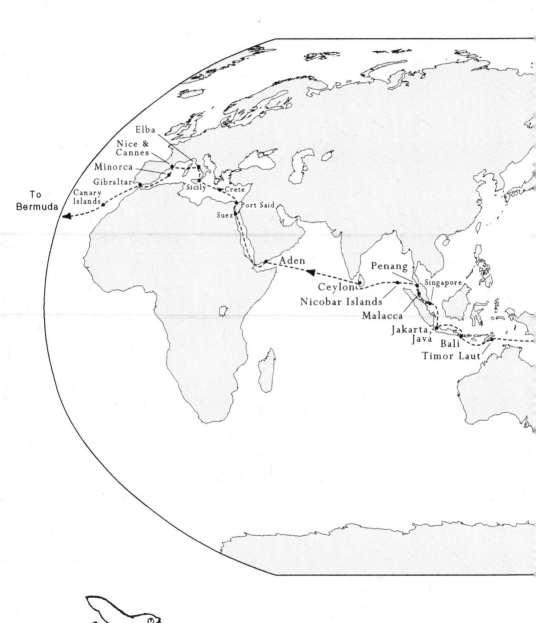

TRACK OF THE SCHOONER *PILGR*

Elba
Nice &
Cannes
Minorca
Gibraltar
Canary
Islands
Sicily
Crete
Port Said
Suez
To
Bermuda
Aden
Penang
Ceylon
Nicobar Islands
Singapore
Malacca
Jakarta,
Java
Bali
Timor Laut